Music, My Life

A Gallimaufry of Musical Memories

'The heart-warming story of a bright Yorkshire lad's 50-year journey from aspiring singer to much-loved broadcaster, choral conductor and national treasure. We meet an assortment of colourful characters along the way, go backstage with the King's Singers, peep into the corridors of the BBC and finally revel in our hero's giant **Messiah** performances at the Royal Albert Hall. Every anecdote is a gem, there are laugh-out-loud moments, and by the end the world seems a sunnier place.'

JOHN RUTTER

'This book has achieved the impossible: it is as charming, as witty, as winsome and good-natured as its author. To lose yourself in its pages is to spend time with Brian himself – what could be more delightful? – preferably with a glass of good wine to hand. Musicians and non-musicians alike will enjoy deliciously funny anecdotes about the most significant musical characters of the last half century. Some will meet old friends: many make new ones. All can share in this wonderful life full of music.'

ANNE ATKINS

'On the page, as in life, Brian Kay is the best company. For someone who has been at the forefront of music-making, and music presentation, at all levels and across the globe, for many decades, he recounts his considerable achievements with candid modesty. Drawing with his infectious enthusiasm on his own rich experiences, and those of his formidable friends and acquaintances whose presence bejewel the book, his warm prose bustles engagingly and joyfully along. This is a delightful read, which will bring enormous pleasure to the many musicians, both professional and amateur, who have worked with him, and to countless other readers who have not had that great fortune.'

JANE GLOVER

Music, My Life

A Gallimaufry of Musical Memories

Brian Kay

UMBRIA PRESS

Published by Umbria Press
London SW15 5DP
www.umbriapress.co.uk

Designed by Louise Millar

Printed and bound in Poland by Totem
www.totem.com

Hardback ISBN 978 1 910074 31 2
Paperback ISBN 978 1 910074 30 5

Contents

Appendices

Life isn't about dawdling to the grave, arriving safely in an attractive, wrinkle-free body, but rather an adventure that ends skidding in sideways, champagne in one hand, strawberries in the other, totally worn out, screaming, "Yee haaa, what a ride!"
(Anon: written on a wall in The Mother Goose café in Bulls, New Zealand 2010)

To succeed as a performer, you need the nerves of a bullfighter, the vitality of a brothel Madam and the concentration of a Buddhist monk. **Jascha Heifetz**

As long as we live, there is never enough singing. Next to the word of God, the noble art of music is the greatest treasure in the world. **Martin Luther**

Tempus don't 'alf fugit! **Frankie Howerd**

No one is a triumph, no one is a disaster. We are put together to get on as best we may.
The Very Rev. Michael Till, Dean of King's College, Cambridge

Since singing is so good a thing, I wish all men would learn to sing. **William Byrd**

I don't sing because I'm happy; I'm happy because I sing! **William James**

It is a tricky business tracing the development of a character along the avenues of reminiscence.
Noel Coward: *Present Indicative*

Music's an excellent thing. It reduces the beast in men. **Joseph Stalin to President Truman**

"Far better to be a big fish in a small pond than a pilchard in an ocean!" **careers advice from Sir David Willcocks**

prodesse quam conspici **Rydal School motto**

Preface

Who am I? What am I? Why on earth have I spent a multitude of precious moments assembling such a self-centred gallimaufry of memories? The first question will be answered in the following pages and as for the third, I've always been a bit of a story-teller and often when I've been pouring forth acorns of memory, generous and tolerant friends have suggested allowing them to grow into an oak of reflection. But let's not get carried away: I can only hope that in trawling through the recesses of distant recollection I might be able to throw some light on the privileges and pitfalls – the great and often not-so-great aspects – of life as a professional itinerant musician and broadcaster.

I've never been one to look back on things that have been and gone – a hazard when it comes to resorting to memory in order to reflect on a life – preferring always to look ahead to what might come next. I've been lucky enough that when one door has closed, another has always opened instead of slamming in my face and for that I shall always remain profoundly grateful. In Dorothy Reynolds' time-honoured words (so tunefully set to music by Julian Slade in the hit 1950s musical *Salad Days*) I can sum up my general feelings thus: 'don't look round, we're outward-bound and we said we wouldn't look back'.

So why am I now doing just that? I take my cue from the autobiographical journal *Full Circle* written in 1982 by my friend and colleague of more than fifty years Dame Janet Baker, in the introduction to which she says this: "As we reach certain mile-stones in life it is a natural thing to do some stocktaking, to step back from activity and evaluate one's situation both personally and professionally". This I have done, though I'm not sure it answers the second of my three questions above: what am I?

Like everyone else I have my likes and dislikes. My relatively modest list of pet-hates includes people who hog the middle lane of motorways unnecessarily, mobile phones, squealing babies on aeroplanes, any form of rudeness, sloppy and careless use of the English language, creepy-crawlies, packaging and anything that reeks of poor quality. But I love tuneful music, home-made shepherd's pie, a warm bed, a good book, winter sunshine, the feeling of a job well done and the good fortune of a loving family.

Did I ever think that a small boy from a Yorkshire village would one day travel the world, enjoy a rewarding and fulfilling life in music, be a member of a world-famous choir and a well-known singing group, spend twenty-five years broadcasting to the nation, conduct at the Royal Albert Hall and even be the answer to a question on Radio 4's quiz show *Counterpoint*? I can't say I did ever think that, but it all happened and I count my lucky stars constantly.

So maybe you can look on this rather self-indulgent exercise as my way of saying thank you to all those who made it happen. There are so many who encouraged, cajoled, disciplined and even listened to me and to one and all my gratitude remains boundless – particularly to my always-supportive and ever-loving wife Gilly to whom these memories are affectionately and gratefully dedicated.

CHAPTER ONE

Antecedents

"Hang it in the downstairs loo." Such is the advice given to people by the Prince of Wales when presenting them with awards. My downstairs loo contains a selection of gold discs (for my association with The King's Singers and the Huddersfield Choral Society) a framed signed letter from Edward Elgar (not, of course, written to me) Certificates for my two Sony Radio Awards (one gold, one bronze), a photograph of the choir of King's College, Cambridge, taken in 1964 and including myself as a second-year bass choral scholar, notification of a ten year conducting award from the Leith Hill Musical Festival and my honorary Fellowship of Trinity College of Music: all in all a clear retrospection on my working life.

There is also a copy of my Family Tree, beautifully crafted many years ago by a distant cousin of my father, which chronicles the Yorkshire Family of Kays from 1675 to the generation into which I was born. It contains some fascinating snippets, starting with Richard Kay (1675-1744) a farmer who came from Langton near Malton to Hall Farm in Marston in the 18th century and produced four sons and a daughter. The second son gave us the first Methodist in the family and he begat two daughters and four sons, one of whom is reputed to have 'read the Bible through twenty times

1

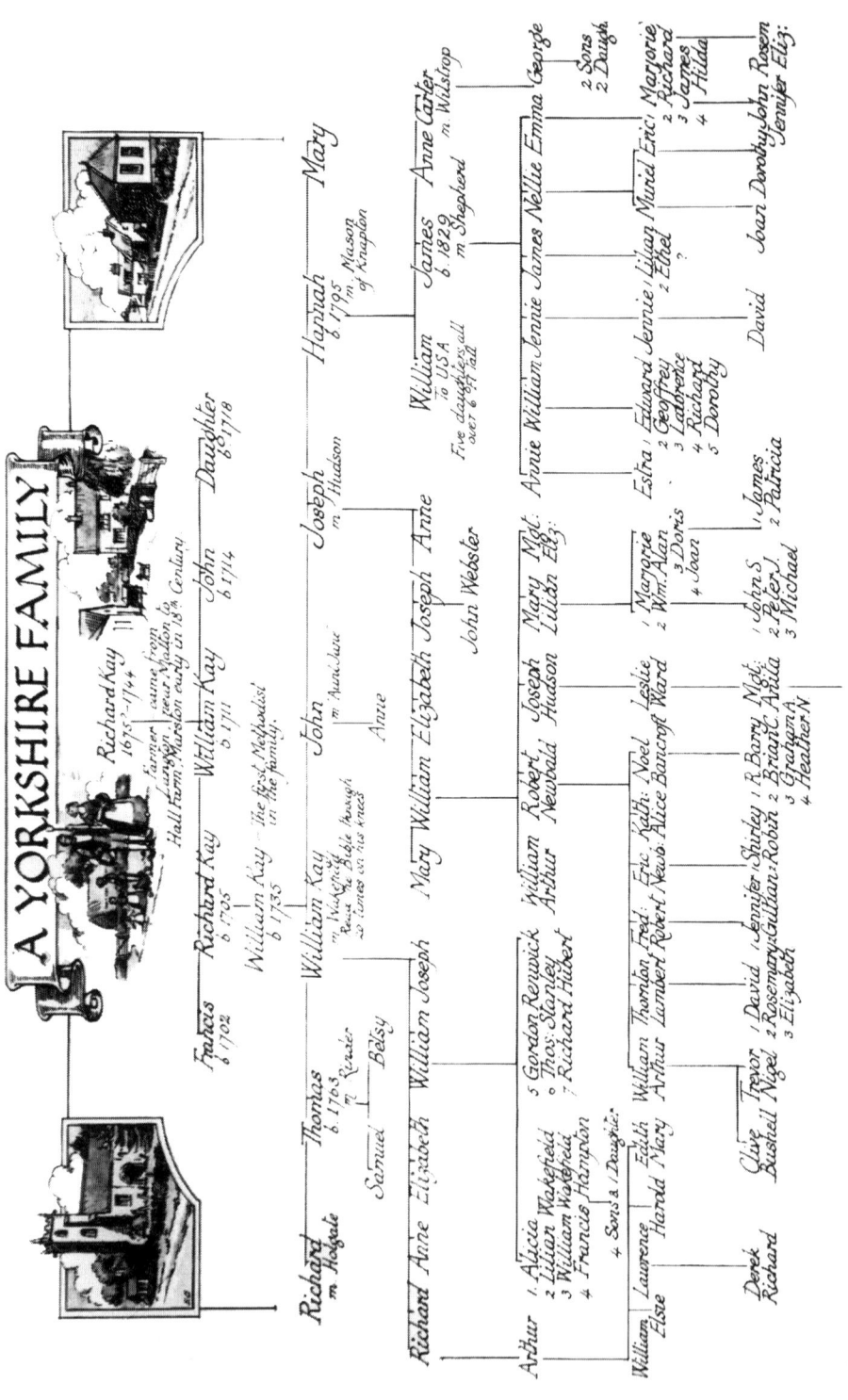

The Kay Family Tree

on his knees'; one of his nephews produced 'six daughters all over 6 ft tall' And so the list goes on, each generation growing ever larger (if not taller), the three sons of another nephew fathering no fewer than nineteen offspring.

One of these was my paternal grandfather – Robert (later Sir Robert) Newbald Kay – some time Member of Parliament and founder of the family firm of solicitors. He died in 1947 when I was three years old, so sadly I have no memory of him. The youngest of his six children was my father and his contribution to the family tree was three sons and a daughter of which I was the second son.

The family home for most of my life was the village of Upper Poppleton, which, together with Nether Poppleton lies four miles to the north west of the beautiful and historic city of York. Poppleton Hall was my grandfather's home and during his time as Lord Mayor of the City it was visited by no less a figure than his political leader. In another room of my house I have a triptych of photos of the Prime Minister's visit to the Hall, surrounded by my grandparents and the rest of the family. As that includes my father as a young boy, I can, with relish and certainty, sing the old song: *Lloyd George knew my Father*. Sadly, the Hall was demolished in the swinging 60s to make way for sixteen houses, now known collectively as Poppleton Hall Gardens.

So, although I was born in Cheshire (during my mother's visit to her parents who lived in Stockton Heath, near Warrington) I have always considered myself a Yorkshireman, or at least, a proud son of a Yorkshire family. My mother's maternal grandfather was a prominent dental surgeon in Warrington and his obituary in the local paper referred to his 'courteousness and kindliness of manner', for whom, 'the eventide of his life, cheered by the sunshine of his nature; the light of past actions, of strength and purpose, of piety and love, had brought a glory which could never waver … He demanded little and so received much.' I wish I'd met him.

My maternal grandfather, Evelyn James Sutton, followed in the footsteps of his grandfather as clerk to Warrington Rural District Council and in 1910 married Elsie Barwick Taylor, the third surviving daughter of the aforementioned dental surgeon. Her sisters had names typical of the period: Ethel, Doris and Nellie, two of whom I remember well, living together all their lives, with Ethel very much the dominant partner, frequently making the rather mouse-like Doris know precisely where she stood in the pecking order. Of course, they loved each other dearly, though Ethel had a strange way of showing it. Grandmother, on the other hand, was the most loving of creatures, with a gentleness and serenity clearly inherited from her father. What a joy it was for all of us when Granny and Grandpa Sutton retired to live in the house opposite ours in Station Road, Upper Poppleton.

Sir Robert Newbald Kay was a devout Methodist and he married Alice Lambert, the daughter of a Methodist minister. It was not surprising, therefore, that my father, followed by my two brothers and me, was educated at a Methodist school – Rydal, in Colwyn Bay, North Wales. Unusually for the time, my grandparents separated, Grandfather continuing to live in Poppleton Hall for a time, while Grandmother had a flat in Scarborough and eventually one near the centre of York. She was a magistrate and a tireless worker for temperance and social welfare within the city.

Part of Grandfather's devout Methodism included total temperance. He never let a drop of alcohol pass his lips. At the time he was Lord Mayor, the newly appointed Duke of York (later King George VI) visited the city and had lunch at the Mansion House, hosted by my grandparents. Sir Robert was so determined that even the smell of alcohol would never permeate the Mansion House during his tenure that he took the train to London for an appointment with His Majesty the King. He made it abundantly clear that – even at a Royal lunch – there would be no drinking. Luckily for him, the King replied that if such was his wish, then so be it. Grandfather would surely not have appreciated the words of Oliver Goldsmith in *She Stoops to Conquer*:

> *When Methodist preachers come down*
> *A-preaching that drinking is sinful,*
> *I'll wager the rascals a crown,*
> *They always preach best with a skinful.*

My father, Noel Bancroft Kay, had four brothers (Arthur, Thornton, Frederick and Eric) and a sister called Kathleen. Three of the brothers trained as solicitors, while Fred joined the Colonial Service in Africa, where he died of a thrombosis in his early forties. A similar fate would overcome three more of the brothers (though rather later in life) including my father. At Rydal School he became Head Boy (as did my younger brother Graham) before studying for the law and joining the family firm.

The first time he came back to the school after leaving, he met a young lady whose brother was then at the school and asked her to dance. It could well have been love at first sight, for Noel and my mother, Gwendoline Mary Sutton, remained together in blissful union until Father's untimely death – at the age of 65 – on board the P&O ship *Canberra* in 1980. He had retired early from the law and possessing generously the gift of the gab and a great sense of humour had taken to lecturing on cruise ships. He also did the rounds of Women's Luncheon Clubs, ably supported by my mother, who herself had been the secretary of the York Women's Luncheon Club for many years.

Before they met, Mother had worked for the Manchester Chamber of Commerce, following graduation from Manchester University. In that capacity she 'slogged away in the typing pool' before joining a delegation to visit Australia, in order to further Lancashire trade, which was being affected by the increasing imports of Japanese cotton goods into Australia. She sailed from Southampton on January 24th, 1936 and spent six months working in each of the state capitals and visiting the Parliament in Canberra: all in all, a tremendous opportunity for a young lady in those far-off days.

At the time I made my first appearance as a family member – towards the end of the war, on May 12th, 1944 – my father was away on active service with the army, rather enjoying his time stationed in Alexandria, as part of an acting fraternity which included Arthur 'Captain Mainwaring' Lowe and the film-star-to-be Martin Benson. My father hardly ever spoke about such times, so when I happened to meet Martin Benson in the 1990s at a charity function, I rather tentatively mentioned Daddy's claim to have trodden the boards with him. It's not that I didn't believe the old man, just that I was hoping for some sort of confirmation. I need not have worried. Martin not only remembered the name of Noel Kay but spoke very fondly of a man who had clearly been the life and soul of the party. How Father would love to have followed in the illustrious acting footsteps of Lowe and Benson. As he possessed a proper sense of duty – not to mention considerable parental pressure – he spent his working life in the family firm of lawyers: deeply frustrating for him in many ways and even more so when two of his children (my sister Heather and me) ended up in the music business.

However, the way Father vented that frustration was through singing and comedy, as a fluent after-dinner speaker and as a prominent member of the York Amateur Operatic and Dramatic Society. He had a light tenor voice (mercifully untrained) and with a natural flair for timing he was a gift to a society such as the York Amateurs. He played the tenor lead – and very well too – in the sort of shows which were so popular in the 50s and 60s: *Show Boat*, *The Belle of New York*, *The Arcadians*, *Rose Marie*, *The Country Girl* and so on. He also became assistant Musical Director and on one glorious occasion had to mount the rostrum and conduct a performance, owing to the indisposition of the MD – a blissfully happy moment for him, no doubt.

His musical pleasures also came from his extensive collection of gramophone records, paid for, he used to say, with money he saved from not smoking. These ranged from box sets of Beethoven symphonies (on 12-inch 78s) to the songs of Tom Lehrer and Paddy Roberts. His favourite music programmes on the wireless were *Melodies for You* and *Friday Night is Music Night*, sadly not living long enough to hear me presenting both programmes for BBC Radio 2, as I did for several years.

There were two other major musical events on radio which he insisted we all listened to each year: the Christmas Eve festival of nine lessons and carols from King's College, Cambridge, and the Vienna Philharmonic's celebrated New Year's Day Strauss-Fest. He was able to experience the King's service at first hand when I had become a choral scholar in the choir, but he'd been long gone before I had the pleasure of presenting the Vienna concert on radio and television, as I did for fifteen years. For him, when it came to appreciating music, familiarity always helped. He used to say "I don't know much about music but I know what I like" and I always rather assumed that he really meant "I like what I know". Good for him.

Mother wasn't particularly musical, as such, but she was a wonderful listener and enjoyed being able to hear so much music through the activities of the rest of us. We would enjoy 'musical evenings' round the family piano. On one never-to-be-forgotten occasion, our neighbour across the road said that a friend of his was visiting and he wondered if we would we like to meet him. As that friend was Donald Adams, the principal bass with the D'Oyly Carte Opera Company, we leapt at the opportunity. Donald came round for supper and then sat at the piano for hours, playing and singing so many familiar lollipops from his extensive repertoire. We had an old Ferrograph tape recorder and as Donald was happy for us to record as he sang, the evening was preserved for posterity, though where the tape might be now is anyone's guess.

And mention of Donald Adams reminds me of a holiday from boarding school in which my father took me night after night to the Grand Theatre in Leeds to hear the D'Oyly Carte in several of the Savoy Operas, thus starting my lifelong love of the words and music of Gilbert and Sullivan. Many years later – in 2010 – Robin Wilson (whose father, Prime Minister Harold Wilson, instigated his boundless enthusiasm for G&S) and I compiled and edited a volume of great G&S choruses and launched its publication at the annual International Gilbert and Sullivan Festival at Buxton.

As I sat waiting for the performance to begin in that wonderful Matcham theatre, a tall gentleman came and sat next to me and asked if I was Brian Kay. He then said: "My name's Thomas Round" – and if there had been room, I could have fallen off my seat. I rather indelicately asked him how old he was and he proudly said "ninety three". "The last time I saw you in the flesh," I replied, "you were singing the part of Frederic in *The Pirates of Penzance* and that was at the Grand Theatre in Leeds in 1953." And there I was sitting next to him 57 years later. In the bygone days of the D'Oyly Carte, every movement and gesture was unchangeable on pain of dismissal; as we watched a splendidly whacky Opera della Luna production of the *Pirates* I asked him what he thought of the way things were done these days. His response: "I just love it and wish we'd been able to enjoy that sort of freedom". He was the first to clap at the end of every scene – still crazy after all those years.

Back to the family: my elder brother Barry was born in 1941 and I followed on three years later. A third son (Graham – born in 1946 on December the 14th – the same date as our father) made the folks wonder if they could ever satisfy their hope for a daughter. Their wish was granted a year later with the arrival of Heather and the family was complete.

CHAPTER TWO

Childhood

One of my earliest memories was the day on which we moved from the family home on the outskirts of York a little further into the country and settled in a house in Station Road, Upper Poppleton which was to be home for all of us until such times as we flew the nest. It had five bedrooms, only one bathroom (how times have changed!) a sitting room, morning room, dining room, double garage, a potting shed, two sizeable greenhouses and a lawn large enough for us to play cricket without breaking too many windows.

People seem to have a habit of remembering that the sun always shone when they were kids, and I really do think summers were rather more reliably warm and sunny in the 1950s. On the day we moved in – this was in 1948, when I was barely four years old – Mother told me to go and do something useful so she could get on with the business of unpacking and arranging the furniture. Apparently, I walked up and down Station Road knocking on every door and proudly announcing to our unsuspecting new neighbours: "Hello, I'm Brian Kay – who are you?" *Precocious, moi?* At least I came home loaded with gifts of sweets and flowers and warm words of welcome.

The village was then quite small and surrounded by fields for walking and playing where there are now rows and rows of houses. The village green was the centre of activity, dominated by a giant maypole, which is there to this day and which was the gathering point for all of us each year for the May Day celebrations. Nearby was – and is – the Methodist chapel, the spiritual and musical home of our childhood years.

Three times on a Sunday we would congregate there and sing our hearts out in a way which (in my humble opinion) only Yorkshire Methodists can. The peculiar smell of harvest festival still lingers in my nostrils as I think of the decorations of fruit and vegetables which covered every available surface – back in the heady days when harvest gifts were genuine produce and not items tinned or boxed. And those wonderful harvest hymns: I have the same tingle these days whenever I play them on the organ in the 900-year-old church next to my home in the Cotswolds.

There weren't too many cars in the village in those far-off days, though we did have a succession of family cars and Father had a very small run-around (Ford Popular – room for two at a pinch!) to drive himself each morning to work in the offices next door to the Mansion House in York. It must have been somewhat nostalgic for him to work next door to the house he had lived in for a year as a small boy when Sir Robert was Lord Mayor. Every morning I used to watch the menfolk of the village as they trudged down Station Road on their way to catch the train to work in York, then more eagerly retracing their steps in the evening. The other method of travel was bicycle and riding round the village and surrounding countryside for hours on end was another of the happiest memories of village life as a child. Sadly, when I began my three years at Cambridge University in 1963, Father drove me to King's College with my precious bike strapped to the top of the car. Being rather un-streetwise, I left it outside the hostel on the first night, never dreaming that it might not be there the following morning. It wasn't, and another favourite childhood passion bit the dust!

Back to the village, and the other form of transport was the giant carthorses which would trundle up the road after a long hard day in the field, inevitably leaving their droppings near to the house, so that our neighbour would run out with a bucket and a shovel and add lustre to his precious roses.

Mother kept the family home warm and clean and provided for our every need. It's just as well she was happy and more than capable of feeding us all plenteously, as Father admitted his uselessness as a cook, referring to himself as 'a culinary thrombosis, or clot in the kitchen'! We grew plenty of vegetables in the back garden, including huge beds of asparagus, and for me there was the regular pleasure of shelling the freshest of peas.

One of Mother's culinary delights we all looked forward to was her own special way with Yorkshire pudding. The origin of this famous delicacy was based on starting a meal with it, swimming in onion gravy and filling up the children so they wouldn't need too much meat. But Mother would bake a large tin full, then cut it up into generous portions and cover it in Tate & Lyle Golden Syrup: heaven.

Father gave us an annual treat when he would drive us all down to London for a weekend's excitement, taking in the latest musicals and each year's Brian Rix farce at the Whitehall Theatre. We would all stay at the Regent's Palace Hotel for a couple of nights and fit in a matinee and an evening show. I can't imagine how much that must have cost him, but those visits left an indelible impression.

On one glorious occasion I well remember seeing Slade and Reynolds' *Salad Days* in the afternoon and Lerner and Loewe's *My Fair Lady* that evening – at Drury Lane with Julie Andrews, Rex Harrison and Stanley Holloway all right there on stage as large as life. With all those tunes rattling round the brain, I don't think any of us slept much that night. Seeing Ron Moody on stage in Lionel Bart's *Oliver* was another unforgettable experience, with Sean Kenny's famous revolving set taking our breath away – and a cast including the young Barry Humphries as the undertaker.

We had one of the first television sets to arrive in the north of England and quickly adjusted our lives to become what Father would call 'slaves to the goggle-box'. Even though it was only a nine-inch screen in a large cabinet showing tiny and not very clear images in black and white, it was new and exciting and we spent so much time in front of it that it rather explains why I eventually grew to like it less and less. Imagine our excitement when one of our London trips included a visit to the filming of two special TV programmes: the *Lonnie Donegan* Show and an episode of the sitcom *The Rag Trade*. To see the inner workings of television was another eye-opener, never believing that one day I too would become involved in that particular medium.

I well remember sitting in front of the telly as a fourteen-year-old watching the news and hearing of the death of the great English composer Ralph Vaughan Williams – that was in 1958. For some reason I was fascinated by the face which appeared on the screen – the famous photo by Karsh of Ottawa – which stayed there for the duration of the news flash – no retrospective videos in those days. Again, who would have thought that one day I would stand on the podium that was built to accommodate Vaughan Williams's considerable girth and conduct from his own antique music stand, as I did for so many years at the Leith Hill Musical Festival?

Another important musical childhood memory concerns my father's involvement in the York Amateur Operatic and Dramatic Society. On the weekly rehearsal nights, we would accompany him to the upper room in York's Rechabite Hall and watch in fascination as bit by bit that year's show slowly gathered strength and we became increasingly familiar with the words and melodies of the popular musicals available to amateur societies at the time. I've always considered those experiences as central to the pleasure I still receive from so-called 'amateur' music-making – that is to say the singing and playing of people who simply love what they are doing, rather than being paid for it. People have often asked me why I enjoy working with amateurs so much and I'm quick to remind them that whereas Noah's ark was built by amateurs, professionals built the *Titanic*!

The camaraderie between the singers, the accompanists and the producers of the York Amateurs gave them all the perfect foil to the rigours of daily life, which in those years following the Second World War was not as easy or straight forward as it might have been. After a hard day's graft at the office or wherever, there was nothing quite like having a good sing with a lot of old friends and even in a much-changed world, the same applies to this very day and hopefully always will. Recognising that fact stood me in good stead years later when I began to conduct amateur choirs and choral societies around the country and in other parts of the world.

Every year at Christmas we siblings would join the village carol singers and, whatever the weather, we walked round Upper and Nether Poppleton, stopping at every few houses to sing one of the relatively small handful of carols we knew, under the watchful guidance of one 'Brough' Walker. He conducted with his walking stick and would proudly announce, in his rich Yorkshire brogue: "Let's give 'em 'ark the 'erald Hangels". The presence of four musical Kay children among the pack almost certainly added a reasonable amount of tone – after all, two of us became choral scholars at Cambridge while our sister Heather became a member of the world famous Swingle Singers.

One port of call was always Poppleton Hall, where we could sing to the residents, Grandfather's old house having become an old folks' home after the war. We would sit on the baronial stairway, freezing cold in such a large and wintry space, singing loud enough to warm ourselves up. At that stage I was hardly aware of the family's connection with what seemed like a mini stately home. It was some years later when I began to go round the wards with Mother, distributing books to the residents, that she was able to tell me what function each of the rooms had once performed. There was the small ante-room to the main mezzanine drawing room, which is where the books were stored: that had been Grandfather's study. There was the grand billiard room on the ground floor, in the corner of which I was told that Father proposed to Mother. There were the family bedrooms and the seemingly immense dining room, where Mother had had to endure the taunts of Father's four brothers when she first came to the hall as a prospective sister-in-law! And the gardens where all those more recent houses now stand reached down to the river Ouse which flowed through the village on its way down to and from York.

There were so many members of the Kay family that there were few houses in the old part of the village which hadn't at some time been inhabited by one or other. That included a small semi in Station Road in which the two maiden aunts Alicia and Lillian lived in sisterly disharmony for many years. They had been antique dealers for a time and I still sit most days to read the paper in the same ancient chair they gave to my parents as a wedding present in 1939. The two sisters were short and rather dumpy and when they walked up and down the road together, Father always said that unless they set off on the same foot, they'd batter each other to bits, as they waddled like a pair of old ducks.

Over the level crossing further down the road lived Miss Wills and it was to her that I was sent to start learning the piano at the age of six. It was an interesting relationship. On day one, she played through a short piece and asked me to recreate it. I did so instantly and very much to her amazement. It was not that I could read music perfectly, it was simply that I could play by ear and having heard what she had played, I was able to play it back to her straight away. Don't ask me how. She played another and, again, I copied what she had done. It was only when the third piece was too long for me to remember that the secret was out and the child prodigy she thought she had discovered turned out to be 'cheating'.

None of this put me off playing the piano, though it might help to explain why it never became absolutely central to my development as a musician. It was certainly a help having the family Bechstein in the sitting room, where it remained until long after we had all left home and was eventually presented to the Methodist chapel for use at the Sunday School.

Family holidays had a delightful sameness to them, certainly for the first seventeen years of my life. Father's oldest brother – Uncle Arthur – owned The Manor Hotel in Scarborough – just across the square from the Grand. As Father did so much of Arthur's office work for him, his reward each year was two weeks free board and lodgings at the Manor for the six of us. It was one of those good, old fashioned family hotels, where we made friends easily, who came back for the same fortnight – the two weeks of the Scarborough cricket festival – year after year. We would hover outside the Grand and the Royal in the hope of catching autographs from our cricketing heroes – Peter May, the Bedser brothers, the great Leonard Hutton, Trevor Bailey and so on. I went back to stay at the hotel for a couple of nights in 2016 and rather wish I hadn't: it's now part of a well-known chain and has lost all the welcoming warmth and friendliness it used to have.

One of the highlights of the holiday (apart from almost freezing to death in the rock pools of the South Bay, even in August) was the weekly talent competition held on the Spa. We were a musical lot, we Kays, and it's fair to admit there was not too much competition when it came to singing.

On one special summer's morning, in the Spa's famous sun enclosure, I had sung Bach's *My heart ever faithful*. Who should be walking past at that precise moment but Scarborough's own 'Mr Music' – the celebrated fiddle player Max Jaffa. He had been the resident music man on the Spa for many years and when he heard me sing, he asked if I would like to have another go in the Great Hall with his orchestra in the evening concert. I didn't take much persuading and the momentous event remains etched on my mind to this day! Max never forgot it either: each time years later I bumped into him in the BBC canteen he would ask: "Do you remember Scarborough?" – Did I ever.

Another treasured memory of the Scarborough holidays is that each year the famous *Black and White Minstrel Show* played at the Futurist Theatre and I would go to hear and see them as many times as I possibly could, even to the extent of knowing all those wonderful choral arrangements inside out from hearing them so many times. The three stand-out soloists – lyric tenor John Boulter, Al Jolson sound-alike Dai Francis and Crosby-type crooner Tony Mercer – were my heroes. Little did I realise at the time that the shows were all *mimed*, which explains why the singers were able to move around so much and to create such a dazzling music-and-movement show.

(We King's Singers never moved around much on stage, which prompted our old friend Miles Kington to describe us as 'the Madame Tussaud's mobile exhibit'!)

Years later – and I'm talking about fifty years down the line – Gilly and I stayed at a wonderful B&B in the Bay of Islands, right at the top end of New Zealand and our hosts were the very same John Boulter (retired and living in 'Godzone' for many years) and his wife Anna Dawson. She had been one of Benny Hill's scantily-clad ladies, running around in manic fashion at double speed on his highly entertaining television shows. John and Anna were the perfect hosts and we all enjoyed two days of nostalgic bliss, with me hardly able to believe I was taking breakfast in his own home with one of my real childhood heroes – well, two of them really.

You never know how your heroes might turn out should you happen to be lucky enough to meet them in a domestic situation. We needn't have worried: within minutes of arriving, we were sitting on their sun-kissed terrace drinking champagne and feeling as if we'd known them all our lives. I hadn't told them about my childhood obsession with the Minstrels until John happened to mention that he'd *"wasted years of his life"* as one of the gang. When I realised that the shows had been mimed, it occurred to me how frustrating that must have been for a singer, longing to give true voice night after night instead of lip-syncing time after time. I hope I was able to convince him that his time was not remotely wasted – certainly as far as one highly impressionable Yorkshire lad was concerned.

Childhood was an immensely happy period, as we four Kay children had enough friends of our respective ages in the village to be able to be self-sufficient much of the time, making our own entertainment. Village life remains as important to me today as it did then, a point made all the more certain by the occasional times I've had to live in a town. But there was no way that idyllic sort of life could go on for ever – as childhood never does – and the end came for me at the age of nine, when, in 1953, I was sent away to boarding school in North Wales. In many ways I moved from one happy state to another and although it would not be fair to say that my schooldays were 'the happiest days of my life' I certainly enjoyed every minute of them, particularly in such a beautiful part of the country, with the sea on one side and the mountains on the other.

CHAPTER THREE

Schooldays

My father, my elder brother Barry and my cousins David and Robin had all been to Rydal, a Methodist school in Colwyn Bay, North Wales, so it was inevitable that both me and my younger brother Graham should follow suit. I had previously been to the school to visit Barry during half term, a small boy sitting in the back seat of the family Ford V8 Pilot somewhat nervous of the tortuous journey across the Pennines, long before the eventual wealth of motorways linking the counties of the red and white roses.

Rydal junior school was then based at Oakwood Park in Conway, a few miles away from the senior school; it had been moved there during the war. But now, in 1953, the year I started as a 'guffy new tick' or 'natty new bug', it had moved back to Colwyn Bay and to an imposing building that had previously been the Pwllycrochan Hotel, a fine Edwardian pile sitting proudly on top of the hill overlooking the bay.

And so it was, in that Coronation year, that a rather timid nine-year-old from a Yorkshire village found himself abandoned at the impressive white gates as the car bearing my parents drove off down the hill leaving me to my own devices. Not unnaturally I burst into tears of loneliness, which lasted but a few seconds. At that point, another new arrival – one Richard Cole – asked what my problem was and I spluttered out my feelings of abandonment; "Don't worry about that," he said, "let's go and explore".

Tears and parents were forgotten in a flash as we began to find out way round the seemingly vast building which was to be our home for the next few years. Everything suddenly had the feeling of adventure: what might we find as one long corridor lead to another in a place that could easily have doubled as Hogwarts! What sort of school food would we be force-fed in a dining room, which seemed unthinkably large to a worryingly small boy? How might I ever find my way to the right room at the right time when summoned by bells?

In no time at all I began to meet the boys who would be my constant companions in the years ahead. We were taken on long walks through the woods above the school and whenever I now inhale that peculiar smell that wet fallen leaves have in the autumn, I'm back there on a school walk. We all joined the Boy Scouts, which allowed us to sleep out in tents – boys learning to be men – and quickly mastering such irresistible skills as dipping twigs in a mixture of salted flour and water and browning them over the camp fire – a culinary delight second only to the daily breakfast treat of crisp deep-fried bread covered with lashings of thick cut marmalade.

We generally towed the line, and when we stepped over it, the housemaster would wreak his ghastly vengeance with six of the best across the backside from a swish of the cane; no chance there of sparing the rod and spoiling the child. We were too busy learning about life. We quickly settled into the routine and began to enjoy the privileged position we found ourselves in. For me, the most important moment came when the music master became aware that I had a voice, one which was loud, pushy and potentially melodious.

21

Music master Ernest Bradfield – 'Brad' to one and all – asked me if I had ever sung. When I admitted my fondness for singing hymns, he asked me to try singing a song. He was about to put together a school performance of Shakespeare's *A Midsummer Night's Dream* and he wondered if I might be able to contribute to the music. I've never quite worked out why – maybe it was all those years singing hymns in Poppleton Methodist chapel – but I was able to read the music he put in front of me and sing the song straight through. He recognised my seemingly God-given ability: I could clearly read music, sing in tune and make a lot of noise. In no time at all, thanks largely to a lack of serious opposition, I found myself top voice in the school choir and my musical journey through life had suddenly begun.

There were other ways in which Brad helped to nurture what seemed like my natural affinity with music. On one unforgettable occasion he invited me, along with a couple of kindred spirits, to watch on television something he thought might be both educational and entertaining. How right he turned out to be, giving me an early glimpse of what was to become a life-long passion for musical comedy. I remember sitting there howling with laughter as Hoovers and hose pipes played music alongside a symphony orchestra in the first of the famous Hoffnung concerts in London's Royal Festival Hall. In terms of its educational value, it must have been the first time I ever saw and heard a symphony orchestra, never dreaming that one day I would end up conducting one. 'Brad' seemed to me then like the oldest man in the world and having kept in touch with him right to the end of his long life, it occurs to me now that he must have been still in his early thirties at the time. But I remain eternally grateful to him for the encouragement he gave me, right from the start.

Another unforgettable experience engineered by 'Brad' came when he took three of us small boys to St Asaph Cathedral to hear a performance of Bach's *St. Matthew Passion*. Now that is a tall order for a twelve-year-old and could have put me off that sort of music for life; but the Evangelist on that night was the tenor Wilfred Brown and his wonderful way with words and his natural gift as a story-teller meant that, sitting there on the front row, I could not take my eyes or ears off this man, so riveted was I by the tale he unfolded. It began a love-affair with this music which lasts to this day, having had the privilege of conducting so many performances of that great work. What Bill Brown did with the text was an object-lesson in communication and one which I have never forgotten. As a singer and later on as a conductor, I used the lesson I had learned on that and many other occasions to great effect, particularly when working with young singers on the art of putting across the text. Only eight years later, as a Cambridge Choral Scholar, I found myself singing the part of Christus in Bach's *St. John Passion*, standing next to the same evangelist Bill Brown, reminding him of that St Asaph experience and starting a friendship which lasted until his untimely death. He was an inspiration indeed and his incomparable recording of Gerald Finzi's *Dies Natalis* remains my number one Desert Island Disc – the one I would keep if the other seven were washed away! His singing of those magical words of Thomas Traherne remains – and surely will remain unequalled.

I wouldn't call myself a model pupil at that age: I was far too busy enjoying life with the Irish Sea on one side and the north Welsh mountains on the other. The most outstanding memory of life in the classroom was when my form master rewrote new words to the old song *The animals came in one by one*, substituting for animals various boys in the class. I assume that my loudness of voice must have had something to do with it, for when he came to 'the second form came in three by three', he proved himself a model of prophesy when he wrote – and the class all sang – *Katie Kay of the BBC*!

Looking back on those prep school days it's an extraordinary thought that as young boys, un-chaperoned and unshielded, we Kay brothers would be dropped off at York station to catch the 10.10 train to Manchester – on our own – then walk the mile-long platform between the stations of Manchester Exchange and Victoria and only then would we be met by a member of the school staff who would take us and the rest of the boys joining there along the coastal ride to Colwyn Bay. In fact, even as young as six years old, when I first went to a pre-prep school in Green Hammerton – some way along the York to Harrogate road – I took the no. 74 bus – on my own – there and back each day. I'm not sure it would be so advisable these days.

Four years after starting at Rydal prep it was time to move on – upwards to the senior school and downwards towards the bottom end of Pwllycrochan Avenue. I was placed in School House, where my father and brother Barry had already spent their Rydal days and where brother Graham would follow. It is always a big moment in a boarding schoolboy's life when he moves from being top of the junior school to bottom of the senior, assuming once again the position of the lowest of the low. One of the first things that happened, perhaps inevitably, was that I auditioned for the school choir.

The Head of choir was sixth-former Richard Barraclough – as it happens, a fellow Yorkshireman – and it was his job to put me through the audition process. After a simple test, he couldn't think of any reason why I should not join the choir and my musical journey continued where it had left off up the road. I often wondered what might have happened had he turned me down! Twenty-five years later, when I was appointed Chorus Master to the Huddersfield Choral Society, there was the same Richard, first as Choir Secretary and then as President.

Music was not, of course, the only subject which fascinated me, though it went on playing the major role in my education. Inheriting perhaps my father's interest in amateur dramatics, I took part in many theatrical presentations – most notably in my final year – 1962. I cannot remember the name of the play, but the occasion is never to be forgotten as the adjudicator for the house drama competition was the already amazingly famous old boy of the school William Roache – well settled even then as Ken Barlow of *Coronation Street* (Jack Howarth, the Street's Albert Tatlock had also had a son at the school).

It was because Bill Roache had been at Rydal that we all watched the first episode of *Corrie* and became immediately hooked on the telly soap to end all soaps. This was the start of the 'swinging 60s' and already, Roache had long hair – not ridiculously so, but long enough to fall down over the collar of his shirt. The day after the drama competition in morning assembly, the Headmaster mentioned how proud we all were that so distinguished an old boy had honoured us with his presence, at the same time reminding us that if any one of us thought of growing his hair to a similar length, he should seriously think again!

The house singing competition was another opportunity to prove the quality of our voices. My father's brother uncle Eric had presented the school with the 'Kay Cup' for solo singing and there was no way we were not going to try for that one. In good time, both Graham and I managed to be the (I hope worthy) winners, keeping it in the family and bringing just a modicum of honour to our house as Trojans (the other houses being Barbarians, Crusaders and Corinthians).

One extra-curricular activity I shall never forget was a system whereby senior boys would visit the old and relatively infirm and try to brighten their lives with a little one-to-one. The best outcome of that was when my contemporary and kindred spirit Jeremy Birkett and I were given the opportunity to visit an elderly blind lady with the glorious name of Gertrude Sumner in order to read to her. We would take the bus up to Old Colwyn and make our way to her tiny terraced cottage in the hope of making her day. In the end, she always made ours, as she turned out to be an utterly adorable old girl with a determination to make our lives a great deal happier than hers.We did read to her, and she was very happy to be read to; but the highlight of our weekly visits was when she insisted that we enjoyed her sherry trifle. She would stand in the kitchen with a bottle in her hand, asking us if she had poured enough sherry into the trifle – not quite, we would add, in the hope that too much was as good as a feast! We would roll back to school – a Methodist School remember! – somewhat determined not to meet any member of the staff with a good sense of smell. It wasn't just the sherry trifle that made us look forward to our visits: we loved her to bits and if she got as much out of our weekly visits as we did, then she would have died happy. In fact, she was finally sent into a home on her 99th birthday and when I visited her the following day, I asked her how things were. "I can't stand it," she said, "the place is full of old people"!

Another fond memory concerns the school matron, a Hattie Jacques type whose remedy for almost every ailment was to apply what we called 'Sister's ink' – the dreaded gentian violet. It is hard to imagine what good it can possible have done when painted on to the offending part of the body, but matron never held back if there was a chance of adding a little colour to whatever the wound or ailment. Her predecessor at the prep school had insisted on inoculating all of us against Asian flu, which was rampant at the time. The result of that was that I caught flu immediately but built up a serious immunity (as apparently did all those who went through the same process in the early 50s) and at the time of writing – over sixty years later – I have never had flu since. As I became old enough to have free flu injections at 65 it was with some trepidation that I agreed to do so in case history should repeat itself. So far so good.

The two greatest influences on my senior school days were Headmaster Donald Hughes and Musical Director Percy Heywood. They were old friends, having met at Cambridge University and taught at the Leys School before ending up at Rydal. They had famously written a cod Gilbert and Sullivan musical all about their passion: cricket. It was called, in best Gilbertian fashion, *The Batsman's Bride*, or *The man who bowled the maiden over*. Hughes's words and Heywood's irresistibly tuneful melodies caught on at the time, so much so that the score was published by OUP and enjoyed considerable success. In fact, many years later

I discovered that a dear friend of ours in New Zealand – the wonderfully-named Dr Hylton Le Grice – told me that he had taken part in a production at King's College in Auckland at what must have been about the time the musical had first appeared.

It was Hughes and Heywood who nurtured the seed for my life-long fascination for words and music, ideally in perfect combination. Donald Hughes was pedantic about correctness in grammar, something which has stayed with me all my life. How he would have hated the way that even the BBC seems to care little these days for such things. He would never have considered splitting an infinitive, placing the word 'only' in the wrong part of the sentence, saying 'different to' referring to 'the only single criteria', failing to differentiate between 'like' and 'as', saying things like 'why does someone hit their partner?' and all the other ghastly grammatical errors seemingly acceptable these days. Call me a grumpy old man, but these things matter and I believe we all have to fight to keep our wonderful language intact. The Headmaster's secretary – one Hester Norris – was quite a character too, driving a yellow MGTF (I've wanted one ever since!) and having been the first woman to climb the Matterhorn.

Percy Heywood was the son of a former Bishop of Ely and had been a choral scholar at King's College in Cambridge in the 1930s. Unfortunately, he could not cope with the rigorous choir training technique of Boris Ord, the Director of Music, and left after a year to become organ scholar at neighbouring Trinity Hall. This meant that he could also concentrate on his beloved sport, something much more difficult as a King's choral scholar in view of the afternoon rehearsal and evensong schedule. Percy went on to be a 'Blue' in both cricket and rugby and this resulted in his being able to inspire hulking sporty types at Rydal to take part in supposedly 'sissy' things, like singing in the school concert choir. Rydal was a particularly fine rugby school: My father had been captain of rugby at the school which produced the famous rugby internationals Wilf Wooler and Bleddyn Williams.

The important thing for me is that Percy taught music almost one to one, aided by his essentially Welsh assistant Elias Walter Jones. At one stage, Donald Hughes wrote to my father suggesting that "Brian seems to have little interest in physics – or chemistry, geography and history. His interest centres totally on music: I suggest he gives up the former and concentrates on the latter." What an opportunity for me to stick to what really interested me and to develop the one educational strand which was clearly beginning to dominate my life.

And so it was that Percy suggested that I might try for a Cambridge choral scholarship and name King's as my first choice. The idea seemed somewhat far-fetched, but as it meant going to Cambridge for a day and missing rugby (for which I had not inherited Father's skill or enthusiasm) I agreed to give it a go, along with fellow students David Humphreys and Geoffrey Harvey. So, in September 1962 Percy drove the three of us to Cambridge on what I imagined would be a fruitless mission. The system was easy: put down, in order of preference, the colleges in which you would like to be considered as a member of the choir. As mine was King's, I was given a room in the college and spent a couple of days in what was clearly an academic wonderland, mainly trying to work out what on earth I was doing there.

Then came the morning when I was summoned to take the audition. This was to be taken by the Director of Music David Willcocks. I entered the rather musty room filled with somewhat shadowy, faceless dons, many of whom would one day end up being my friends. Mr. Willcocks (as he then was, later Sir David) asked me to sing the bass part of a motet by Thomas Tomkins. I had been well enough brought up to do what I was asked and so I did. He then asked me to do the same in Stravinsky's anthem *The Dove Descending*. This was a more daunting task, but somehow I was equipped to make a reasonably decent fist of it.

After a few simple ear-tests, the last part of the audition was to sing an aria in the King's chapel. The very idea of singing in that iconic building was beyond every possible imagination for a boy from Upper Poppleton but that was the requirement. As it happens, the chapel was closed for renovation and I was told to report to the chapel of St John's – arch rival to King's and a short walk down Trinity Street.

The organ scholar at St John's at that time was Brian Runnett, clearly a star in the making whose life was tragically cut short in a motor accident eight years later. He accompanied me in the aria *Mighty Lord* from Bach's *Christmas Oratorio*. We aspirants were asked to report to the Junior Combination Room at King's where the results of the committee would be announced. There were Eton and Winchester boys and many others from privileged musical backgrounds who might well have assumed that choral scholarship places were theirs for the taking. We rather more modest hopefuls approached the JCR meeting with never a serious hope that our lives were about to change somewhat dramatically. Among my fellow hopefuls were Alan Opie (who was to become one of our leading operatic baritones) and Robert Key, a future Minister of State. Each of them was given a choral scholarship. Then came the big moment: the Dean of King's, Alec Vidler, thanked us all for coming and then said: "These are our decisions: King's Kay, St. John's Humphreys". Neither David nor I can remember the rest as we were in a state of total disbelief. Our little Methodist school in North Wales had beaten the big boys and confounded our hopes and beliefs. David Willcocks walked over to me, shook me by the hand and said (exact words I shall never forget): "So much looking forward to having you with us. Now go and get another A level." That was all I had to do, though it proved anything but easy.

The academic requirements in those far off days were far more modest than they are now and choral scholarships were a good way – like sporting prowess – of by-passing the need for academic excellence. Quite rightly those days are long gone. But without that slightly open door my life would have taken a very different turn. I found a phone box in market square and passed on the good news to my incredulous but delighted parents, before contacting the school to make sure that our good fortune would be made known in the following morning's assembly.

CHAPTER FOUR

And places where they sing

*"Undergraduates owe their happiness chiefly to the fact
that they are no longer at school. The nonsense which was
knocked out of them at school is all put gently back at Oxford
or Cambridge."* **Max Beerbohm in** *Zuleika Dobson*

*"Prime Minister, we're going to have to do something
about the universities – both of them."*
Sir Humphrey in Yes Minister!

There was a major problem for me. As a Yorkshire Methodist
I had never sung a psalm, I didn't know the form of Evensong,
Matins or Eucharist, and I was about to join a choir famous
throughout the world for its singing of those church services.
It was naturally assumed that I would have more than an
inkling as to how to proceed. This was a serious worry, for
me certainly, as it would have been for David Willcocks, had
he but known of my ignorance in such matters. It was time for
action and I did what little boys from Upper Poppleton were
not expected to do: I dialled the phone number (surprisingly
not ex-directory) for York's musical 'Mr Big' – Dr Francis
Jackson, the celebrated organist and director of music at York
Minster. I explained my situation and asked – straight out – if
I could possibly spend two weeks sitting among the basses
in the Minster choir, in order to learn my trade and quickly.

He was only too happy to oblige and so it was that a couple of possible career-saving weeks were spent singing between Andrew Carter (then a bass in the choir and later a distinguished choral composer and dear friend) and a retired miner called Fred Jones. The experience I gained in those two weeks was both invaluable and hugely enjoyable and my gratitude to Francis and his jolly bunch of singers who made this young interloper feel so welcome remains incalculable. I was thus able to turn up at King's with far more confidence and know-how and able to hold my own in the distinguished company of the established choral scholars and choristers and, of course, the illustrious Director of Music. I was delighted to be able to remind Francis of his major part in my life when he celebrated his 100th birthday in 2017.

It is an extraordinary moment when school finishes and university begins: that sense of relative freedom and of life having moved on a notch more than makes up for the fact that once again one is starting at the bottom of the pile, hoping that the only way is up. I was one of three new King's Choral Scholars in 1963 along with the counter-tenor Martin Lane and the tenor Neil Jenkins, together with a young first-year organ scholar from Watford Grammar School called Andrew Davis (later Sir Andrew).

We were about to embark on three of the most amazing years of our young lives. It is hard to explain the feelings one has when singing in that choir, in that building and under the direction of one of the world's leading choral directors. Even now, more than fifty years later, those feelings come flooding back every time I enter the building: the dark winter afternoons and evenings spent in the candle-lit womb of the chapel, long before general electric lighting was installed; the privilege of such a working environment, with an acoustic to die for, in spite of the difficulties of reverberation; the sense of being part of a tradition which reached back to the 15th century; the knowledge that you were only ever as good as your last sung note and that the ears of all – most particularly the remarkable ears of the Musical Director – were upon you every time you opened your mouth.

The choir consists of sixteen boy choristers and fourteen undergraduate adult voices, twelve of them choral scholars with two extra bass 'volunteers' – auditioned voices which may or may not belong to a member of the college, but which hopefully add extra warmth at the bottom of the choir in an acoustic – like all the great cathedrals and college chapels – famous for favouring upper voices.

The system for choral scholars was basically straight forward: each of us would go to the chapel in the morning and collect his pile of music for the afternoon service. It was then his responsibility to spend time studying the music and thus being in a suitable state of preparation for the afternoon rehearsal, which began each day at ten past four. Naturally enough, one was never allowed to be late for rehearsal or service and one was not expected to make mistakes, however difficult the music may be.

In rehearsal, if you happened to go wrong, you were asked to raise your hand, so that Mr. Willcocks knew that you knew that you had made a mistake, thus enabling him not necessarily to stop the rehearsal every time he heard something inaccurate. If, on the other hand, you made a mistake in service, you had to proceed to the organ loft before leaving the chapel and grovel your apology. This happened to me on one notable occasion and when I explained to David, he admitted that he had, of course noticed and added: "Dear Brian, don't worry: everyone makes a mistake – ONCE!"

One inevitable fact about the choir at King's is that a large percentage of choral scholars and choristers leave the choir at the end of each academic year. This means that every October, the Director of Music has to start again with virtually a new choir and to work fast, in order that just three months later, the choir is on top form for the famous Christmas Eve Festival of Nine Lessons and Carols, which has been broadcast globally since 1928.

That service is, for so many people all over the world, the start of Christmas, that heart-stopping moment when one chorister sings – all alone and unaccompanied – the first verse of *Once in Royal David's City*. For those of us singing in the choir at that service, it is a moment of great tension, though as soon as we all join in the second verse, it is possible to relax and enjoy simply singing another of the many services which form the basis of our life at the time. Nonetheless it is impossible not to spare a thought that so many millions world-wide are hanging on our every note. In my final year – Christmas 1965 – David Willcocks asked me to sing the baritone solo in the carol *The Three Kings* – a gift for a baritone and a privilege to be asked to sing it. In the morning rehearsal for the BBC, David asked me to make sure that, when the time came, I should stand on my kneeler, in order that I might be a little closer to the microphone to help the balance of my singing against the might of the King's choir. That was no problem, until the moment came, late on in the broadcast service. What we had failed to realise was that by the time that carol came round, it would already be dark and that with only candlelight to guide me on my way, I would find myself holding a copy which was *above* the candles and therefore impossible to see. Fortunately, I knew the carol by heart and was able to muddle through, though it was a relief to think that only 800 million people were listening at the time!

Each year during the Christmas Eve service one of the men has to read the choral scholar's lesson. Again, in 1965, I was asked to do this on the televised service and of course I was delighted to do so. The following morning, our Irish verger greeted me with appreciation of my reading: "your voice, if I may say so," he said, "has a certain *residence* to it"! A lived-in quality, I suppose, though I knew what he was trying to say and was grateful for the thought.

For only the second time, television came to King's for the Carol Service in 1963, my first year, and that added a certain *frisson* to proceedings. It was fascinating to see how television – still in its relative infancy – coped with the cosiness of the choir stalls, where most of the singing inevitably took place. These days, with the advance in technology, it is possible to turn the whole chapel into a variable stage set, with cameras wherever the director wants, though things were not so advanced back in those comparatively dark ages. But the very idea of people being able to see what they had been able only to hear for so many years was a significant and welcome advance.

We made LP recordings during the summer when we had returned during our university holidays to keep the music running. This was another privilege and one we always looked forward to. It used to make me laugh whenever we made a recording of Christmas carols while June was busting out all over. This was inevitable in view of having to get the recordings ready for the Christmas market all those months later. But it amused me to think that when tourists came to King's and stood outside the chapel listening through the walls, they must have thought that if the choir was busy singing Christmas carols in June, no wonder they sounded so good by Christmas Eve!

I had decided to read music for my degree, which meant that every day as I sang works from so many different centuries, I was constantly learning, on top of the weekly routine of lectures and tutorials. On one shameful occasion when I woke on a Monday to realise that I had not written an essay for my supervision that morning, I hurriedly took down Grout's *History of Western Music* and copied out large chunks of it, in the hope of getting away with it.

When I presented my humble efforts to my tutor, Philip Radcliffe, he quietly read through what I had written and did indeed look impressed. He then calmly walked over to his bookcase, took down his own copy of Grout's book and turned to the appropriate page remarkably quickly. As my worries began to mount, he read quietly through what Grout had written and without a flicker said simply: "I think you'll find that Grout agrees with you" before adding: "a remarkably similar turn of phrase too if I may say so." Nothing else was said. It was not necessary as I had been well and truly rumbled, though one of the benefits of education is that one learns from one's mistakes: I never tried that particular ploy again. Now, every time I look at Grout's book on the shelf in my shed I still shiver in appropriate embarrassment!

One year at Christmas we choral scholars were invited (I was never sure why) to attend, with free tickets, the opening night of the pantomime at the Arts Theatre. This featured the popular entertainer and poet manqué Cyril Fletcher (he of the 'odd odes' on Esther Ranzen's popular television programme *That's Life*) and we thought we should accept and relive memories of childhood, at the same time as having a good laugh. This we certainly did and howled the place down: so much so that this became an annual event, our enthusiastic (though somewhat deprecating) response having set the panto off to such a good start.

One particularly delightful side-line to our normal duties was when six of we King's Choral Scholars enjoyed singing light-hearted close harmony arrangements at parties, at the famous Footlights Club and on university rag days. Generations of former choral scholars had collected such arrangements and handed them down from year to year. Little did we realise then that our doing so would eventually lead to our forming a group that would (with gradual replacement of members) go on to sing all over the world for over half a century. When we began singing regularly as a group we gave ourselves the distinctly unmanageable name of the *Schola Cantorum pro musica profana in Cantabridgiense*! Not surprisingly, and certainly wisely, we quickly changed that to *The King's Singers* and the rest, as they say, is history.

Eight of the choral scholars joined the King's College boat club and formed a choir boat in the May Bumps. Although we had a pretty poor technique at the oars, we all shared a corporate sense of rhythm and, setting off at about 120 crotchets to the minute, we bumped every boat in sight – hence the old oar with our painted names which still hangs proudly in my garden shed/study at home.

We would stand on the riverbank before each race and sing (naughty, but nice!) *Forth in thy name, O Lord, we row*. News of this got round and featured in William Hickey's column in a national newspaper. We received letters from 'disgusted of Tunbridge Wells' or wherever (and quite rightly too) for abusing our great privilege by changing the words of a well-known hymn to suit our somewhat juvenile pursuits. But the exercise and the camaraderie of eight men in a boat takes some beating, even if the good it did for our bodies was soon undone after each outing by a few pints down at the old Bull and Bush.

Each year, on Lammas Day, the college provided for the Director of Music and the choral scholars a seven-course breakfast, which we enjoyed in a private room at the college, well out of sight of our fellow students. It was a gargantuan affair, ending with a pint of particularly strong Audit Ale. As we drank the amber nectar, David Willcocks, with immaculate timing, would say; "Anyone for a game of squash?"

His own technique was not all that good, but he was so quick, he could get to wherever the ball was and beat everyone in sight; all, that is, with the exception of choral scholar and later my King's Singer colleague Alastair Hume, who happened also to be captain of the University Squash team and – as a Blue – the only one of us who could give David a run for his money, even after such a massive meal.

The choral scholars always sat together on the same table in hall for the gown-wearing dinners which were still in those days very formal affairs with a long Latin grace and procession of distinguished Fellows to the High Table. One of our fellow students – intensely musical though not reading music – was a young man called John Eliot Gardiner and he rightly criticised the fourteen of us for keeping ourselves to ourselves, rather than using this great opportunity to mingle with people who were reading other subjects, thereby far

39

more greatly enriching our privileged education. Everyone remembers where he was when President Kennedy was assassinated and sure enough, we choral scholars were sitting at our usual table and talking to ourselves.

That same John Eliot Gardiner decided to put on a performance of Monteverdi's *1610 Vespers*, a work of which he had – already as an undergraduate – made his own edition. He assembled assorted friends, choral scholars and singing colleagues from elsewhere, and was given permission by the college to put the performance on in the chapel. We King's choral scholars were naturally invited to swell the ranks of the altos, tenors and basses and on a never-to-be-forgotten day in 1964, the performance took place. I must honestly admit that the excitement of the preparations for what turned out to be a remarkable display of student music-making exceeded anything I had ever experienced before: a Damascene moment for me if ever there was one.

The performance was outstanding and it was followed by another in neighbouring Ely Cathedral. What might have been a one-off event ended up being anything but, as Gardiner called us the Monteverdi Choir and fifty years later, it remains one of the finest choirs in the world. John Eliot knew exactly what he wanted to do with music which, in those days, was rarely performed and in so doing, he sowed the seeds for a professional choir which has employed and doubtless inspired generations of young singers, only too keen to be part of a musical outfit of such distinction. Little did we imagine, on that day – March 5th 1964 – that many of us would meet again fifty years later (March 5th 2014) to recreate the magic under Sir John Eliot's masterly baton.

That was only one part of the mind-bogglingly rich quantity and quality of music available to us all in Cambridge at the time. Many of my contemporaries had been members of the famous National Youth Orchestra and they would get together on rag days and similar occasions and sit anywhere – in the college grounds, the streets, the pubs – and make music, giving ad hoc and masterly performances of the Mozart wind serenades and much more besides. Having so much enjoyed playing together in this way, many of them stayed together on leaving Cambridge and formed the London Sinfonietta, arguably the world's finest ensemble for performing contemporary music.

Next door to King's, at Clare College, a fellow undergraduate reading music had already started on what became his lifelong career as a composer, principally of choral music: none other than John Rutter and I can well remember sitting in my study one morning pretending to work, when one of his choral scholars from Clare knocked on my door, breathless that I should hear a tape the choir had just made of some of John's carols. The first few notes I heard made me sit up and recognise immediately that this was the breath of fresh air which carol singing needed, as the words and notes of John's *Shepherd's pipe carol* filled the air – a recording with orchestra which the Clare choir had made and which is still very much available – now on CD – fifty years later. We were all astonished at John's skill as composer, orchestrator, choral director and first-class musician, all the more so as that first carol I heard had been written while he was still at school.

Among many other musical movers and shakers was our King's Organ scholar Andrew Davis (like Gardiner, later knighted for his distinguished services to music). On one typical occasion, he asked me if I was doing anything after college dinner. He had got together a group of wind players and booked the Music School concert hall to make music and was putting together a programme at this eleventh hour. "Do you know?" he asked me, "Michael Tippett's Songs for Ariel for baritone and wind ensemble?" I admitted my ignorance, but this was not enough to deter him. He had the necessary wind players and the music and all he needed was a baritone who could sing them without rehearsal.

Such was the fearlessness of youth and the God-given talents we all had we were able to perform these three far-from-simple songs on one quick run-through. This was absolutely typical of the way things were done and gave us all a tremendous opportunity to enrich our music lives, thanks to people like Andrew and to the trust we all had for each other that we could bring it off without too much embarrassment.

Other fellow students who worked similar feats of magic were two who were clearly fascinated by the world of 'early music' – still in those days something of a rarity. It came as no surprise that they both went on to have a massive influence world-wide as the explosion of interest in so-called 'stone-age music' spread across the globe. David Munrow and Christopher Hogwood, like Andrew Davis and John Eliot Gardiner, simply made things happen and gave the rest of us the opportunities to sow seeds for our own musical futures. David wasn't even reading music, but his boundless enthusiasm was quite overwhelming. He could produce musical sounds out of blowing on a blade of grass, so no wonder all those exotic early instruments appealed to him so much – he simply had to play whatever he could lay his hands on.

42

Mind you, the livin' wasn't always easy: in my first year I had 'digs' in the Garden Hostel of King's College – a short walk across 'the backs'. In my second year I moved into college and into a ghastly area of the College known as Chetwynd Court. I had a bedroom and a sitting room but had to walk across the open courtyard – in all weathers – to a bathroom, and believe me, the one I had was as basic as they come.

Just like the boy scouts at school we were – in theory – learning to be men. There was a piano in my room – a perk for choral scholars – and it was against a wall which made the rest of the room basically unworkable. I tried to move it! It weighed a ton. I simply could not even lever it away from the wall, let alone heave it to another part of the room. I called the piano movers and they humiliated me by asking where I'd like it, lifting it off the ground, holding it there in mid-air and asking 'where would you like it, Gov?' Luckily for succeeding generations, those rooms have long since been demolished.

It was not surprising that we King's choral scholars should be given ample opportunity to develop our skills as solo singers. Many of the colleges put on concerts and would invite us to take part, helping us hugely to gain experience in standing at the front of the platform and contributing to the performance of great choral and orchestral works. On one notable occasion I was asked to sing the part of Christus in Bach's *St. Matthew Passion* which took place in King's chapel. What made this a somewhat daunting prospect for me was that the tenor who had been booked to sing the role of Evangelist was none other than Benjamin Britten's partner Peter Pears.

In rehearsal (a February performance) he kindly warned me that it was likely to be extremely cold the following day and that I might be well advised to go across the road to A.E.Clothier and buy a pair of *Long Johns*. I gratefully complied, assuming that this was advice based on many years of experience. All went well until I stood for my first recitative as Christus, only to discover on standing that the Long Johns had stuck to the trousers of my tailcoat and exposed a great expanse of white leg! The entire recitative was spent trying to shake the trouser leg down in the hope of regaining my dignity! I never wore them again.

As I mentioned earlier, I was also lucky enough to sing the Christus part in the *St. John Passion* on another occasion, also in the chapel, when the Evangelist was the same Wilfred Brown who had so fascinated me in the St. Asaph performance of the *St Matthew* all those years before. He was tremendously supportive and just before the performance he showed me the inside front cover of his exceptionally well-used copy. There was a letter from his father, written many years previously, wishing him well in his chosen career. I remember it ended with the words: "thine, Dad". Bill said he never sang a performance without re-reading it as an inspiration.

Bill Llewellyn, Director of Music at Charterhouse, told me that he had once engaged Bill Brown to sing two performances of the *St. Matthew* two Sundays running at the school. At the first, Bill proudly announced that this was his 149th performance as Evangelist. The following Sunday Bill Llewellyn suggested some celebration for this, Bill's 150th, only to be told that this was the 154th: he had sung four performances that week between the two Charterhouse outings.

Back at King's, there was always a large and interested crowd at evensong, keen to hear this famous choir for real, rather than on radio and recordings. On one occasion we couldn't help noticing that the congregation included a young Richard Briers, already famous for his many wonderful TV programmes like *The Good Life*. He was there in Cambridge to appear at the Arts Theatre in *Arsenic and Old Lace*, alongside Sybil Thorndyke, her husband Lewis Casson and Athene Seyler. On leaving the chapel I plucked up courage and asked him if he might care to join us for a drink in my room, which was conveniently close to the chapel. He seemed happy to do so and out came the bottles of cheap South African sherry. Along with other Choral Scholars, I spent a very jolly time hearing all sorts of stories about his fascinating life in the theatre. It was only when someone asked what time his performance was due to start that he realised he had outstayed his welcome and had five minutes to get to the theatre for curtain-up.

Well fuelled by sherry, we all made our way to our audience seats and were amazed by his performance, clearly un-fuddled by the experience or the sherry. Years later, by which time he had a small house in the Cotswolds near to ours, I found myself standing behind the same Richard Briers in the queue at the local butchers. I again plucked up courage and asked him if he remembered the Cambridge occasion. "Oh my God," he replied: "it was you!" He had clearly not forgotten.

Among the distinguished Fellows of King's – many of them given rooms for life in return for their unique distinction – was the novelist E.M. (Morgan) Forster. He would frequently attend musical events in the College, particularly if an orchestral concert included what he once told me was one of his favourite works – César Franck's *Symphonic Variations*. On one notable occasion, my old pal Tom Wheare and I asked Forster if he would care to take tea with us when convenient. He gracefully accepted and we spent a fascinating afternoon chatting about everything under the sun, including his working relationship with Benjamin Britten. At one point, he suddenly announced that he had had a dream the previous night and had written it down on a piece of paper. Could this, we wondered, be the start of a new epic novel, with us in at the beginning? After much fidgeting and fumbling, he found the scrap of paper in a pocket and slowly read out: "Let us taste of Eastern promise, my dear". That was it, and it clearly left little room for development. But he was a great man and it was a privilege to be in his company. I still think back to that time whenever I re-read one of his novels.

Talking of Britten, he came to King's during my last year and, together with David Willcocks, conducted a performance of his recently composed *War Requiem* – to me a work of genius and very much his choral and orchestral masterpiece. Peter Pears (for whom they were written) sang the tenor solos and the soprano was Heather Harper, who had famously stood in for the first performance in Coventry Cathedral when the Russians refused Galina Vishnevskaya an exit visa. Heather was wearing a hat, as women did in church in those days (even in the 'swinging 60s') and a pretty odd-looking one at that. Years later, when I was presenting the *Cardiff Singer of the World* competition for BBC TV, she was one of the jury. After a few drinks and a good dinner, I mentioned to her that I had a photo I had taken of her and Pears outside the chapel of

King's. She begged me to let her have a copy, as she had sung with him so many times and had no photo of the two of them together. I said I would try and dig it out but warned her that she was wearing a rather ghastly hat. Once home, I found the photo, had it copied and sent it to her. She was thrilled and wrote that it was already framed and on her piano, adding "you were right about the hat!"

It is hard to put into words the feeling of singing in the King's choir at that supremely impressionable age, the sensation of standing where hundreds of years of choral scholars have been lucky enough to share the same good fortune, contributing each in his own way to a tradition which began way back in the middle of the fifteenth century. But a wonderful feeling it undoubtedly is and certainly was in my case. It reminds me of my asking James Galway what it was like being a member of the Berlin Philharmonic in the days of Herbert von Karajan, when Jimmy was principal flute: "like being part of a Rolls Royce engine" was his enthusiastic reply.

Not only was it an immense privilege simply being there, it also sowed so many seeds for what might hopefully lie ahead as a professional musician: that sense of discipline, the camaraderie, the warm glow of being a member of a tightly-knit team, the art of self-sublimation to the general good, learning how always to give of your best regardless of how you might be feeling, and the sheer thrill of being able to use your gifts in the service of music. All these qualities remain with me to this day and my three years at King's were the best possible schooling I could ever have hoped for.

With so much music of top quality all around us in Cambridge, not to mention the many college choirs which were keeping going the great tradition of choral services day in and day out, it is hardly surprising that so many of us felt inspired to think seriously about making music for the rest of our working lives. Having said that, I was by no means sure in 1966 what might be in store when my three immensely privileged years at King's were over. But one had to do something and go somewhere – where better than the City of Dreaming Spires?

Intermission One

It's the funny things that brighten up our lives and for musicians, there's never any shortage. Like the time that great conductor John Pritchard went to Buckingham Palace to receive his knighthood from Her Majesty the Queen. He was on his way to his holiday home and he knew that half-decent toilet rolls were almost impossible to come by in his part of France. So he wisely filled the boot of his car with a plentiful supply. He arrived at the Palace to be faced with inevitable security checks and as the officer in charge opened the boot of Sir John's car and saw his remarkable collection of loo rolls he was moved to ask – in that wonderful way policemen have always had in questioning someone: "Nervous are we Sir?"

The tenor Ian Partridge told me the story of a very distinguished bass singer who was to sing the role of Elijah in Mendelssohn's famous oratorio. This was in the north of England and unfortunately, this particular soloist was rather fond of the sauce. The performance was accompanied by organ alone and when it came to that wonderful bass aria *It is enough*, the singer had already spent the interval filling himself with Dutch courage. The organist played over the intro to the aria and the singer failed to come in on cue.

The organist decided it was best to have another go, though sadly with the same result. Having assumed that 'third-time lucky' might work, he bravely tried again and to save the situation, the great Isobel Baillie (soprano soloist on that occasion) graciously got up and sang it for him! 'It is enough' was clearly not writ large in that particular singer's vocabulary!

A critic was once asked to review yet again a play he'd seen several times and had loathed more on each occasion. He thought he would give it one more try. In the end, his review consisted of simply this: "Hebrews, chapter 13, verse 8". Everyone rushed to his Bible to see what the reviewer had in mind and sure enough read the famous line: "Jesus Christ, the same yesterday, today and for ever".

Our dear pianist friend George (later Sir George) Shearing was blind from birth but took his disability lightly. On a television programme he was asked if he'd been blind all his life and he answered: "not yet"! In the days when you used to be able to take a guide dog on a plane in America, his journey to California was interrupted by a re-fuelling stop mid-west. The pilot told George that he need not disembark with the other passengers but added that, no doubt, his dog would like to do what a dog likes to do. George gratefully accepted the situation and the captain did the honours. The dog returned and settled down and George prepared for the continuation of the journey. There was clearly a delay and when George asked the steward what the problem was, he was told that the other passengers were refusing to re-board the plane as they'd just seen the pilot walking around the airport with a guide dog!

The great composer and pianist Rachmaninov was accompanying a famous violist in a concert in New York's incomparable Carnegie Hall. This particular player prided himself on never using music, preferring to be more impressive by always playing by heart. He had therefore learned the new work which Rachmaninov had written for him. All went well in the first movement but in the slow central section the player suffered a senior moment and lost his way. Still playing – making it up in the composer's romantic style – he wandered over to the piano and in a stage whisper asked: "where are we?" Rachmaninov replied: "Carnegie Hall"! When Rachmaninov died, the mourners at his funeral were invited to file past his open coffin. Those included Sir John Barbirolli, who couldn't help noticing that "he looked a lot happier in death than he ever did in life"!

As part of my duties as Principal Conductor of The Really Big Chorus I'm lucky enough to conduct concerts two or three times a year in London's Royal Albert Hall, always with a cast of thousands. Four thousand singers converge in that great gladiatorial ring every Advent Sunday to perform – without rehearsal – Handel's *Messiah*. One year we decided to see if people would come and sing Karl Jenkins' much-loved Mass for Peace: *The Armed Man*. Three thousand said yes, including a group of schoolgirls from Northern Ireland. I stood on a podium at the back of the arena with the Promenaders' area full of a massive orchestra. The choir reached up the stage on either side of the mighty organ, halfway round the hall from floor to ceiling and the Irish girls were on the top shelf to my left. Amazingly enough, they had learned the entire one and a quarter hour work by heart and had not even brought copies of the music with them. After the performance I walked through the stage door to find them standing there in their little black frocks, "You're the Irish girls" I fondly suggested. "We are that too", came the reply. "It was so good having you there", I added, "knowing the entire work by heart, as you were the only people who watched the beat throughout". "Great," they said: "who are you?"

Then there was the conductor who was talking to a particularly non-musical friend who found his company somewhat unsatisfactory. They were chatting quite happily about obesity and diet. This prompted the conductor to ask his friend what he thought might be the ideal weight for a conductor. His friend's reply: "two and a half pounds, including the urn!"

On one occasion, when I was suggesting to the music committee of the Leith Hill Musical Festival which pieces we might offer for the choral competition the following year, I mentioned a madrigal by Richard Edwards with the rather unusual title *In going to my naked bed*. My predecessor and fellow committee member Bill Llewellyn always had some amusing anecdote about almost anything and he wasn't going to miss this one! He reminded us all that years ago he had received from a London music publisher a list of available madrigals, including, as the brochure said: *In going to my naked bed (with or without accompaniment)*!

When William Walton's ballet *The Wise Virgins*, based on arrangements he made of music from Bach's cantatas, was in rehearsal, there was some doubt as to whether or not the preparations for the premier would be completed in time. The posters which advertised the opening night simply referred to *The Wise Virgins (subject to alteration)!*

On one of the annual occasions at the Leith Hill Musical Festival when I conducted a performance of Bach's *St. Matthew Passion*, the massed choir had been prepared (in my absence on an annual visit to New Zealand) by Richard Stangroom, famous in the area as an outstanding conductor himself. He was a distinguished looking gentleman with a grey beard, and having trained the choir for this particular performance, he was given a seat on the front row of the gallery. At the end of the performance, I turned to gesture to him, so that he could take his well-earned bow as Chorus Master. On leaving the hall, an elderly lady was overheard saying to her friend: "and wasn't it lovely having the composer in the audience"!

On another occasion, when I was presenting my weekly BBC Radio 3 programme *Brian Kay's Sunday Morning* – 'live' from a hotel in Exeter – I put on the next CD and went, as they say, to press the flesh, talking to members of the audience and networking hard on behalf of the Beeb. A lady stopped me in my tracks and said how much she enjoyed my Radio 4 music programmes on Saturday nights. "But", she added, "I have a problem, 'cos Saturday is my bath night, see, and I always turn on the taps just as your programme's about to start; so would you mind always starting with something loud, otherwise I can't hear it." Oh the joys of one-to-one broadcasting!

Another lady wrote to me saying that "like everyone else" she listened to Alistair Cooke on a Sunday morning on BBC Radio 4, coming over to *Brian Kay's Sunday Morning* on Radio 3 the moment he had finished his *Letter from America*. "The trouble is," she went on, "you're always in the middle of a piece of music and I've no idea what it is until you tell me at the end; so would you mind always starting a new piece just after Alistair Cooke has finished, so I know what I'm listening to?"

I was interviewing Sir Thomas Armstrong, the former Director of the Royal Academy of Music, for a television programme celebrating his 90th birthday. He couldn't resist telling me about the time he was asked to be an adjudicator at the Moscow Piano Competition. He gladly accepted the invitation and was duly visited at his flat in London some weeks before the competition by some heavy Russian officials keen to make sure everything would go according to plan – even to the extent that, as they said to Sir Thomas: "We understand the winner is to be a man called Ashkenazy"!

That campest of comedians Frankie Howerd was cast, perhaps surprisingly, as the drunken jailer Frosch in a London production of Johann Strauss's opera *Die Fledermaus*. As Howerd was making tea for the prisoner, he milked it – the scene and the tea – for so long that a bejewelled Glyndebourne-type lady in the third row shouted out: "For goodness sake get on with it". There's no way Howerd was going to be upstaged by this particular heckler so he staggered to the front of the platform, stared at her in his unfriendliest fashion and boldly suggested: "Shut your posh gob, lady: I know your sort – all mink and no knickers"! How the orchestra ever managed to play anything after that is hard to imagine.

André Previn told a marvellous story about his association with the Vienna Philharmonic Orchestra. He thought that with such a world-beating string sound, they were sure to know the Vaughan Williams ravishing *Fantasia on a theme by Thomas Tallis*. He was amazed to discover that they did not and programmed it for them to play at the earliest opportunity. They were, of course, knocked out by the beauty of the music and asked Previn: "Did he write anything else?" One of the players even asked: "This guy Tom Tallis, was he a friend of Vaughan Williams?" Ah well, they are very good at playing Strauss waltzes.

I've never liked any feeling of pomposity in music or musical presentation, ever since I saw Percy Grainger's wonderfully unstuffy way with performance instructions – calling chamber music 'room music' for example and instead of *accelerando poco a poco* saying 'faster, lots'. William Walton enjoyed having a go at that sort of thing too, giving a mood-marking to one of his stirring marches: *con prosciutto, agnello e confitura di fragile*: sounds impressive, though all it means is 'with ham, lamb and strawberry jam'!

CHAPTER FIVE

The Other Place

By 1966, a tradition had developed whereby 'retiring' King's Choral Scholars would 'put off the evil day', enjoying more time at tax-payers' expense by spending another glorious year at Oxford and studying for a Diploma in Education. The tradition was so well established that when my turn came, it was relatively easy to gain a place on the course, with the absolute intention that I would end up being a teacher. The added bonus was that there was an open gateway to sing in the choir of New College in order to earn one's keep.

And so it was that I ended up in Oxford, determined to continue a university existence while thinking that I could bring to the Oxford choral scene some of the experience I had gained at King's: oh the arrogance of youth. It was instantly fascinating to compare the two university cities, each in its way unique, bearing in mind that I was joining the Oxford fraternity having already had the experience of three years at Cambridge. It was a joy to find myself in a new, if similar environment, with the pressure of gaining a degree already behind me.

My old friend from Cambridge – Tom Wheare, who had been a bass volunteer in the King's choir with me, and who was to end up years later as Headmaster of Bryanston School – came with me to Oxford to study for his Dip. Ed.

His father – Sir Kenneth Wheare – happened that year to be Oxford's Vice Chancellor and Rector of Exeter College. So, I was lucky enough to find myself with some of the finest 'digs' in Oxford, in a spare bedroom at the Rector's lodgings in Exeter College.

My enjoyment at being in Oxford was greatly enhanced by the fact that not only was I singing in the famous New College choir, but that also I found myself deputising for a bass in Christ Church Cathedral, who was taking time off ill. So, along with the counter-tenor James Bowman, I managed two evensongs a day: Christ Church at five minutes past five and New College at six o'clock – having run down the High Street between – before the two of us ended up at seven o'clock in the snug bar of the King's Arms – every night for a year! What a life.

The teacher-training year fell into three parts: the first and third terms consisted of lectures and tutorials. Our psychology lecturer – one Sprent by name – began the first lecture of the third term (after we had all been off to many parts of the country for teaching practice) with the word 'and', as if we had deserted him mid-sentence at the end of the first term. I wish I could remember more about him and his lectures.

The middle term, as I said, was spent in the gory business of facing classes of pupils and as I was, during that year, singing in those two college choirs, it was not possible for me to be sent to some far-flung part of the country to try my hand at actual teaching. Instead, I was assigned to Magdalen College School – then as now among the finest in the country and seemingly stuffed with dons' incredibly bright offspring. The school also supplied the boy choristers for the college's fine choir.

My problem was that my Cambridge degree was in music and the Dip Ed course did not allow for the teaching of music at that time. When I arrived at Magdalen College School, the Headmaster asked what else I could do apart from music and as I could speak reasonable English, he decided that that was what I would teach. Oh Dear. First off, he sent me into the lions' den: Advanced English to the sixth form where the boys were studying Shakespeare's *Anthony and Cleopatra*.

As I entered my first session with those terrifyingly bright boys clearly longing to make my life a misery, I started by bravely asking if any boy would like to summarise the play for me. "Sir hasn't read it" came the reply and I had to resort to a non-existent plan B. We staggered along as best we could – bearing in mind that I must have been only three or four years older than those highly intellectual sixth formers – though this was clearly going to be an uphill struggle. In my own schooldays, I had never looked forward quite so much to the bell which indicated the end of the lesson. Although I did not greatly enjoy that teaching practice experience, it taught me enough to be able to pass my Dip Ed and to find myself at the end of the academic year officially qualified to teach. It is greatly to the advantage of generations of potential pupils that I never had to resort to standing in front of a classroom again.

I was able to enjoy the continuing musical experience which I had begun in Cambridge, by singing as much as I could whenever asked. It was during my teaching practice term that my old King's colleague, the tenor Neil Jenkins, asked me to sing the bass solos in a performance of Michael Tippett's *A Child of our Time* which was being performed at Marlborough College, where the director of music was Neil's old school musical director from Dean Close in Cheltenham, Graham Smallbone.

I was busy with my teaching term and singing in those two college choirs, so I did not spend much time learning the bass solo part. As a former King's choral scholar I believed I was sufficiently well equipped to 'muddle through' without too much preparation: again, the fearlessness of youth, and how distinctly unwise. I arrived at Marlborough for the afternoon rehearsal and made as good a fist of it as possible, imagining that nobody was likely to know right from wrong, should I happen to come adrift in performance. Come the evening and we trooped in with the conductor and took a bow. Graham suggested we remained standing for a moment and I was just beginning to wonder why when the great west door of the chapel opened and Michael Tippett walked somewhat ceremoniously into his seat! I learned a very valuable lesson that day. Years later when I met Tippett again, I reminded him of the occasion and was relieved when he told me that his memories of that particular performance were nothing but good.

New College was my official address during that academic year, even though I was also singing at Christ Church, teaching at Magdalen and living in the Rector's Lodgings at Exeter. The choir was then largely made up of lay clerks, several of whom had been there quite some time. Next to me was Frank Green, a man short in stature, but who had in his youth been a very fine and experienced professional soloist. One of the altos was Michael Groser, who carried out his trade as a stonemason during the day and famously carved many of the magnificently sinister gargoyles which adorn so many of Oxford's oldest buildings.

The other bass was Willoughby Pountney, whose son David would go on to be one of our leading opera directors. On one occasion, when one of the tenors was having trouble with his voice, Willoughby suggested he knew someone who could help, though he lived some distance away in Banbury. After evensong, the hapless tenor jumped on his *Lambretta* and chugged his way hopefully all the way to Banbury, only to find when he got there that the suggested help turned out to be a vet!

The choir at Christ Church was similarly equipped with lay clerks, none of whom (apart from James Bowman) was in the first flush of youth. But I was happy carrying on the daily business of singing evensong and being part of a musical outfit built on many years of tradition. It began to look as if I might be spending the rest of my life as a lay clerk in a cathedral choir and maybe teaching in a choir school. This was something I would greatly have enjoyed and when my Oxford year came to an end, it was this sort of life that I had very much in mind. The aforementioned James Bowman was teaching at the Christ Church Choir School and clearly happy in his work, along with his singing in the two college choirs. But word got round in pretty lofty musical circles that there was a countertenor in Oxford who had a voice potentially large enough to be heard at the back of an opera house. Benjamin Britten, no less, had written the role of Oberon for Alfred Deller when he composed his opera *A Midsummer Night's Dream*. Deller had resurrected the male alto voice from centuries of relative obscurity and put it firmly back on the musical map. It had always been there in cathedral choirs, but it took a charismatic performer such as Deller to create a niche for the voice in the concert hall.

Deller's voice, beautiful as it was, was not particularly large and as his acting experience as such was pretty limited, so he ended up singing the operatic role of Oberon from the pit, while the role was acted out on stage by another.

Now along came James Bowman and all that changed. At first James was very reluctant to dig himself out of his cosy Oxford existence in order to audition to Britten, but he was eventually persuaded. Once again, the rest is history, as he transformed the public's conception of the alto voice and opened the floodgates to many distinguished countertenors who followed in his illustrious footsteps.

One nice side-effect for me was that in 1967, Britten asked James to join Peter Pears as a soloist at the opening by Her Majesty the Queen of the concert hall on the South Bank which bears her name. James managed to get hold of a couple of tickets to the grand royal opening and along with the choir school's matron Mabel Chadwick I was able to be there in the audience for that glossy occasion. Little did I realise then that quite soon after that ceremonial opening, the Queen Elizabeth Hall would become a second home to we six founder members of The King's Singers as we performed our official London debut concert there on May the 1st 1968. For several years after that we were back in the hall to present our annual 'spring collection' when we announced our new repertoire to our ever-growing audience. Although James was reluctant to give up his teaching to pursue a solo singing career, I had no such regrets when it became clear that I might not be destined for a life in the common room after all.

CHAPTER SIX

London Calling

And so, in the autumn of 1967, the big wide world beckoned after four years of a seemingly unreal Oxbridge studentship. I was more than ready for it. During my Oxford year I had been several times to London to audition for conductors of the sort of professional choirs which I hoped might find room for someone like me with a voice like mine. As luck would have it, two vacancies occurred almost straight away for Lay Vicars (professional voices) in the choir of Westminster Abbey – an alto and a bass – and as James Bowman had also moved to London in the hope of moving on, we both applied to the organist and Director of Music Douglas Guest, sang to him and were duly appointed. My time in church music was clearly not yet over. This was a salaried post, with the glorious income of £600 a year! My father had told me, when I moved to London, that if I could earn a thousand pounds a year I would be more than able to survive. In my first trading year I did precisely that and in many ways have never felt richer. Young people these days find it hard to believe that I was paying £4 rent per week for a one-bedroom flat and that the ride to the Abbey on the number 88 bus cost me six old pence each way from my flat in the South Lambeth Road.

That reminds me of an occasion when I was asked to sing a song recital at a music society in Liverpool; I was billeted with a wealthy lady who kindly agreed to put up this young upstart for the night in her rather grand house in the city. Over a sumptuous dinner served by her butler after the performance, she regaled me with stories about her flat in Curzon Street and her villa in Morocco. When it was my turn to tell her where I lived (my one-bedroom flat just off the South Lambeth Road in Vauxhall) her reaction said it all: "Yes, I suppose these days one can live south of the river"! – clearly something she would never consider doing herself. She was probably one of those subscribers to the old debutante's dictum: "Darling, the thing is, one simply shouldn't be seen in London after July 31st" – hence the villa in Morocco.

The Westminster Abbey choir in those days was filled with relatively 'mature' singers on jobs-for-life contracts and to be brutally frank, some of them had clearly seen better days. As a result, the music was not perhaps top quality, though we all laughed a lot and thoroughly enjoyed each other's company, as well as the privileged position in which we found ourselves. The Abbey was such a wonderful building to be in and I felt it a great honour to be part of another great tradition, having had to sign my name on appointment in the same book as had been signed centuries before by Abbey organist Henry Purcell.

Two of the lay vicars – Ken Tudor and Bill Hepworth – had, like me, spent some time in the choir of York Minster and my joining them at the Abbey gave rise to some friendly publicity in the Yorkshire newspapers. My immediate next-door-neighbour in the choir stalls was Harry Barnes and on one occasion when The Queen Mother presented the royal Maundy money in the absence abroad of the Queen, Harry turned to me as she walked between the choir stalls and said "I sang at her wedding". That was in 1923 and there he was, still singing in the same choir. There were many great state occasions when most if not all the royal family would be present and once a year, the Judges service, when all the senior legal figures on the land would assemble, dressed in their finery and closely resembling a scene from Gilbert & Sullivan.

The combination of an Abbey salary and enough freelance professional choir work meant that I was earning enough money not to have to worry about where my next meal was coming from. It was a lovely way to carry on living the sort of life I had enjoyed at Cambridge and Oxford and as long as it lasted, it was increasingly clear that I was not going to have to fall back on my teaching diploma.

The professional choirs were full of seriously experienced singers and it was from them that newcomers like myself were able to learn so much. The John Alldis Choir was one of the finest. Josh (as he was affectionately known) was a King's-man and was always happy to bring fellow King's-men into the fold. He was able (I'm not sure how, but money must have come into it) to put on remarkable concerts of largely contemporary music – the sort that no other conductors would touch with a bargepole.

I well remember an entire evening of Stockhausen's extraordinary music at the Victoria and Albert Museum (recalling Sir Thomas Beecham's famous comment when he was asked if he had heard any Stockhausen. His reply: "No, but I think I might have trodden in some"). We might well have wondered what we were doing singing such incomprehensible 'music' but it was a living and the living was reasonably easy.

The Alldis Choir gave me my first introduction to the mighty BBC. There was a series of evening concerts – so-called Invitation Concerts, though known to us as 'Irritation Concerts' as they were *live* at ten o'clock on a Tuesday evening in the Concert Hall of Broadcasting House. The Alldis Choir was asked to present a concert entirely made up of 'squeaky-gate music' – items by living composers which might otherwise never see the light of day, and wisely so.

We rehearsed in the early evening and then retired to the Green Room to don our DJs and pretty frocks in order to inflict on an unsuspecting 'Third Programme' audience the works which had been selected for that particular programme. Five minutes before the start time, the producer came into the room and announced: "Bad news, I'm afraid: there's nobody there. So please go out and sing the first piece, then put down your music and CLAP"! And so we did, giving undeserved music a warmer reception than any audience could possibly have given. I looked across at the green baize table to where the great radio announcer Alvar Lidell was sitting, resplendent in his tuxedo. He was laughing so much that he had tears rolling down his face, before pulling himself together and giving a standard *Third Programme* back announcement. I watched and listened, thinking to myself that this was a job I would like one day to do, never dreaming for a serious minute that I would end up doing precisely that.

Another unforgettable association with the Alldis choir was when we were asked to provide the backing group for the Pink Floyd album *Atom Heart Mother*. It was an extraordinary experience – certainly for one so much involved in church music. The printed scores from which we sang were not exactly notated as we were used to, but we managed to make some sense of them.

We made the recording in Abbey Road studio 2 (home to the Beatles) and then joined in the 'fun' performing at the Hyde Park rock concerts and at Shepton Mallett. Standing in front of a bank of speakers designed to propel our combined sound to the other end of the Edgware Road was a sobering experience and could well have led to premature deafness, had this become a regular gig. On top of that, it was dangerous to breathe in at any time, so thick was the air with the smoke of unfamiliar substances! But it was indeed a great experience.

It's amazing to think that in those distant days, you could park the car anywhere on the street in London without having to worry about meters, wardens or yellow lines. On Sundays between the morning and evening services at the Abbey, we lay vicars would simply drive up to Broadcasting House in Portland Place, calmly walk in (no security then!), make our way up to the BBC canteen on the eighth floor and enjoy cheap and cheerful food.

One of the perks of the job at the Abbey was also free parking within the confines of Dean's Yard, a central London location for access to which people would kill these days. We all had to have a sticker on the windscreen to be allowed in and on one occasion when I changed cars, I threw the old sticker in the fire before handing the car over to its new owner. I then applied to the Receiver General for a new sticker, only to be told that I could have one only when the old one was produced. He could not accept the fact that I had burned it and said it must be presented in order for a new one to be issued. I had no choice but to bring in a bag full of ash from the fire, dump it on his desk and hope that that would do the trick. Not really, though I had made my point and a new sticker was grudgingly provided.

Freelance singing in professional choirs gave me some wonderful experiences, singing for some of the great names which were coming to the end of their lives and careers. The first of these was the great German maestro Otto Klemperer. The Alldis Choir was employed to provide the chorus for Klemperer's recordings of Mozart's *Marriage of Figaro* and Beethoven's *Choral Fantasia*. The extensive piano part in the Beethoven was played by the young Daniel Barenboim and it was fascinating to watch these two outstanding musicians – years apart in age – finding common ground in interpretation. Klemperer could not walk at that stage and had to be carried on to the podium. With a simple flick of the wrist the music would start and thereafter it was largely a matter of watching the orchestral leader in order to get things together. When the big man became too ill to carry on, his place was taken by Sir Adrian Boult and it was such a privilege to be able to sing under another musical giant.

It was the same Sir Adrian who apparently conducted at the famous Three Choirs Festival on one occasion, with a vast choir assembled against the west wall of Worcester Cathedral, accompanied by the BBC Symphony Orchestra. Halfway through the rehearsal Sir Adrian stopped everything and said that there was a lady behind a pillar who could not possibly see him. "It's all right," came the reply: "I saw you last year"! One of Thomas Beecham's famous put-downs of the great man summed up his uncomplimentary feelings: "Here comes Adrian, reeking of Horlicks"!

Another major conductor with whom we sang was Sir John Barbirolli: we rehearsed with him on the afternoon of the day he died. These great men had so much experience to share with relatively young singers and although styles of singing have changed dramatically in the years since, it was a special privilege to be able to be in their presence at – for us – such an impressionable age.

The Alldis choir frequently joined members of the Covent Garden chorus to record operas, usually in the Walthamstow Town Hall, which was large enough and had a sufficiently good acoustic for that purpose. One morning at 10 o'clock we all assembled to record Puccini's *Il Tabarro*. People were talking about a young tenor who had flown through the night to be with us, having sung Wagner the previous evening at Bayreuth. Everyone agreed that such crazy scheduling would soon destroy a wannabe tenor. The young man walked in, asked for a cup of tea and then sang. Those hardened opera chorus members who had sung with all the greats were amazed by the sound he produced so early in the morning, after flying through the night. But they concluded that, unless he found a better agent, this star-in-the-making would probably burn out in no time at all. How wrong could they have been: the unknown young man's name was Placido Domingo!

Round about that time, Martin Neary was the Director of Music at St. Margaret's, Westminster, next to the Abbey (where he later became organist). His wife, Penny, was one of the daughters of Prime Minister Edward Heath's doctor and this established a relationship with that most musical of Prime Ministers, to the extent that Martin was frequently asked to provide entertainment at No. 10, Downing Street.

On one notable and indeed unforgettable occasion I was asked to join Martin's group of singers in order to provide after-dinner music for the Heath and his distinguished guests. It happened to be the 80th birthday of the former Prime Minister Sir Alec Douglas Home and Heath wanted something appropriate to this rather special dinner. With Douglas Home's Scottish connection, Martin cleverly decided that one of the items sung round the dining table in No 10 would be the Vaughan Williams arrangement of the old Scottish song *Loch Lomond*. Now, as it happens, this includes a lyrical baritone solo, which meant that yours truly got to sing the big solo in Downing Street.

Judging by the overall conviviality of the evening it is doubtful that anyone present remembers a note of what I and we sang; but it was, certainly for me, an unforgettable moment: the only time I ventured into the hallowed precincts of No 10 Downing Street. Even better than that – among the guests was former Prime Minister Harold Macmillan and as I turned up in that most famous of addresses (in those days you could simply walk up to the front door without any security – imagine that!) Macmillan turned up at the exactly the same time. Having been properly brought up, it seemed only decent for me to stand aside and let him enter his old home first.

In another account in Michael McManus's Heath biography, MP Kenneth Clark recounts a similar occasion – one on which I could well have been singing. Clark admitted that: "I enjoyed it enormously, but I won't mention which colleagues, looking round, were subjected to agonies by the experience." *In vino veritas!*

A last John Alldis Choir memory concerns the soprano (later mezzo soprano) Felicity Palmer (later Dame Felicity).

She had sung, for six months, as the top voice in the fledgling King's Singers (now there's a thought!) while we waited for countertenor Nigel Perrin to come down from King's. On one occasion she asked Josh if she could be released from an afternoon rehearsal, though she never gave the reason for the request. The next morning, she turned up again as if nothing had happened. It was only during the rehearsal break that one of the choir read in the newspaper that Felicity had won the coveted Kathleen Ferrier Award the day before. She had never mentioned she was in for it and she never said that she had won it: there's star quality.

One rather good way of supplementing the weekly earnings was to be on the deputy list of the BBC Singers – the Beeb's professional choir. This meant that from time to time (in fact quite often) I would be asked to sing as a bass in the Daily Service, which in those days was broadcast 'live', frequently from the church of All Souls in Langham Place, next to Broadcasting House. It was particularly good to be invited to sing on a Saturday morning as the moment the service was over, we were handed another set of music and straight away recorded the evening service for later that day. This gave us a take-home pay of twice the normal rate – ie £18 instead of just £9. When you are paying £4 a week for your rent, that is a very useful addition to funds.

On another never-to-be-forgotten occasion, Michael Howard's professional choir *Cantores in Ecclesia* made a commercial recording of Thomas Tallis's famous 40-part motet *Spem in Alium*. Ace fixer Geoffrey Mitchell provided the voices and we dutifully turned up at a north London church and did the honours. It was only when the Producer announced himself happy with the final result that someone pointed out that there were only 39 of us! It became a prime example of what used to be called – for easy-learning purposes – Music Minus One.

At the same time that all this freelance work was taking place, the six King's Choral Scholars who had so much enjoyed singing together while in Cambridge were beginning to consider staying together and seeing if there might be a market for a close harmony group such as ours. Neville Marriner had taken his fledgling Academy of St. Martin in the Fields to a minor stately home south of Salisbury to perform in the drawing room of Hale Park for its owner David Booth-Jones. When David asked about other possible performers, Neville graciously mentioned the six of us, having heard us sing when the Academy had come to King's to make records with the college choir. We were, he suggested, cheap and available and might be glad of the opportunity.

So began a delightful chapter in our lives as we did indeed perform at Hale and enjoyed a few days living off the fat of the land in such beautiful surroundings. So much so that when we were asked a few years later to make a film for BBC television, we were only too pleased to suggest Hale Park as a suitable venue for recording some of the scenes. The big house had been built for himself by the architect Thomas Archer, shortly after he had completed one of his outstanding London buildings, the church of St. John's Smith Square in Westminster.

David Booth-Jones's inevitable connection meant that he was in charge of the Friends of St. John's, which quickly established itself as a major new concert venue, as well as a regular place for the broadcasting of BBC Radio 3 lunchtime concerts. As I had begun singing in the Westminster Abbey choir, just round the corner, David asked me if I might be remotely interested in the job of caretaker at St. Johns. The big plus was that there was a flat at the church, which could be made available to me. Tempting yes, until David told me that the job included moving six hundred chairs around regularly and keeping this magnificent building clean. A lovely idea bit the dust and a golden opportunity to have a pretty neat central London address rent-free passed me by.

Taking stock, it looked as if church music was going to continue to dominate my life at the same time as trying to establish The King's Singers and enjoying the life of a freelance professional singer. But there was one more area which began to contribute to my musical well-being. As I answered the phone one day, a familiar-sounding voice at the other end said: "hello, my name's Donald Swann". My parents had been to the Fortune Theatre in London while I was still at school and seen Flanders and Swann in their immensely popular show *At the Drop of a Hat*. They had bought the LP and during school holidays I had listened to it – no exaggeration – several times each day, until I knew every word, every note and every comic gesture by heart. For me this was a supreme example of the perfect marriage of words and music and I loved every minute of it.

To hear that highly individual voice in my ear, clearly wanting to speak to me, was the most unexpected and pleasant surprise: so much so that I assumed it was one of my friends having a laugh at my expense. Nonetheless, it really was Swann and he wanted to invite me to join a quintet of singers to appear with him on stage in the autobiographical revue *Between the Bars* which had begun to dominate his life after his partnership with Flanders had come to an end. Could I possibly come and see him? Well this was too exciting for words and as soon as he told me he lived in Albert Bridge Road, virtually round the corner from my flat, I was able to say that I would be with him in a matter of minutes. And so I was, thereby beginning another wonderful chapter in my musical life and another special friendship. We drank tea and talked for a long time, with me hardly daring to believe that I was in the company of another of my childhood heroes. What made this whole idea even better was the fact that he had also asked my sister Heather (she being also by now an aspiring session singer and eventually a member of the famous Swingle Singers) to be part of the quintet as well. Having spent so many years in the rarefied atmosphere of college and cathedral choir stalls, here was an opportunity to sample another area of music-making altogether, in the hands of an expert whose theatrical experience had taken him all over the world for eleven years of tremendous Flanders and Swann success. The experience for all of us was a real eye-opener as well as sheer pleasure. I suppose we must have been paid something for our efforts, though we were so busy soaking in the delights of it all that I really can't remember. It was not going to take over my life, but it certainly enriched it. Of this, more anon.

One more excitement came in the form of my taking an audition for an organisation called *Youth and Music*, which offered young singers the chance to study abroad. I am not sure that it was quite what I wanted to do, but nothing ventured, nothing gained. I was asked to appear at the grand Mansfield Street apartment of Sir Robert Mayer, the man who spent so much of his life and his fortune giving a helping hand to young musicians and who proudly told me, among other things, that as a young boy, he had sat on Brahms's knee! The listening panel must have had a combined age of goodness-knows-what, including Sir Robert himself, who lived to be 104, the dramatic opera soprano Dame Eva Turner and Roy Henderson, the baritone who had famously taught Kathleen Ferrier. All I had to do was to sing a couple of arias and answer a few questions and bingo: they offered me a year's free tuition in Italy with any singing teacher of my choice.

This was a problem, with all the other exciting things happening to me in London. It would mean giving up my salaried position at the Abbey, forsaking the pleasure of the Swann connection and curtailing the idea of developing The King's Singers – at least as far as I was concerned. In the end, grateful as I was for the offer of this golden opportunity, I turned it down and stuck to the current *modus vivendi.* I've often wondered what difference it might have made had I accepted the offer, though I can't help thinking that there were so many good young singers around with frankly better prospects than mine that I was better off sticking to my guns.

Years later, when I was asked to write and present a BBC radio programme on the 35th anniversary of the death of the much-loved singer Kathleen Ferrier I interviewed Roy Henderson at his home in South London. After we had done the business he took me into his study and showed me his collection of photographs. The main one, suitably framed and hanging on the wall in prime position, was of the sixteen soloists for whom Vaughan Williams had composed his ravishing *Serenade to Music.* This had been written to celebrate Sir Henry Wood's golden jubilee as a conductor, most famously of the Proms. Roy Henderson – 'Prof' to all his singing pupils – pointed out Vaughan Williams and Sir Henry and added that there were only two of the original sixteen soloists still alive – himself and Eva Turner. He then added – clearly with some relish: "the tenors all went first"!

I carried on at the Abbey, remaining a member of the bass section until 1971 at the same time as beginning to make serious developments in the life of the fledgling King's Singers. David Booth-Jones, having enjoyed our performance at his home at Hale Park decided that he would like to do something more for us. He organised and promoted two concerts with the organist (and our fellow King's-man) Simon Preston in the cathedrals of Salisbury and Winchester. Those were so well received that David decided to go the whole hog and hire the Queen Elizabeth Hall in London to bring together the musical friends he had made. This concert on May the 1st 1968, turned out to be the official London debut of the group, as well as giving a platform to Neville Marriner and his merry band of players in the Academy of St. Martin's. Simon Preston also joined us and largely thanks to an appreciative audience of friends and a hugely supportive review from Stephen Walsh in *The Times*, The King's Singers were up and running.

One other solo singing experience I was able to enjoy before The King's Singers took over my life altogether was taking part regularly in the BBC schools programmes called 'Singing Together'. This involved reporting to the sub-basement of Broadcasting House at an unreasonably early hour on a Tuesday morning and trying to get the voice going. The programme was presented by a variety of people who could easily and fluently talk to children about singing songs. There would be a choir there and there would be me, singing the songs to the best of our ability and hopefully inspiring school children everywhere to join in. The presenters (whose job I rather envied) included such luminaries as children's favourite Johny Morris, superstar rugby player Cliff Morgan and the tenor, critic and popular 'My Music' panellist John Amis. Adding considerable lustre to our efforts was that great man of the so-called kitchen department – banging every conceivable instrument – Nigel Shipway, who was, until his death in 2017 still very much at it and frequently playing in concerts I'm privileged to have conducted: a man of endless charm and good humour, whose stories were as entertaining as they appeared to be limitless.

On a personal front, my time at Westminster Abbey provided another crucial life-changing situation. There was at the Abbey Choir School a young assistant matron by the name of Sally Lyne. I am not sure exactly where and when we first met, but I was certainly well aware of her presence with the boy choristers whose time in the choir gave them the advantage of free schooling right next door to the Abbey in Dean's Yard. Many of them as middle-aged men now remember being bathed by the future Mrs. Kay as Sally and I were married in 1970, not long before we both left the Abbey family and set up home in Kingston upon Thames.

Young singers these days often ask me how I ever managed to buy a home on the sort of money I was earning at the time. They find it hard to believe me when I tell them that my first rung on the property ladder was a two-up, two-down detached house near to Richmond Park and that it cost me the princely sum of seven thousand pounds. Not so long ago I found myself in the area and paid a nostalgic visit to Borough Road to find my old house somewhat gentrified and probably now worth half a million – and the rest!

That remained our home for three years, which saw the birth of my son Jonathan in 1973. We then moved to Ewell Village near Epsom and it was there that Charlotte was born in 1975 to complete the family. After a few years there it occurred to me that it was taking me as long to drive from there to central London as it might from somewhere far out in a more beautiful part of the country and that was how my still continuing presence in the Cotswolds came about.

Funnily enough, the estate agent in Ewell initially said that he would be embarrassed to charge me commission on the sale of the property as it was such a perfect house for a commuter and would sell in no time at all. This was also a detached house – three bedrooms this time – at the quiet end of a cul-de-sac and within easy walking distance of the main railway line into central London. The hapless agent failed miserably in his efforts to attract a commuter, selling the house after six months hard labour to Tony Connor, the drummer in the group 'Hot Chocolate'!

But I'm jumping ahead, when there are still areas of life as a freelance singer to recall, before the time when The King's Singers completely took over my life.

Intermission
Two

The leading early 20th century English composer Ralph Vaughan Williams was asked, late in his career, to visit Cornell University in America to offer some advice to budding composers. He was already a great age and held in appropriate veneration State-side. He nobly sat through all sorts of efforts by compositional hopefuls until one particularly adventurous wannabe showed him his latest score. To his eternal credit, RVW patiently read through the 'music' before him, filled to the brim as it was with ghastly bangs, crashes and wallops. In the end, with a stunning display of diplomacy, he offered the most touching advice: "If a *tune* should ever occur to you," he said, "please don't hesitate to write it down"! No wonder RVW's music is better known and more loved universally than that of his would-be student.

When the film maker Tony Palmer wanted to make a film about Vaughan Williams, he approached the Music and Arts section of BBC television to see if they might be interested in showing it. The gist of the reply he had from a member of the Music and Arts team beggars belief, suggesting that the department was interested to hear the proposal though it didn't quite fit in with current thinking. However, if Mr.

V. Williams was doing anything interesting they might like to see, he should not hesitate to get in touch again. RVW by this time had been dead for fifty years.

When my sister Heather was touring with the Swingle Singers, they found themselves in Sydney and about to perform at the famous Opera House. Who should pass by but a young Kiri te Kanawa. The one particular thing Heather remembers of that particular encounter is that Kiri was wearing a T-shirt bearing the legend I AM STILL A VIRGIN. On the back when she turned round it said THIS IS A VERY OLD T-SHIRT.

My two professional double bass playing colleagues in The King's Singers – Alastair Hume and Simon Carrington – were for a time members of the bass section in the old BBC Northern Symphony Orchestra (now the BBC Philharmonic). When they were playing for a performance of Handel's *Messiah* the conductor had a go at the double bass section, suggesting that everything was not quite in order. The leader said to his number two: "Pass us the resin Fred and I'll show him who's King of Glory!"

The same player was battling against the sheer number of notes in the double bass part in Handel's *Israel in Egypt*. So much so that after a particularly traumatic section he was heard to pass the thought that "if there had been as many bulrushes in Egypt as there are notes in my part, they'd never have found bloody Moses"!

That top-of-the-range professional adjudicator Sir Thomas Armstrong was doing his duty at the Llangollen International Musical Eisteddfod at the tender age of approaching ninety. I was then 'fronting' the Eisteddfod for BBC TV and as such sat in on the main adjudications. There were six thousand people sitting in the massive marquee which hosted the events in those days, everyone eager to hear the words of extreme wisdom which inevitably dripped from Sir Thomas's incomparably diplomatic tongue (remember that it was his equally distinguished son Sir Robert who, as cabinet secretary to Margaret Thatcher famously termed the phrase 'economical with the truth').

One of the choirs had sung Handel's Coronation Anthem *Zadok the Priest* and Sir Thomas had clearly enjoyed the performance. "Hearing it, he said, "reminded me of the occasion when I sang it as a member of the choir at the Coronation". The crowd of people from all over the world cheered in excitement at the thought that he was old enough to have sung at the Coronation. They were then stunned into even more silent admiration when he quietly added: "in 1911"!

He had even sung at the lying in state of Edward VII. When I interviewed him for a 90th birthday television tribute I did so at his home in Olney in Bedfordshire. I was, of course, thrilled to be in the presence and I made absolutely sure that I was there on time for the start of the filming: so much so that I had time to visit the antique shops in the village. I saw and bought a beautiful framed print of *The Apotheosis of Handel*. It is a famous etching and I was delighted to have it, particularly as it was very nicely framed. After I had done the day's filming with Sir Thomas, he showed me round the house to which he had retired some years previously. I noticed prints of famous composers and then told him how thrilled I was to have found the Handel print in the local antique shop that very morning. "Yes," he replied, somewhat soulfully: "it belonged to me, but when we moved here, a whole lorry-load disappeared and most of it ends up in the antique shops". I was so sad to hear that and my response was as immediate as it was inevitable: "It's in the boot of my car." I offered, "and you shall have it back". "Not at all," was his response: "I'm ninety years old, there's no room on my walls for any more pictures, and there's nobody I'd rather have it than you." Imagine my delight. Every time I see it now I think of him and the fact that it might well have originally hung in the office of the Director of the Royal Academy of Music. Such a great man and so lucky for me to have enjoyed such a special day's work.

He then took me round his garden and I was intrigued by a number of statues – busts of what were clearly great composers. When I enquired about their origin, Sir Thomas told me that they were originally to be found on the outside of the Queen's Hall, which had been catastrophically bombed in 1941, having been London's best-loved concert hall and the birthplace of the Proms. When I got home, I checked my old photos of the Queen's Hall and, sure enough, there they were, large as life as ornaments around the outside of the building. It seems that, after the bombing, the remnants had been given to the Royal Academy of Music and that when Sir Thomas retired from the Directorship, the busts were given to him. So, there they were: history encapsulated in a Bedfordshire garden.

I've always been intrigued by misprints! The famous ones like Mussorgsky's opera *'Doris Goodenough'*, Haydn's oratorio *'The Cremation'* and countless others. With The King's Singers, we were once misprinted in the press as 'an all-male grope'. A newspaper review which took the biscuit for me was when a reviewer came up with the classic response to our performance: "Going to a King's Singers concert gives one a feeling of *déjà vu* – particularly if you've seen them before"!

A bassoonist friend was stopped by the police when, as a student, he was driving his old banger on the road between Oxford and London. The officer walked round his car a few times then began to regale him with the things that were legally unacceptable: only one break light, a flat offside tyre, a missing windscreen wiper and a passenger door which didn't close properly. "Do you have anything to say?" asked the policeman. The student's brilliant reply: "I'll say it when you've gone"! Oh to have had such presence of mind.

I love the review in a New York newspaper which referred to a young soprano as having 'a small but unpleasant voice'.

Then there was the occasion when the most unlikely 'dumb blond' starlet Pia Zadora was cast (I'm not making this up) as Anne Frank in an American dramatization. She, Pia, was so unspeakably awful in that role that at the crucial moment when the SS came knocking at the door in search of Anne, the audience shouted: "She's in the attic"!

When Sir David Willcocks was on tour in Canada in his position as Director of Music at King's College, Cambridge, but also as a distinguished organist, he gave an eagerly awaited recital to members of the Royal Canadian College of Organists. It hardly seems possible, but in the middle of a Bach fugue, his pedal work came adrift and he soldiered on manfully to the end. When the bemused audience applauded wildly, he stepped forward and announced: "there was a moment in that fugue which reminded me of a familiar verse in the psalms – although my foot hath slipped, thy mercy, O Lord, hath held me up".

And on another occasion, I was conducting a concert in Cheltenham in which our guest singer was the wonderful Dame Felicity Lott. As an encore she sang just the *Alleluia* from Mozart's famous motet *Exsultate Jubilate*. Now there are moments during that when it could be the singer or the strings who get the tune ... sure enough, Dame Flott took a wrong turning and, of course, received a riotous reception at the end. Even more so when she proudly announced: "at least I got the words right"!

My sister Heather was, for a time, a member of the famous Swingle Singers: in fact it was as part of the English group Swingle 2, which founder and director Ward Swingle formed after the demise of his original French group. When the original album *Jazz Sebastian Bach* came out in the early 60s, the assembly of mainly French singers were billed as Les Swingle Singers. No wonder, then, that Ward was often called Les! And what a great start in life for a jazz arranger and singer to have been born with the real name 'Swingle'.

The last time I performed in public as a baritone soloist I had already started working for the BBC and was determined that this would be the right time to concentrate on speaking rather than singing. I was asked to appear as bass soloist in the performance of Haydn's *Creation* in Nottingham, conducted by my old friend John Morehen. It was the perfect work to end on, with those wonderful duets between Adam and Eve and I gave it all I'd got – really sang as well as I possibly could, determined to give a good, final impression. The next day, John kindly sent me a copy of the review in the local paper. 'The soprano', it said, 'sang with exemplary beauty of tone, perfectly capturing the character of the part. The tenor brought a tremendous sense of drama to his many recitatives and the bass, Brian Kay, sang with all the clarity of diction one would expect from a Radio 3 announcer': It was clearly time to stop.

CHAPTER SEVEN

Swanning Around

It was such a pleasure to meet and become involved professionally with Donald Swann. I have already mentioned my admiration for his immortal partnership with Michael Flanders and my tremendous fondness for all their songs and sketches. One thing easily overlooked when listening (again and again) to their recordings is what a glorious touch Swann had at the piano. Flanders dominated the stage so splendidly, his rich bass-baritone voice the perfect foil to Swann's light tenor. But careful attention to the piano playing is rewarded with an object-lesson in how to accompany two singers whose freedom of rhythm was a vital part of their entertainment. Donald's touch at the piano was exemplary and remains a joy to hear, so many years later.

He was an essentially modest man who suddenly found himself part of a hugely successful partnership which dated right back to their time together as boys at Westminster School. I love the story of how, when they decided to try and launch their two-man show *At the Drop of a Hat* on the London stage, the theatre-owner they approached said that it sounded like a good idea, though he wondered who might be in it! When Flanders and Swann rather shyly said they thought they would do it themselves, he said that as they were paying the rent for the theatre they could do what they liked. Luckily huge audiences all over the world liked it too and the show ran (with its sequel *At the Drop of Another Hat*) for eleven years worldwide. It's sad that a third projected show (cunningly to be called *Hat Trick*) never came off, as they both decided that so many years on the road were quite enough.

The King's Singers later worked with Michael Flanders when he wrote with the composer Joseph Horovitz a light-hearted romp called *Captain Noah and his Floating Zoo*. Jo had attended one of our early concerts – at the Kensington Music Club – and he came round to the dressing room afterwards to ask if we might be interested in performing this piece, if he were to arrange it for our six voices with jazz piano. We readily accepted the idea and went on to give the London premiere and to make a recording which is still available all these years later, now on CD. I well remember Flanders coming to Jo's house in Notting Hill to hear how we were getting on. There is a steep set of steps up to the front door and it was our job – the six of us – to carry Michael up the steps in his wheelchair. He was a big man.

When Donald put his show together with our vocal quintet, we wanted us to be known as Donald Swann and the Cygnets, but for some reason he decided against it. Maybe it went back to the time his name was similarly abused when his wedding was announced in the papers under the heading 'Swann hooked in Battersea'. The show involved Donald telling his life story interspersed with musical extracts – songs, duets, ensembles and even a couple of times when he and I played piano duet. He had written a jolly little number while he was still a student at Christ Church, Oxford and he used to say "I think you'll know what sort of piece it is when I tell you I called it *The*

Outskirts of Warsaw Concerto. The tempo-marking, he added, is *Liberace ma non troppo*! It was fascinating to hear his memories of touring the world with Flanders – never more so than in the list of hotel notices he had jotted down 'If you haven't paid for the second bed, don't sit on it' was one, along with 'please ring for the maid for the consummation of your desires'.

The show also involved intricate dance routines, which for those of us more used to donning a cassock and surplice (Madame Tussaud's mobile exhibit again!) came as a bit of a shock. It was all good knockabout stuff and we had terrific fun taking it to a number of relatively small theatres up and down the country. It was never going to rival the *Hat* shows but it gave Donald the chance to carry on in the theatre. He was, however, a shining example of the clown who wanted to play Hamlet, always wanting his more 'serious' music to be as well accepted as his popular songs. This was another reason why both Flanders and Swann brought their on-stage partnership to an end, as they both felt that joint success frustrated their individual creative abilities. 'Stardom' never interested Donald: in order to entertain full houses at the Theatre Royal in the Haymarket he travelled every night from his home in Battersea by bus.

He used to tell how when Westminster Abbey celebrated its 900th anniversary, the two of them asked the Dean and Chapter if they could perform in the Abbey, recalling their young days at Westminster School. When they were turned down, Flanders brought to mind their most famous song when he said: "I suppose all they want is God, God, Glorious God"! When Swann was asked to preach a sermon at St. Paul's Cathedral he was stuck for a text. Flanders, as usual, came to the rescue: You tell 'em this," he said: "we're all cast in the same mould, but some are mouldier than others".

When Flanders died in 1975, Donald asked me to help him arrange – along with Michael's widow Claudia – the music for his memorial service at St. Martin in the Fields. The three of us sat in the garden of the Flanders family home in West Kensington and worked out a possible 'programme'. The two young Flanders daughters would be running around, none of us imagining at that stage that Stephanie would one day end up as the BBC's great economics guru and – for someone like me, quite hopeless in understanding money matters – the only person I know who can almost make me work out what it is all about – her delightful television and radio persona consequently known, with affection and respect as Stephanomics.

My last association with Donald came with one of his more 'serious' musical moments. He had set to music words by the Poet Laureate Cecil Day-Lewis called *Requiem for the Living* and this involved soprano and baritone soloists, four-part choir, Donald on the piano, an extensive part for cimbalom (to be played by Heather Corbett, who ended up as percussionist with the BBC Scottish Symphony Orchestra) and the whole thing narrated by the poet's wife, the actress Jill Balcon with her husband sitting in the front row. We gave two or three performances and then recorded it, though I fear it has largely disappeared without trace in the intervening years. More's the pity.

The other three singers joining me and sister Heather for Donald's autobiographical show *Between the Bars* were Catherine Martin, Virginia Broadbent and Alastair Thompson. As Alastair and I were both becoming increasingly busy with

The King's Singers, it was perhaps inevitable that we would eventually be replaced. And so we were, my replacement being Roger Cleverdon, my old next-door-neighbour in the bass section of the Westminster Abbey Choir. The show eventually petered out, though not before we had all learned a fair amount about life in the musical theatre, as well as having had a seriously good time.

CHAPTER EIGHT

The King's Singers

"It's a good idea and worth a try, but it will never work". This was the advice given to us by our esteemed Director of Music David Willcocks in 1966 when we asked him if six of us former Choral Scholars should form a full-time singing group in order to make a living. When The King's Singers celebrated their 40th anniversary in 2008, I reminded Sir David what he had said. His response was equally positive: "Yes and I would give the same advice today". He was, I am sure, genuinely proud of what we had achieved as well as carrying the name of King's all round the world. But he was a practical man and to be fair, full-time singing groups were pretty thin on the ground in those days – particularly all-male ones.

It was a tricky idea, setting ourselves up as a feasible outfit, back in the later years of the 'swinging 60s'. But in many ways, we didn't have much to lose. We could have gone on singing in Cathedral choirs (three of us in the choirs of Westminster Abbey, St. Paul's Cathedral and St. George's, Windsor) with another two playing double bass in the old BBC Northern Symphony Orchestra. But we had youth and enthusiasm on our side and we decided that a couple of years 'on the road' might be worth the risk.

That official London debut on May the 1st 1968 had gone better than we could ever have hoped and the many Music

Clubs around the country sat up and took notice: so much so that the offers began slowly pouring in. I have talked about David Booth-Jones's Hale Park connection and the thanks we owed to Neville Marriner for giving us a vital leg-up with David and his concert series. Once again it was Neville who spread the word – this time to the far-flung corners of the globe. His Academy of St. Martins had toured Australia under the auspices of an organisation down under called Musica Viva Australia. He dropped the name of The King's Singers and we were approached by a lovely man called Ken Tribe who was looking for groups who were 'cheap and available' and might enjoy the chance of touring Australasia.

Ken and his wife Joan came to London, made contact and accepted an invitation from me to have dinner at my (four pounds a week) London flat. I picked them up at the rather smart Westbury Hotel in my cheap and cheerful one and a half litre 1952 Riley and drove them south of the river and together with my colleague Simon Carrington gave them dinner. In spite of its singular lack of quality, we forged an immediate friendship as a result of which The King's Singers were offered a three-month 35-concert tour in 1972, which gave us the perfect opportunity to take that ultimate risk and give up our regular jobs. I can't remember what food and wine we served that night but it must have done the trick. And so began a relationship with the other side of the world which lasted throughout the 70s with absolute delight – I would like to think – on both sides.

How does a group like the one we wanted to become develop? It's a good question and well worth considering. Whenever a number of people want to form a musical unit – a string quartet, a Lieder partnership between singer and

91

pianist, a wind ensemble, a singing group or whatever – there has to be a basic chemistry between the potential members – both as human beings and as musicians.

For us, that first hurdle was already long since overcome, as we had been soul mates at King's Cambridge. We knew each other extremely well and we simply wanted to stick together: first hurdle sorted. We had also sung together in the college choir – an environment which suited each of us perfectly. All we had to do was to find a suitable repertoire, work exceptionally hard largely at our own expense, and then try to sell ourselves. And that is precisely what we did.

Most of us were recently married and that, perhaps inevitably, added a strain on relationships within the marriages and within The King's Singers. But we were, maybe selfishly, determined to make this thing work. We applied ourselves to the task a hundred percent and allowed it to overwhelm our lives. More fool us in some ways, but then there has to be that sense of absolute determination if any sort of musical entity is likely to succeed.

Over the years we enjoyed a variety of agents, who helped to channel our efforts and establish our name. Most of these were 'classical' agents until the moment when we were approached by the Noel Gay Organisation. Noel Gay (born Reginald Armitage) made his name and his fortune writing popular songs and musicals, *Me and My Girl* being the most famous: think *Lambeth Walk, Leaning on a Lamppost, Run Rabbit Run* and many more. His son Richard ran the family firm and clearly took a shine to us six young men, recognising that there was something there which might have serious potential.

At our first meeting with him, he said he assumed that we would like to cut our workload by half at the same time as doubling our money. This seemed to us a cunning plan of Baldrickian proportions and Richard immediately set about making it happen. Those were the days when television audiences enjoyed what was bracketed under the heading 'Light Entertainment'. The Noel Gay Organisation had considerable clout in that area, thanks to having on their books TV stars of the magnitude of, for example, David Frost and Russ Conway. Say no more! The direct result of this was that we were suddenly flavour-of-the-month with television directors, particularly those who wanted a reliable and relatively cheap act to supplement their variety shows.

One of the first to express an interest was Barney Colehan, famously the producer of that old TV warhorse *The Good Old Days*. This olde-time music hall show filmed at the City Varieties in Leeds was hugely popular and of course we would love to have taken part. Barney happened to be (or probably arranged to be) in York at the same time that we were giving a concert in the city. He asked us to sing to him the following morning and we nervously trooped up the stairs of a rather unsavoury looking building to be greeted by the Big Man.

We sang a couple of songs and that was enough to convince him that we were suitable material for his popular programme. We went on to appear dozens of times over the years and to love the experience of finding ourselves 'Music Hall stars'! We shared the miniscule and singularly ill-equipped dressing rooms with all sorts and conditions of fellow thespians, including on one notable occasion, the comedian Les Dawson. The sight of him in his underpants, warming up by cracking jokes constantly while preparing to tread the boards, haunts me to this day.

One of the most generous TV producers who gave us so many wonderful breaks was Yvonne Littlewood, who asked us to appear regularly on the series she was producing with the lovely and much loved Greek singer Nana Mouskouri. That started in 1974 and opened the gates to a brave new world for the six of us. It was a joy to work with Nana and her incomparable Musical Director Peter Knight, as we did on a number of series. We did, however, have a problem: we had trained as choristers and as such could sight-read music straight off without any trouble. The worry with that is that, as there was never any need to remember anything, being able to sing at sight, our memory muscles were somewhat under-developed. This really didn't help matters when taking part in a major series such as this one. We would meet with Nana and Peter on a Friday and discuss what six or so songs we might sing with Nana in the following show. Half of them would be in Greek (and the only Greek we knew was *Kyrie Eleison*!). Peter would then work through the night making arrangements for we six and Nana and then we would meet again on the Saturday morning and sing them through. We would then go off to various far-flung corners of the country to sing our own concerts, then on Monday we would have to perform those arrangements – BY HEART – 'live' on BBC television. See what I mean about not being able to memorise at speed … we had to learn fast how to learn fast and we did. Otherwise we would have been out on our ears.

But we had such fun making those series and working with so many superstars who also appeared as guests on the programmes. I remember asking Yvonne one week who the big names were to be and when she said – this was in 1974 – Cliff Richard, we all said: goodness, is he still around? That

94

My paternal grandfather
Sir Robert Newbald Kay

Prime Minister Lloyd George's
visit to Poppleton Hall surrounded
by my grandparents, uncles and –
as a small boy – my father

My mother, Gwendoline Mary
Kay (née Sutton)

My father, Noel Bancroft Kay

Angelic, moi? – and all that hair!   All ready for prep school circa 1950

We four siblings
– Barry, Brian,
Graham and
Heather circa
1950

Sixty-four
years later
at my 70th
birthday
celebrations,
May 2014

Graduation day 1966 with my parents, brother Graham and sister Heather

Cantoris choral scholars at King's, Cambridge, 1965 *L-R:* Robin Pegna and then three eventual King's Singers – BK, Simon Carrington and Alastair Hume.

with the King's Singers UK tour bus, 1980

Six stout-hearted men, with Dame Hilda Bracket (Patrick Fyffe)

Bright young things – the King's Singers in the 1970s

Forty years on at the 50th anniversary lunch, January 2018 L-R: Nigel Perrin, Alastair Hume, Alastair Thompson, Anthony Holt, Simon Carrington, BK

My high forehead made me a shoo-in for Elizabeth the 1st in the Dutch television entry for the *Prix d'Italia*

with Queen Elizabeth the Queen Mother at the King's Lynn festival, 1980

On the *Brian Kay's Sunday Morning* roadshow – and they call it wireless!

Presenting the Vienna New Year's Day concert in 2010 from the studios of Austrian television.

The Radio 3 presentation team in 1983
Back row L-R: Donald McLeod, Peter Berg, Douglas Reith, Tony Scotland, BK
Middle row: John Holmstrom, Jon Curle, Malcolm Ruthven, Peter Barker
Sitting: Elaine Padmore, Cormac Rigby, Susan Sharp

Brian Kay's Sunday Morning on BBC Radio 3

In full conducting mode at the Leith Hill Musical Festival

Conducting the annual Huddersfield Choral Society *Messiah* performances 2006

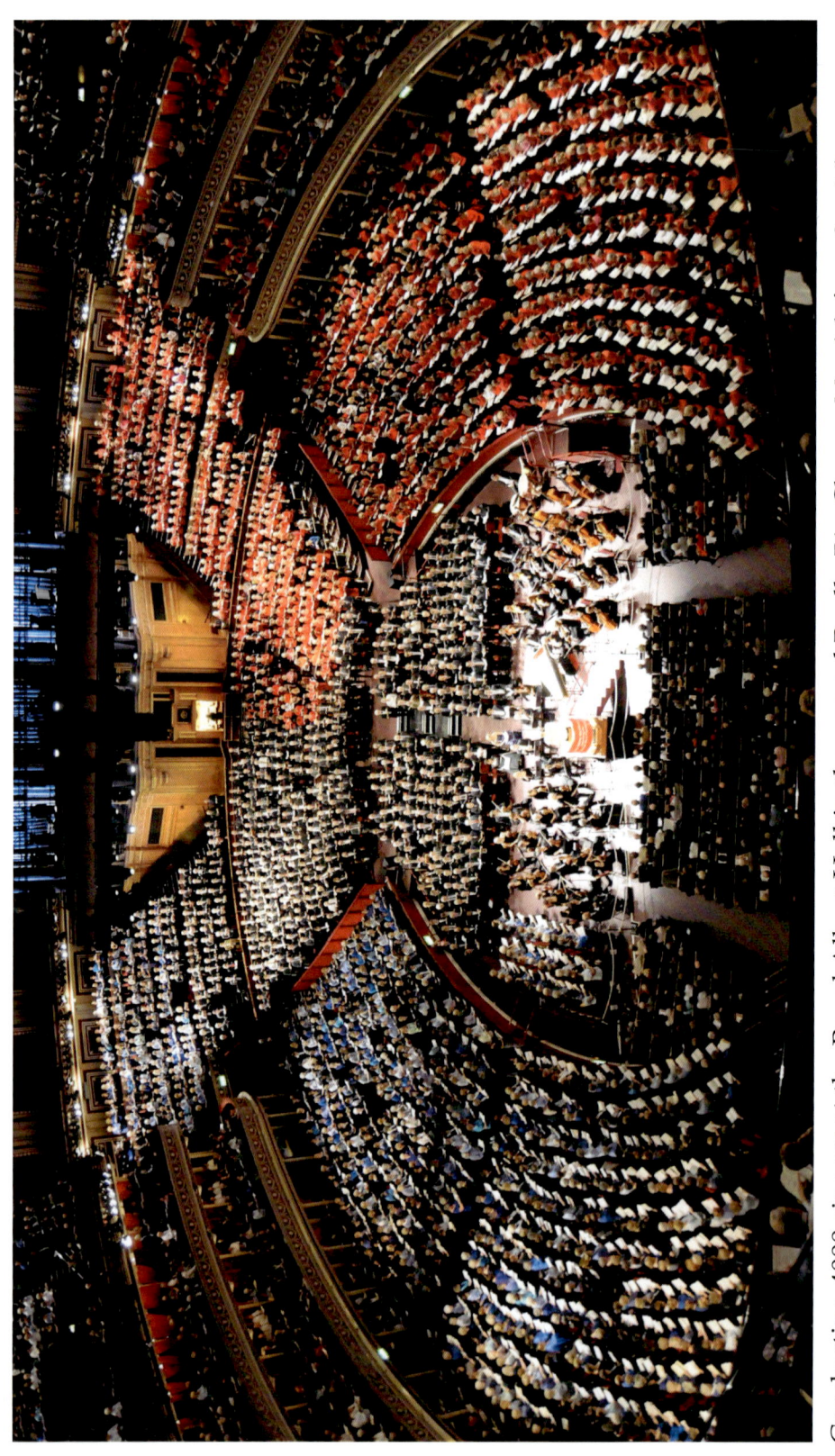

Conducting 4000 singers at the Royal Albert Hall in the annual Really Big Chorus *Messiah from Scratch* (photo credit: Chris Christodoulou)

was over forty years ago! And who would have thought that we Kingsmen would end up rubbing shoulders with the likes of Vera Lynn, Charles Aznavour (brilliantly lampooned by Morecambe and Wise as Charles Az-no-voice!) Demis Roussos (the singing tent!), Shirley Bassey, Kenneth McKellar, Jimmy Galway, Dudley Moore, Hinge and Bracket and many other 'light entertainment' superstars? Well, we did – lucky us. Dudley Moore composed a crazy operatic *scena* for himself as prima donna and us as a singing orchestra. I still have it on DVD and can hardly believe we were privileged to work with the former Oxford organ scholar who became a Hollywood superstar. Terrific pianist, funny man.

Yvonne also produced countless programmes of the Val Doonican series and, again, it was such a joy to work with that nicest of lovely men. Val had been a member of a 'boy band' in his youth and seemed to be glad to have us around as backing and as guests. He would sing in the middle of the group, making us a septet, and add his rich, warm voice to the ensemble, thanks again to the magnificent arranging skills of people like Musical Directors Peter Knight, Alyn Ainsworth and Ronnie Hazlehurst.

The important thing about these TV appearances is that they generated an audience for us which then spilled over into the concert hall. People would see and hear us on these prime time shows and want to witness us in the flesh. In that way we found quickly that our audiences grew by internal combustion and all we had to do was to make sure that when they came to a concert hall, we made it well worth their while.

Mind you, when they did come to our concerts, they did not necessarily get what they might have expected. They will have seen us appearing, for example, as the Six Wives to Harry Secombe's Henry VIII (since you ask, I was Anne of Cleeves). They would then come along and have to sit through 16th century madrigals and motets, serious and light-hearted contemporary music and much more besides, before eventually hearing the sort of thing they had been expecting all along.

Our hope was that we charmed them into submission. Mention of Harry Secombe brings to mind the fact that although he had such an enviably fine tenor voice, he always sang sharp. We prided ourselves that we could sing in tune and this occasionally made life tricky. Harry knew about this: he admitted on one occasion that he had been to a singing lesson and had been told, after singing an aria, that he had sung the whole thing a semitone sharp. His reply: "You think that's easy?" Such a funny man and such fun to work with.

On another occasion we were recording Harry's show at Yorkshire Television when there was a union dispute mid-filming. The lights suddenly went out and the producer asked what the problem was. He was told that there were fleas in the curtains and the whole place would have to be fumigated before filming could continue. Tensions began to rise as television filming costs a fortune per minute. Enter Harry, who asked what the problem was. As soon as he was told, he burst into song: "Oh, fleas a jolly good fellow – and so say all of us"! Everyone had a laugh and got back to work.

One of our more bizarre television experiences came in the form of a programme produced by Wilhelmina Hoedemann, the then Dutch wife of Paul Taylor, a professional singing colleague of ours. She decided to make a programme as the

Dutch TV's entry into the annual television prize the *Priz d'Italia*. As we were The King's Singers she came up with the whacky idea of turning us into six kings (or rather five kings and a queen, as my already lofty forehead made me a shoo-in for Elizabeth the 1st!).

Minka, as she was affectionately known, created a crazy scene for each of the royal personages to fool around in, at the same time as using our singing talents to make the appropriate musical noises, singing all the dialogue. One, for example, was Frederick the Great and for his scene, recalling a famous visit by Johann Sebastian Bach, the entire script was made up of titles of Bach's cantatas! The script was put together by all of us, simply sitting around, making it up and having a ball. We spent hours each morning in make-up, producing facials suitably idiotic for the appointed task and then filming the rest of the day. I cannot begin to imagine how much it all must have cost, but it ended up as a sizeable waste of money, totally failing to excite the adjudicators for the prize. But for us it was tremendous fun.

Back in the real world, away from the television cameras, I try to imagine what it was that endeared us to our audiences. These were the 60s and 70s and the world was changing: maybe it was our clean-living image which appealed to people, with well-cut suits, tidy hairstyles, a sense of fun we shared with our audiences and the fact that (I would like to think) we could sing well and create a well-balanced and perfectly blended vocal ensemble. This did not just happen: for the first few years we toiled endlessly on sound, style and repertoire, working out what sort of music our audiences might like to hear. I say 'audiences' as there was obviously the Music Club circuit which enjoyed the more 'serious' side of the repertoire and there was the television audience which leaned more towards the populist end.

The way we built programmes reflected those needs. In the early days our programmes were musically weightier but would always end with what we called 'arrangements in close harmony' – popular songs, comic songs, folk songs, classical music send-ups, that sort of thing. Later on the musical selections became lighter in tone and it is fair to say that the lighter they became the more we began to lose the more serious end of our supporters. Many years down the line the current group has splendidly redressed the balance, much, I believe, to the benefit of its audience. The point we consistently tried to make was that there need not exist barriers between the various types of music, the idea being to approach all sorts of music in the same well-rehearsed and polished way: the important thing was the sound of The King's Singers, regardless of what sort of music to which that sound was applied.

We liked the idea that a television audience which had seen us sitting in six baths and singing a Flanders and Swann song would come to a concert and before they got what they were expecting, they had the chance to experience sixteenth century madrigals and motets, Victorian part-songs and a wealth of contemporary music written specially for The King's Singers' sound. The very idea that some of the world's leading composers would want to write for us suggests that they were fascinated by that sound: Penderecki, Berio, Ligeti, Richard Rodney Bennett, Menotti, John Rutter, John Tavener, Paul Patterson and many more. Also great arrangers: Gordon Langford, Daryl Runswick, Ron Goodwin, Richard Rodney Bennett again, Goff Richards, George Martin and so on. Lucky us.

After the excitement of that first three-month Australasian tour, the internal combustion which had brought us thus far swung into top gear and for the rest of my time as the bass singer in the group we were on the road almost constantly. I performed over 2,000 concerts worldwide during my fifteen years; it was a wonderful way to see the world and to be able to share our collective gifts with audiences of so many different kinds.

Belfast became one of our favourite ports of call, particularly in those troubled times of the 1970s. We were invited each year to sing in the Cathedral, where we were well looked after by the Dean, the Very Revd. Sammy Crooks. Every time we sang there the cathedral was packed. There was not so much 'live' entertainment in Belfast in those days and we managed to build up a great audience over the years. Sammy would go out before each concert and welcome everyone, including us. The last time we went he came into the vestry before the concert and admitted that he could not think of anything new to say about us. We encouraged him to try and out he went: "Ladies and Gentlemen", he began, in that great Irish brogue of his: "it's a great pleasure to welcome back our old friends The King's Singers. I heard them rehearsing this afternoon and if they're no better tonight you can get your money back on the way out." Follow that!

The 70s saw us touring in Australia five times, New Zealand four times, Japan twice, South Africa four times, North America most years and throughout much of Central Europe, as well, of course, as venues all over the UK. Germany produced particularly appreciative audiences and indeed the last concert I performed with The King's Singers

99

(November 8th, 1982) was in the Berlin Philharmonie: not a bad place to bow out.

The first Australasian trip in 1972 was a real eye-opener for all of us and a joy from start to finish. Having said that, it is hard to realise how out of touch we felt during the three months we were there: those were the days when even making a phone call home was a major operation, long before the days of mobile phones, faxes or Skype. If we wanted to talk to our nearest and dearest, we had to book a call – through the operator – for whatever time was suitable, often several hours ahead. Then when we eventually got through, there would be a terrible delay on the line, meaning that whenever we said something, over the top of what we were saying was the delayed reply from the other end. It was all very uncomfortable and as a communication tool was best avoided altogether.

Our first concert in New Zealand was in the north island town of New Plymouth. We did not know anyone who had been to the country before so we were all agog to find out what our audiences might be like. We decided that the best way to get some idea, in advance of singing to them, was to read the local newspaper in the hope of learning something about the local people before inflicting our singing on them. In New Plymouth our luck was in as our visit coincided with the 80th birthday of a lady whose principal joy was going to the movies. In celebration of this major milestone in her life, she had been given free tickets to the local fleapit for a year, a bottle of fizz, some flowers and a full-page interview in the local rag. This, we thought, might throw some light on the population. In the middle of the interview, she was asked – remember this was 1972 – if she thought there was too much sex and violence in the cinema these days. Her reply – again,

I'm not making this up! – "As I always sit on the front row I never know what the rest of the audience is doing."

Our first concert in capital city Wellington was obviously important in terms of likely publicity and we were naturally concerned as to how our type of mixed programme might be received. The concerts organised by the Chamber Music Federation of New Zealand normally consisted of string quartets, violin and piano concerts, Lieder recitals and such erudite material. And here we were – six young Englishmen with a mixture of unaccompanied ensemble music from the 13th to the 20th centuries, serious in part but always ending with some good, clean fun! The reaction to our Wellington debut was encouraging: on the way out of the concert, a staunch member of the federation was heard admitting to her friend "I'm rather afraid I enjoyed that"!

Wherever we went on our travels, we were always fascinated by other all male vocal close harmony groups and avidly collected their LPs. An American male-group 'groupie' called James Stewart (not that one!) held a party at his home in Chicago to celebrate our visit when we performed at Evanston University. There we met three of the four members of the Singers Unlimited – the delectable Bonnie Hermann, Don Shelton (who had previously been a member of the HiLos) and the amazing Len Dresslar, the bass to end all basses. I stayed with the Dresslars and still have a photo of the two of us, well oiled at party time, each clearly trying to sing a lower note than the other. Len won by about an octave and a half! Also there were members of The Four Freshmen, The Polka Dots and assorted barbershop quartets. We were in heaven.

A German group from the 1930s and 40s was one whose singing we particularly enjoyed – six men who had a huge following as The Comedy Harmonists. When we sang in Berlin I managed to find two double albums of their remarkable recordings and eventually, Daryl Runswick made arrangements for us of five of their most famous songs. We premiered this set in the Philharmonie and the songs went down a storm: clearly the Comedy Harmonists were fondly remembered and much loved. During the interval there was a knock on our dressing room door and two elderly gentlemen introduced themselves as Erwin Boots and Bob Biberti – the only two members of the original group still alive. We could hardly believe it and were knocked out when they said – with tears in their eyes – how thrilled they were to hear our affectionate tribute to them, so many decades after they had stopped singing.

Touring in America was particularly hard work: we had to self-drive thousands of miles over regular lengthy tours, initially as part of the series known as Community Concerts. Nobody had heard of us, so there was not a great deal of interest. Those who came to the concerts – largely because they had paid their annual sub and wanted their money's worth – were appreciative enough, though clearly this was not the way to make a mark in such a large country. The daily routine was not perhaps as glamorous as people think. After breakfast we would self-drive all morning and sometimes into the afternoon to get to the next place, grab some lunch, rehearse for a couple of hours, grab some tea, perform the concert, grab some supper and go to bed. That pattern followed day after day, five days performing each week for six weeks on the trot. We seemed to be getting nowhere fast.

Mind you, we did have some interesting experiences on our American travels. On one unforgettable occasion we sang in Nashville, Tennessee – the home of country music, where we were invited to join the audience at the Grand Ole Opry. What an eye-opener that was. We were used to hearing some sort of country music pumped out of Broadcasting House in London, but this was the real thing. The first time we went, the programme still came from the old, somewhat dilapidated hall, one for which any suggestion of 'health and safety' had clearly never been considered! There we saw some of the most famous old-timers: Roy Rodgers, yo-yo man Roy Acuff, Tammy Wynette and many more. Also on the bill was a tall, thin, amusing and apparently very well-known character called 'Stringbean'. He would do an amazing trick with his hat and end each song with his famous catch phrase: 'When you're hot, you're hot; when you're not, you're not'.

Our agent in California had booked us into the Hermitage Hotel, obviously one she had picked out of a brochure from the 1930s. Talk about faded glory: it had clearly seen far better days – certainly up on the eighth floor where my room was located. The room was filthy and I discovered to my discomfort that I was all alone on that top floor. This became even more worrying when I turned on the local TV programme on returning from the Grand Ole Opry to hear the news that the very same Stringbean had been shot dead on arriving home from the performance we had just seen. I tried to get to sleep, only to be disturbed in the early hours by the sound of someone walking along the corridor trying each door with a key. I leapt out of bed, rushed to my door, connected the rape-lock and gave it a gentle tug, to make sure it was strong enough. To my ever-growing horror, the entire architrave fell over my head into the room, leaving me holding onto a door which could no longer shut! You couldn't make it up! When I eventually calmed down and looked out of the space where my door had been, I saw a lady with her trolley, simply making up the rooms which were unoccupied.

When we got to Memphis, I decided to drive out to Gracelands, the house where Elvis Presley had died a couple of weeks before. I found a crowd of women beating their heads against the perimeter wall in despair and could not help wondering how anyone could have been so moved as to go to such lengths. After seeing as much as I could I got back into the car and turned on the radio. The lunchtime news mentioned that Bing Crosby had died on a golf course that very morning: I felt like going back and joining the distraught ladies.

Our fortunes in the States changed dramatically in 1982 when we were asked to appear on a coast-to-coast TV programme as guests of the famous Boston Pops Orchestra. We had previously sung to the orchestra's legendary conductor Arthur Fiedler in his suite at the Savoy in the hope of a big break. By the time we did the show – 'live' in Symphony Hall in Boston – Fiedler had retired and his place had been taken by the great film composer John 'Star Wars' Williams. This was to be his first major concert as Pops conductor and he was understandably nervous about sharing the platform with six English guys of whom he had never heard.

We trooped into his dressing room at Symphony Hall and found him welcoming but clearly desperate to be impressed. We gathered round his piano and he asked us to sing something. Within a few bars, it was wonderful to see a broad grin spread across his face as he realised that his fears had been in vain. It was another of those great moments, working with such a man and it is amazing to see snippets of that career-changing moment still available on YouTube nearly forty years later. That nationwide TV coverage did the trick and started a whole new life for The King's Singers: too late for me, as I left the group a few months later. Maybe flogging round all those community concerts had not been a waste of time after all.

Back home we were the lucky ones for whom so-called Light Entertainment on BBC TV gave us immediate access to people's homes. Forty years on, that sort of exposure sadly no longer exists. But there was a possibly down-side for us, as already mentioned, in that the more popular The King's Singers became on telly, doing frankly rather silly things, the more the original *modus operandi* failed to appeal to those of our audience who had so much enjoyed our more 'serious' side. The world of unaccompanied vocal groups was widening, to include such superstar groups as The Sixteen, the Tallis Scholars, I Fagiolini, and so on. As I've already said, the great thing is that the current group of King's Singers has concentrated on the more 'serious' side (I hate that term, but you know what I mean) and have continued to keep the brand name more than ever alive worldwide by being perhaps more true to our roots.

Memories of our visits to South Africa are rather shrouded in the fact that this was the 1970s and the horrors of apartheid were still very much in evidence. Nonetheless we loved the country and gradually built up our audience over four major tours. We were touring for the Performing Arts Council of the Transvaal and to begin with, our audiences were exclusively white. When we were asked to come again, we agreed to do so only on the condition that the doors would be opened to all people, regardless of colour. It was agreed that a certain percentage could enjoy this facility and it was only on our fourth tour in 1980 that it was agreed that the audiences could include people of any colour. That wasn't going to change the political situation overnight, but it could at least be considered one small step.

On the last day of the 1980 trip, following our concert at the Nico Milan Theatre in Cape Town, the British Ambassador kindly invited us to his residence for a post-concert party. He greeted us at the door and offered us two alternatives: we could go into a small room which housed the largest collection of malt whisky in the country, or we could proceed to the larger room where a great crowd of people were waiting to meet us. No prize for guessing which room we tried first. We then made our way into the drawing room where the Ambassador introduced me to two people he was sure I would like to meet – none other than Anne Ziegler and Webster Booth. This hugely popular singing duo – the English Nelson Eddy and Jeanette MacDonald if you will – had retired to Cape Town and had been at the concert. I was thrilled to meet them and we chatted happily for some time, all of us enlivened by the copious quantities of delicious South African wine on offer.

After a while we were asked to sing one song for the benefit of the embassy staff members who had not been able to get tickets for the concert. As it was the last night of the trip, with some time off to come, we agreed. After that I asked Anne Ziegler and Webster Booth if they would sing for us. They half-heartedly refused, claiming that they had not sung in public for a long time. When I told them that I happened to know the piano part for one of their most famous duets – *The Keys of Heaven* – they generously agreed to sing if I played. And so they did, quite splendidly. I have a photo to prove it. When I went back to thank them afterwards, a very small bald-headed man joined us and thanked me for playing, adding that he used to play that same piece for Clara Butt and Kennerly Rumford! He turned out to be Ivor Newton, one of the UK's finest piano accompanists of the generation before Gerald Moore.

All in all, we were having the time of our lives. How else could we bright young things have enjoyed the opportunity to travel all round the world at someone else's expense? We were relatively young, hugely enthusiastic, determined and anxious to spread the word: and so we did, year after unrelenting year.

But there comes a time in one's life when one has to take stock and decide if it is the one thing each of us wants to do. The problem is that one is part of a team and that team depends on everyone being there with all cylinders firing all the time. For me, as an example, constantly being away from home put tremendous pressure on family life: so much so that the family unit faced the dilemma well-known to so many in this sort of job. My wife Sally inevitably found the pressure too great and understandably sought solace elsewhere, taking the children (Jonathan, then aged six and four-year-old Charlotte) to what she hoped might be a better life. I can and did completely understand and deeply regret that situation, as nothing mattered to me more than the sort of joys of family life which my own parents had instilled in all of us. There was this ghastly struggle between making a go in the music business and yet keeping the family unit intact. This should never be a struggle if you believe in the sanctity of family life, as I did and do: but it was and became increasingly difficult to keep the balance right.

And so I found myself living alone and moving from our family home in the Cotswolds to a one-bedroom flat in Camden Town. In a way this made work easier, as I could virtually walk to the BBC and the major London concert halls and even getting to Heathrow was less of a problem. But coming and going from a lonely flat in order to entertain audiences all over the world became for me a very difficult situation to come to terms with: the whole idea of that itinerant existence seemed suddenly rather pointless. I put up with it for some time, though I am quite sure I became a difficult colleague, less able to apply my old enthusiasm to the task.

I soldiered on, trying to make the best of some of the more exciting engagements which were coming the way of The King's Singers. We were asked to sing at a major gala concert for Princess Grace of Monaco, sharing the platform in Monte Carlo with some pretty unlikely people, including Telly Savalas, famous throughout the world as 'Kojak'. We appeared at the Royal Variety Show, apparently at the special request of The Queen Mother, who had enjoyed us in concert a number of times. We managed to confuse a Palladium audience by singing excerpts from Her Majesty's entry in Debrett's Peerage set to Anglican chant! Benny Green's newspaper review found it utterly unspeakable, but The Queen Mother herself was clearly delighted, even to the extent of asking for it again next time she came to one of our concerts.

On one remarkable day of tele-recording, we managed to contribute to two major programmes – one with Spike Milligan and the other with Terry Wogan. On Spike's programme, we sang a lovely setting by our old friend Gordon Langford of one of Spike's own poems and the director said that at the end, we should simply bow – low and slow – and that they would then feed in the applause of our non-existent audience. We rather wondered why they had insisted that we wear clothes from the BBC wardrobe, rather than our own flash suits. All became clear as we raised our heads from taking the bow: Spike and five others rushed at us with custard pies! The ghastly stuff went everywhere – up our noses, in our ears and eyes and needless to say, all over the clothes which, mercifully, were not our own. Twenty minutes later, after hosing us down, we were in the next-door studio recording with Wogan. We could still taste and smell the zinc ointment which had made up the so-called custard pies! Terry joined us and stood on the end of the row, next to me. I had already announced to the others that I would be leaving and I happened to mention this to Terry, asking if he had a good, strong bottom C in case he might like to take my place! Without a single thought, he sang a resounding bottom C – bang on the note. I often reminded him since what a great opportunity he turned down by not joining the group. I wonder what happened to him.

Two brief memories of meeting people on tour: one happened during one of our early Australasian trips. We had a day off in Sydney and someone told us that there was another harmony group in town, also keen to make a name for itself. We had just heard of them, as their first hit record – Burt Bacharach's *Close to You* – had already been released in the UK. They were Karen and Richard Carpenter and we managed to get tickets for their late-night performance.

There were not many there and when the show (amazing as it was) was over, we wandered backstage in the hope of meeting them. That was no problem: we simply knocked on their dressing room door and introduced ourselves to them.

They invited us in and we had a long and delightful chat, comparing notes about the relative state of our developments. It is hard to imagine having that sort of opportunity these days and I look back on that strange meeting with the Carpenters with particular pleasure. Theirs was an amazing close harmony sound, achieved largely thanks to the skill of multi-tracking – overlaying their own voices again and again in order to create a sound that was so perfectly blended – very much the same sort of approach we were working on ourselves. In that concert, Karen also played the drums as well as making that gloriously rich, warm sound with her deep, mellifluous voice.

On one of our visits to New York we followed our performance by being invited to a club where actors and musicians of various kinds would meet after the day's work and chill out together. As each person arrived, he or she gave a name to the man on the door, who then shouted it out over the Tannoy so that everyone knew who was there. Clearly the name of The King's Singers meant nothing to everyone so we sat quietly enjoying a few drinks on our own. After a while, in came Barry Humphries, whose one-man show was not at that stage exactly the talk of the town – mainly because it was a bit over-the-top for the relatively prudish New York audiences; so much so that the doorman announced Mr Humphries, currently appearing as Dame *Ethel* Everage! He sat a couple of tables away from us, with nobody talking to him, so we ventured to join him, particularly as we had recently been working in the UK with his great mate (and ours) Willie Rushton. That was sufficient introduction for him to start talking – very loudly indeed – about himself, making sure that by the time he left the club, everyone would be aware of his presence and his achievements.

Another extraordinary event comes to mind and that one found we King's Singers performing on a German television programme fronted by the operatic tenor Renee Kollo. He was joined by a fine trio of similar status singers: soprano Lucia Popp, mezzo Brigitte Fassbaender and the baritone Tom Krause. As if that weren't enough excitement for us all, the instrumental guest was none other than Benny Goodman, who played the slow movement of the Mozart Clarinet Concerto. That reminds me of a story of Benny Goodman, who was not perhaps the most generous of musicians! He was giving a lesson to a young pupil in his New York apartment when she suggested to him that it was getting rather cold. Asking her to hang on for a moment, he left the room and returned wearing a sweater!

Well, in 1982, I made the decision to leave the group and try to have a go at something else. I was not sure what that something else might be, but I knew that, with the passage of time, this essentially young man's way of life had become less attractive than it had been at the start. I had performed over 2000 concerts worldwide; I had had a terrific time travelling all over the world and making many friends in the process; I had without doubt hugely enjoyed being part of such a successful ensemble, one which had started out as a fun way of keeping together with old friends at the same time as 'doing the what comes naturally' – making music. I was and remain very proud of what we had achieved, setting standards for similar groups and refreshing the male voice repertoire with arrangements and compositions which are still widely performed in many parts of the world by any number of groups inspired by what we did.

In the back of my mind was something I had first thought

of when I was very young. I used to listen to Eric Robinson presenting *Music for You* on the BBC radio and thinking that that sort of thing was just what I would like to do, one fine day. It was a ridiculous dream for a village boy from Yorkshire, but something had clearly sown a seed in my mind and with the experience of The King's Singers behind me, as well as having had the opportunity to meet so many people in radio and television, I began to think that this sort of thing might be the next step forward.

And so, on November the 8th, 1982, I sang my last concert as a King's Singer and after it was over – as I said, in the Philharmonie in Berlin – the rest of the group, with my replacement Colin Mason, travelled on to their next destination while I flew back to Blighty as a 'free man'. It was an extraordinary experience and the feeling of being on my own after so many years was wonderfully refreshing.

One of the first calls I had was from the bass Terry Edwards: six foot nine and a former colleague in the session singing world. The young Simon Rattle had been asked to direct the summer South Bank festival and had come up with a typically revolutionary idea. He asked Terry to fix a group of singers to perform, over five nights in the Purcell Room, all sixty five madrigals by the late 16th, early 17th century English composer John Wilbye alongside the complete unaccompanied choral music of the 20th century French composer Francis Poulenc. Terry charmed me by saying that as I had spent all those years singing bass parts which were really too low for me I might like to try singing some baritone parts which might well be too high for me. After some considerable time I agreed, thinking that the project might be a lot of fun. It was much more than that, as it was to change my life for ever.

I had always been very conscientious when it came to things like punctuality and for the first rehearsal I turned up good and early in the hope of getting to know my new singing colleagues before we started making music together. Some of them I already knew from my previous professional session singing days; but there was one who was new to me and who also liked to turn up in good time, rather than risking being late. Terry immediately introduced me to the soprano Gillian Fisher, none of us able to imagine that within a matter of months, Gilly and I would be married. More of that happy situation later, though there and then it became blissfully clear that, in all sorts of ways, life was about to begin all over again.

Starting a new life post-King's-Singers could have been difficult, as I had no concrete plans and would inevitably have to start earning money again. Gilly had read Law at Warwick University and had then moved on to the Royal College of Music in London in the hope of becoming a singer rather than a lawyer. She had a very beautiful, crystal clear soprano voice (mercifully preserved on many outstanding CD recordings – see Appendix VII) which was perfectly suited to the rapidly developing world of so-called 'authentic' or 'historically-aware' performance of Baroque music. In no time at all, I became a 'kept man'. Gilly was suddenly singing all over the world, from Sydney Opera House and Tokyo's Suntory Hall to New York's Lincoln Centre, London's Royal Albert Hall and all stations in between. I could afford to take my time working out what on earth to do next.

CHAPTER NINE

Katie Kay of the BBC

Remembering back to that remarkably prophetic description of this loud-mouthed nine year old by his second form master at Rydal Preparatory School, I had the feeling that if I was lucky enough, the opportunity might arise for me to approach the BBC.

I did not need to wait long: one of the last concerts I sang with The King's Singers in the UK was at the Cheltenham Festival. For our appearance there the festival had commissioned for us *Seven Deadly Sins*, asking seven distinguished composers to choose a sin each and to set a suitable text to music. For one of these, the text – a spoof Edwardian melodrama – was wonderfully written by the incomparable Willie Rushton and set to music by top film and television composer Carl Davis.

The whole thing began with me, off stage, breathing into the microphone, in a suitably breathy tone, a typical old-style 'third programme' announcement. The entire evening was being recorded by the BBC World Service and during the interval, the producer – Jimmy Burnett – told me that he had heard that I was going to leave the group. What, he wondered, was I going to do? I admitted that I had no real idea, but that I just wanted to stop being a King's Singer. "Have you ever considered", he asked, "becoming a radio announcer?" He thought I had made a good job of pretending to be one and asked straight out if I might be interested in presenting for the World Service all the concerts from the festival that year. Needless to say, I leapt at the idea and a couple of weeks later found myself in a BBC studio reading scripts prepared by Jimmy and feeling completely at home.

The other producer for that series of programmes was Paul Reading and he immediately called BBC Radio 3 and asked if they might be interested in my auditioning for an opportunity to present a long-running afternoon programme with the crazy title *Mainly for Pleasure* (who on earth came up with that one?). This had a number of presenters who took turns to choose their own music and present it at the five o'clock slot each weekday afternoon. The executive producer of the programme was Gareth Walters and he took me on board, offering me the opportunity to present a number of programmes. It was a terrific way in for me and started me off on twenty-five years of constant radio and television work. This was in those far-off days of long playing gramophone records and although I had a fair collection, I had to start spending many hours in the BBC Gram Library in order to create programmes of sufficient variety to fill an hour and a half's programme and I loved it.

After a while I wanted to do more than this one particular slot and I asked if there were any other outlets in which I could develop my experience. As it happens, the Head of Presentation for Radio 3 at the time was Cormac Rigby and as he had been a regular member of our audience at King's Singers concerts he was well aware of my speaking voice, as I used to introduce our programmes from the stage. He invited me to come to the studio and read a five-minute news summary and weather report so he could play it to the Controller, with a recommendation that I join the team as a staff announcer. I must have made a decent fist of it as I was immediately offered a full-time job. On my first day I was taken to the office to meet the distinguished presenters who were about to become my colleagues. I knew all their voices well enough and was able to identify each of them the moment they said hello.

I was to replace the immensely popular and gloriously voiced Patricia Hughes who was about to retire. It was she who taught me how to play the gramophones (this was well before the advent of CDs) and on one occasion in studio when she had introduced some music, started the LP and closed her microphone fader, I plucked up courage and asked her how long she had been working for Radio 3. Her reply, in that wonderful, almost baritonal voice: "My dear, I was here before tape"! It was so good to be joining such a jolly team of enthusiastic and immensely experienced presenters – Peter Barker, Malcolm Ruthven, Tony Scotland, Jon Curle, John Holmstrom, Elaine Padmore, Cormac Rigby himself and, like me, recent newcomers Donald Mcleod (later to become the outstanding perennial presenter of *Composer of the Week*), Susan Sharp (the truckers 'through the night' favourite) and Douglas Reith (years later to star in the global television success *Downton Abbey* as Lord Merton).

My first experience on air was a tricky one. The newsroom clearly knew that there was a new kid on the block and decided to see if I was any good. At seven o'clock in the morning on my first day I had to read a five-minute news summary and ten seconds before I was due to read it, there was no sign of it. It was only during the six seconds of 'pips' that the door suddenly opened and the text was thrust into my seriously sweating hands. There was just time to look at the first sentence before I sight-read the entire thing, 'live' on air. The blood drained from my face as I saw the news folk had handed me a somewhat challenging first sentence. It was one I shall never forget: "*Father Jerzy Popiełuszko, Poland's most popular pre-solidarity priest, has been murdered*". Try saying that when your nerves are on edge and an awful lot of people are listening to you. Luckily, I was able to stagger through that particular tongue-twister, after which the rest was kids' stuff.

And so began a couple of years as a staff announcer and a marvellous opportunity to see the inner workings of the BBC at close quarters. I was able to meet so many of the people who make the whole thing work and to learn the basics of radio presentation including the techniques involved in improvising trails for programmes, playing the LPs and tapes and developing my own way of doing things, very much within the 'house style' appropriate to Radio 3. I learned largely by listening to others and by watching them at work. The old Radio 3 presentation studio had a glass wall in front of the presenter's chair and on the other side was Radio 1. I could sit there watching the likes of Tony Blackburn and Kenny Everett doing their stuff in a rather different way.

It was at about that time that my old friend Miles Kington wrote an article in a national newspaper all about BBC Radio, the climax of which was when he described the Radio 3 announcer as having "the voice, the phrasing and the patient enunciation of someone who knows that nobody's listening to him" – naughty but nice. After I had been on the staff for several months, someone in the personnel department noticed that I never officially applied for the job, with the result that there was no information about me on the staff list. I was asked to fill in an application form so that the omission could be corrected. Having dutifully done so, I had a reply from the department saying that there was currently no vacancy as a Radio 3 announcer, though they would be in touch if such an opportunity arose! Perhaps nobody really had been listening.

I loved the work, but there was a down-side and it eventually led to my deciding to leave the team. The problem for me was that, as an announcer, the job consisted of reading out scripts which had been written by the producer of each programme, regardless of whom the presenter might happen to be on the day of the broadcast. It was therefore difficult to introduce any sense of personality into the presentation. If I had any serious thoughts about a career in broadcasting I wanted to be a 'presenter' rather than an 'announcer'– in other words, someone who could choose his own musical material, write his own script and present it in his own way. This is not the way things were done at Radio 3 in those days and for those who had announced in that way for so many years that was fine. For me it was just not enough of a challenge and the fulfilment was not sufficiently great.

So with some regret I called it a day and went back to working as a freelance presenter available for whenever there might be an opportunity. This also meant that I could be free to work for Radio 2 and Radio 4 if the occasion arose. And indeed it did. I was on holiday in New Zealand when a fax appeared from Christine Hardwick at the Beeb. Richard Baker had presented a regular Radio 4 programme for many years, first as *Baker's Dozen*, then as *These you have Loved* and more recently as *Music in Mind*. He had decided to give up that particular strand and Christine asked me if I might like to be part of a team of presenters, taking turns to deliver the goods. Of course I was delighted by the prospect as this really did mean making my own programmes and presenting them with the freedom to do things in my own way. I was given the opportunity to kick-start the process by presenting an entire quarter – thirteen weekly programmes each of forty-five minutes on a Saturday night leading up to the 'God slot' just before ten o'clock. I must have started well as I ended up presenting *Music in Mind* without a break, every Saturday for nine years! My producer from the start was Sarah Devonald and it was she who would also go on to start and help me to develop the most important programme of my broadcasting career.

When Nicholas Kenyon was appointed Controller of Radio 3, I happened to bump into him in the lift one day and offered my congratulations. He immediately suggested that it would be good if we could meet as he wanted me to come up with some ideas. As it happened, Frances Lyne, the Controller of Radio 2 had recently moved that much-loved Sunday morning programme *Melodies for You* to Sunday evening and the huge audience for that slot suddenly had to find something else to listen to on a Sunday morning – one of the best times of the week for listening pleasure. I suggested to Nick that it might be worth considering that particular audience and coming up with something to bring them on board. He liked the idea and said he would think about it. My hope was maybe an hour's programme of musical 'all sorts' carefully chosen for the time of day and the time of the week.

I went off to Australia to be with my wife Gilly as she sang as soprano soloist in several performances of Handel's *Messiah* with Harry Christophers and The Sixteen. By the time I returned Nick had decided on a programme called *Brian Kay's Sunday Morning* and that it should last for three-and-a-quarter hours, 'live' from nine till twelve-fifteen every Sunday for the foreseeable future. When I asked what sort of music he wanted he generously said that I should include anything I want as long as it added up to a good morning's listening. All my Christmases had come at once.

I was not entirely sure how I was going to be able to build a long weekly programme unless I moved into Broadcasting House and spent most of my time in the gramophone library. Help was at hand in the form of my producer Sarah Devonald, with whom I had so much enjoyed working on my Radio 4 programme. We would meet early in the week and discuss ideas and gradually we worked out a formula which we hoped might satisfy Nick Kenyon's instruction.

He had also decided that, as my programme coincided with the birth of the BBC Music Magazine, it would be good to have a tie-up between the programme and the magazine. With only a few short weeks to go until the start of both, I was asked to put together what the magazine called *Brian Kay's Starter Collection*, the idea being that I might select half a dozen CDs each month in order to encourage people to build up their collections. The great benefit to me of this idea was that all the major record companies started sending me their new releases, in the hope that they might make it into the *Starter Collection*. This also meant that my own relatively modest CD collection rapidly grew into something far more substantial, from which it would be so much easier for me to build Sunday Morning programmes at home. As the programme and the column ran for nine years, I ended up with well over ten thousand CDs and an impressive library of recorded music on which to draw.

The programme quickly built up a large and seemingly appreciative audience. There were those who thought that this was not the sort of musical melange that Radio 3 – or perhaps I should say 'The Third Programme' – should be encouraging, though they were far outnumbered by those for whom a carefully-chosen selection of musical 'all sorts' clearly hit the spot. It was, for me, a fascinating way of communicating my own musical enthusiasms to as large an audience as possible and it was a particular excitement to be rewarded on two occasions by being awarded a Sony Award as *Music Presenter of the Year*, including the coveted Gold Award in 1996.

Once the programme had settled and the audience had become established, it was decided that we should occasionally take the show on the road. This turned out to be an excellent way for Radio 3 to do some serious networking – reaching out to its devoted audience and hopefully beyond. We would move to venues in various parts of the country and broadcast from there with a mixture of 'live' musical inserts as well as a selection of CDs. We set out tables with gingham cloths and served teas and coffees and the Sunday papers, so that those who came could relax and listen, as we hoped they normally did at home. I have fond memories of places as diverse as the enormous tent at the Llangollen Eisteddfod (where I had presented the television coverage all week), the Floral Hall at the Covent Garden Opera House and fine halls in towns and cities as far apart as Truro, York,

Exeter, Cheltenham, Edinburgh (at festival time), Manchester (to celebrate the opening of the Bridgwater Hall), Oxford, Cambridge (where we persuaded The King's College choir to perform 'live' either side of their Sunday morning service!) and many more.

The most extraordinary away-day took place in Vienna. Radio 3 was celebrating what it called a 'Danube Week' and decided to include *Brian Kay's Sonntags Morgen* in the schedule. We broadcast from the canteen of the Austrian Radio building, which I knew well from my many years of presenting the New Year's Day Concert. Unfortunately, on a Sunday morning there is virtually nobody working in the building and we found it rather hard to create a real atmosphere of an audience having the time of its life! When we included a 'live' performance, we had to encourage the kitchen staff to join us in order that there might at least be some applause! To say that they were somewhat bemused is a classic understatement.

We had asked the Vienna Philharmonic to recommend a suitable zither player, in order to create some local colour and memories of *Harry Lime*. They found an old chap who had clearly been playing all night in various clubs and who, like the kitchen staff was blissfully unaware of what the programme was all about: that was until I told him that, although there were very few people in the room, there were countless thousands all over the UK who would be hanging on his every note. At mention of that, the blood drained from his face and he began frantically trying to re-tune his rather battered zither!

Back home in London's Broadcasting House, the routine was the same each week. I would drive up to London from my home in the Cotswolds on Saturday night (not daring to risk Sunday morning traffic) and stay at the hotel next door – built on the sight of the old Queen's Hall, which had been bombed in 1941 and sadly not rebuilt. I would go to my studio and sort out the CDs. This meant lining up the appropriate tracks on whichever of the three players each CD would eventually be broadcast. After I found the exact place on the CD where the music would begin, the machine would then memorise that place, so that when I put the same CD in the same machine the next morning, it would automatically go straight to that precise place, ready for action. After a good night's sleep, I would make my way to the studio first thing in the morning and prepare to do the business. I began to have a brief chat 'on air' with the presenter of the previous programme (Paul Guinery's *Sacred and Profane*) in the same way that Radio 2 had introduced this technique involving Terry Wogan and Jimmy Young. This gave us a chance to preview what was coming up in my programme. We tried to make it as informal and entertaining as we could (again, no doubt, to the distaste of the old-school Third Programme listeners) and perhaps we succeeded too far. After some months of doing this, a message came through from Nick Kenyon suggesting – in a prime example of BBC-speak – that 'these entertaining conversations between Brian Kay and Paul Guinery must become increasingly infrequent'! They did, but nowadays, everyone does it.

Sitting alone in a studio and broadcasting 'live' for three and a quarter hour takes a fair amount of concentration. One false move and everyone knows. Even with hours of thorough preparation, mistakes can happen – the right CD in the wrong machine or the wrong CD altogether, forgetting to open a microphone fader when announcing the next music, or forgetting to close it when you've finished speaking – very dangerous that! But I soon got used to it and found that the time passed pretty quickly. It was at least an hour and a half's drive back home after the programme and by the time I arrived I was certainly ready for a large gin and tonic and a good lunch.

Each year I was allowed four weeks off during the summer and when I made my annual pilgrimage to New Zealand, I recorded programmes; that was handy, though never the same feeling as broadcasting 'live'. My stand-ins in those summer breaks made an interesting and somewhat eclectic bunch: the first was Patricia Routledge – then hugely popular as the television star Hyacinth Bucket, though, of course, well remembered as a singer on the West End musical stage. Then came my dear friend and colleague as conductor of the Huddersfield Choral Society Jane Glover. She was an avid *Archers* fan and admitted to listening to that long-running radio series instead of me on Sunday mornings – even to the extent that on her first programme at the appropriate hour, she included in the programme a recording of the signature tune! Husband and wife Tim West and Prunella Scales (also friends and colleagues) had a go and ended their last with Pru suggesting to Tim that they should repay the privilege by asking me to stand in for Tim in some production or other. They were slowly and cleverly faded out as Tim suggested I might take over in his current production as *King Lear* before both agreeing that I was too bald! Sadly, the only person who turned us down was Judi Dench, claiming that she didn't know enough about music. But when you have a voice like that, what difference does it make?

I mentioned staying in the hotel next door to Broadcasting House. This reminds me that when I was on the staff as an announcer, if I was closing down the network at midnight and opening up again at six o'clock in the morning, I had to go over the road to what is now the extremely plush Langham Hilton, but which was then a rather clapped-out studio block with a handful of bedrooms for this precise purpose. It was like jumping aboard the *Marie Celeste* – a ghost building full of low lighting and long corridors, not perhaps for the faint-hearted. I would make my way to the Radio 3 announcer's room – large and sparsely furnished – a brass bed, a locker and a wardrobe. I would fall into bed and get to sleep quickly, only to be woken up – every time – when the Radio 4 announcer came into the room next door after closing down his network much later than Radio 3. The crazy thing was that with so many rooms to choose from in this vastly under-populated building. these two rooms were adjacent.

In the end, we all complained and in their infinite wisdom, the Radio 4 room was moved and replaced – by a bathroom, with the lavatory cistern immediately behind where I would be attempting to sleep. This could well have been another reason I decided that being a staff announcer was not quite the thing for me.

Back to my Sunday Morning programme and after nine years of building up a large audience, I had a call from Controller Roger Wright asking if we might meet for a cup of tea. I dutifully turned up at his office, only to be told that we were going over to that same Langham Hilton for that cuppa. We chatted happily – largely about cricket – for about twenty minutes, until I realised that this was not all he had in mind. I fed him the appropriate line: "Still happy with the programme?" He said that he was, but that he was going to take it off. In fairness to Roger, he gave me not only nine months' notice, but also two new programmes in lieu.

But it was a sad moment for me, as the programme was so popular and I could never get from the Controller the real reason for his decision. However, I had had a good run and was in no position to complain. The idea of having uninterrupted weekends at home suddenly appealed to me and I resigned myself to an enforced change of direction. The saddest thing about it, however, was that the programme was replaced by one which simply did not work – even though it was presented by the lovely Stephanie Hughes, at that time also very popular as a TV music presenter. The audience which I and my producers had so painstakingly built up over nine years quickly disappeared, largely because much of the music had been 'gifted' to the BBC by the European Broadcasting Union, with the idea that it should all have been performed and recorded during the week before the broadcast. Details of the music had to be committed to in the Radio Times, before the recording had been heard. The result was no quality control and a lot of music-making of distinctly inferior (and frankly unacceptable) quality. No wonder a discerning Radio 3 audience lost interest.

Mind you, they gave me a great send-off. Radio 3 booked the famous concert hall of Broadcasting House for a final 'live' three-hour programme and allowed me to suggest a selection of musicians who might take part. We settled on The King's Singers, who were only too keen to be involved (and sang wonderfully) and the young up-and-coming soprano Sally Matthews. She had already sung for me at a number of concerts and I was well aware that she was a star in the making: and how right I turned out to be. She had recently won the coveted Kathleen Ferrier award (as a member of the jury that year, I had done my best to make sure she triumphed) and together with the pianist Iain Burnside, she delighted the audience and indeed the presenter. I also persuaded my old friend George Shearing to take part – a huge thrill to have him playing so beautifully and amusing the audience with his anecdotes. In a sort of preview for the Light Music programme which I was about to embark on, we also enjoyed the pleasure of a splendid palm court orchestra: all in all a terrific collection of 'live' performers, intermingled with carefully chose recordings.

Of course, I included one of my favourite Gillian Fisher recordings – her exquisite rendering of the aria *Guardian angels O protect me* from Handel's oratorio *The Triumph of Time and Truth*. And when it came to the big finish – well, I couldn't resist Gracie Fields' *Wish me luck as you wave me goodbye*! The whole thing was followed by a champagne reception in the Council Chamber after which I took the family over the road for an extremely jolly lunch.

The two programmes which I was given in replacement could not have been more different. One was a Sunday afternoon listeners' request programme – *3 for all* – and the other was what Roger Wright told me was something particularly close to his heart – *Brian Kay's Light Programme*. So-called "Light Music" has always been looked down upon by those for whom "serious music" is more their thing. However, there is a massive audience of enthusiasts for whom this easy-listening form of tuneful (largely orchestral) music is so much loved.

How do we define 'Light Music'? I like to use the famous phrase penned by a former BBC Head of Light Music (they really did have such a position for many years) who defined it as "music where the melody is more important than what you do with it". That sums it up perfectly, though it gives no credit to the superb tune-smiths whose craftsmanship and melodic instinct created so many classics of the genre – Eric Coates (the 'King of Light Music'), Robert Farnon (first called 'The Guv'nor' by Frank Sinatra, no less, and then by everyone else), Ernest Tomlinson, Ronnie Binge, Edward German, Trevor Duncan, George Melachrino, Roger Quilter, Richard Addinsell, Albert Ketelby and many more. In all, I featured the music of no fewer than 700 composers over the seven years the programme ran. I still have a recording on my answerphone machine of the last message I had from Bob Farnon before he died: "Brian, I just want to say thank you for playing so much of my music on your programme". He then paused before adding: "It's the listeners I feel sorry for!" Great and lovely man, wonderful composer, incomparable arranger.

The Light Programme was not broadcast 'live': I would build the content in my garden shed at home and write the script, bringing the CDs and the script to London once a month and recording four one-hour programmes in a day. That is quite hard on the voice, but it made far more sense in terms of time and cost to do it in that way. In the early days of the programme, there was not a great deal of appropriate music available on CD – plenty on old 78s and LPs (Gram Library again) though not much of that on my shelf at home. Gradually, as the programme gained in popularity, record companies latched on and began putting together compilations from old records as well as recording newer music which had never made it onto disc. If anyone should doubt the popularity of this music, he should just take a look at the enormous quantity (and quality) of recordings which have appeared in the last twenty years – an absolute treasure-trove of melodic gems which well deserve to be there for posterity, as they now are. One adventurous company has already produced well over 100 light music CDs and clearly would not have done so had the demand not been there.

I suppose my good fortune at being asked to present the Vienna New Year's Day concert for radio and television ran very neatly in tandem with the Light Music programme. The reason it came my way was simply that my distinguished colleague Richard Baker, who had presented it for many years, 'defected' to *Classic fm*, which meant that he could no longer present music programmes for the BBC. I was asked to step in for what I assumed might – with luck – be a year or two and ended up spending fifteen consecutive New Years in Vienna, enjoying one of the great perks of music presentation.

The only trouble was that for my first year – 1996 – BBC television had agreed to broadcast a major concert conducted by Sir Georg Solti and left the New Year's Day concert in the hands of Radio 2. It was the first year for decades that it had not been seen 'live' on TV and there was, inevitably, an uproar. Nonetheless, I went to Vienna with my producer David Gallagher and hoped that everything would run smoothly, as he had already produced the programme previously with Richard.

For some reason, the Vienna Phil clearly decided that if we – the BBC – were not prepared to televise proceedings, then we did not deserve to have the usual tickets for the first of the three performances. Even more unkindly than that, they told us that the performance would begin at 10.30, whereas in fact it started at 10.15. Luckily David knew the back way into the Golden Hall of the Musikverein and as we crept along corridors en route to the standing area at the back of the hall, we heard music. Only then did we realise that we had missed the first few minutes. This was deeply frustrating, though we did manage to hear the rest of the programme, standing at the back with members of the armed forces, all of whom had been given access to the performance and most of them clearly wishing they were somewhere else.

Whenever I had previously watched the concert on television (we always had an open-house party at home on New Year's Day and the instruction was to turn up as soon as the Vienna concert had finished) I wondered where on earth Richard Baker must be sitting in the hall. I soon found out, as he was not in the hall at all! First thing on the morning of the broadcast, David and I walked from our hotel close to the Musikverein to the studios of Austrian Radio. There I would set up at a normal presenter's desk, with a small television set and a script and do the honours from there.

There is nothing quite like the sound of the Vienna Philharmonic playing Strauss in that finest of all concert halls and every year I thanked my lucky stars that I had been given this opportunity so many times. Shortly after the first time I had presented it, I went to a Sony Award dinner in London and was worried when I saw Richard Baker making a beeline for me. I need not have worried: he simply wanted to let me know how well he thought I had done the job. That was a wonderfully generous gesture from a man who might have felt aggrieved at being replaced.

After fifteen glorious years, during which we got to know Vienna and all its restaurants, watering holes, parks, concert halls and historic buildings very well, I too was replaced, when Radio 3 decided that they would use only in-house staff presenters. I had had my turn and remain profoundly grateful for that, as a privilege accorded to very few. Each year had been different, depending on the variety of conductors. During my time, these included Riccardo Muti, Zubin Mehta, Lorin Maazel, Nikolaus Harnoncourt, Seiji Ozawa, Mariss Jansons, Daniel Barenboim and my own personal favourite, Georges Pretre.

It's a tall order for any conductor, with three performances of a very demanding programme within 48 hours. Most of them did not use a score and to retain those waltzes, polkas and gallops, with their variety of repeats, is a real *tour de force* – particularly so when you think that Maestro Pretre was 83 and 85 years old when he conducted his two occasions. The joy on his face throughout radiated through the responsive orchestra to the global audience of hundreds of millions – and one extremely lucky presenter.

The concert is one of those very special events which have the power to give people all over the world a kick-start to a new year and it is that aspect of the occasion that I always tried to convey. It is by no means just another ordinary concert and it has its own unique atmosphere. There was even talk at one time of the presenter simply sitting in a studio in London and talking over the pictures, but that simply wouldn't work – not as far as I'm concerned. You have to be there in Vienna and experiencing the magic of it all at first-hand in order to complement the music in an appropriate way.

131

One place we headed for most years, just round the corner from the Cathedral, is the Mozart House, formerly known as the Figaro house, as it was there that Mozart wrote his most popular opera. The house has been beautifully kept as a museum, though wisely the rooms are all free of any kind of furniture. On the walls of each room, a small section of the layers of paint have been meticulously stripped back to reveal the covering that would have been there at the time the Mozarts rented the apartment.

At that time, the house belonged to the court plasterer and the ceiling in the bedroom is testament to his skill: it's easy to imagine Wolfgang and Constanza gazing at that same ornate plasterwork as they settled down for the night. It's also easy to reflect on the fact that Haydn, Beethoven and Hummel all visited Mozart at the time. The very idea of Mozart and Haydn playing string quartets together in those very rooms gives a certain *frisson* to the visit. Sadly, it is the only house remaining of the nine that the Mozarts inhabited during their years in Vienna. Add to all that the homes of Beethoven and Schubert and the dozens of musical star-shaped memorials all along the pedestrian road of the Kärtnerstrasse, commemorating all sorts of famous musicians (rather like the Hollywood stars) and it's impossible to forget that you are in the most musical city in the world.

Presenting for television is a very different thing from the relative anonymity of the radio studio. I never fancied my chances on the small screen: as one BBC TV executive producer once told me – straight out! – 'you're the wrong age, the wrong sex and too bald'! But that was long after I had enjoyed a few years presenting concerts, competitions and the Llangollen Eisteddfod for the BBC based in Wales.

It all started with a phone call from the BBC's Welsh Head of Music Mervyn Williams, a wonderful guy and a joy to work with. He was about to launch a new major singing event, to be called the *Cardiff Singer of the World* – this was in the early 80s – and he was looking for someone new and hopefully musical to 'front' the television coverage. I was, of course, delighted to be asked and went on to present the first three competitions, in 1983, 1985 and 1987. At the same time, he kindly invited me to present the daily coverage of the Llangollen International Musical Eisteddfod – a week's work doing 'live' presentation throughout the day, interviewing singers and dancers from all over the world, every day for a week, at the same time putting together a special look-back programme for BBC 2 at the weekend.

It was special to be involved in such a wonderfully worthwhile and hugely enjoyable enterprise and the years I spent in that beautiful part of Wales remain among my fondest memories. The very idea that a field in North Wales should become – for one week every year – the musical centre of the universe, bringing together kindred spirits from all around the world, was the perfect way to remind people that the difficult world we were living in could be united in peaceful endeavour. When the Eisteddfod took place for the first time shortly after the Second World War, a German choir was invited and naturally there were backstage nerves as to how it might be received when it walked out on stage. In a moment of divine inspiration, the platform announcer setting the scene welcomed onto the stage "our friends from Germany". The ice was broken, the choir was warmly received and ever thereafter, the phrase 'our friends from …' was used to introduce all musicians, wherever they came from. It remains one of the many unifying factors of a unique organisation and one which is increasingly important in a troubled world.

The *Cardiff Singer of the World* was something else, which was equally enjoyable, and which has since developed into one of the most important solo singer competitions in the world today. Back then it was virgin territory and nobody knew how it might work. Singers from around the world would send in tapes of their voices and on that basis alone, each country put forward a representative. Later on my old Cambridge friend Julian Smith (Puccini expert and conductor most closely associated with Welsh National Opera) would travel the world, hearing singers in the flesh before agreeing to their inclusion in the competition.

Any doubts that the venture might work were dispelled immediately when, on the first night of the first competition, singer number one was a 22-year-old Finnish soprano called Karita Matilla (affectionately known to us as 'Matilla the Finn'!). The moment she began to sing, we knew we were onto a good thing. She was the first person I interviewed at the beginning of the week. When I talked to her again before the final a few days later, I asked if anyone had contacted her since she had appeared on the first day of the week. She told me that Covent Garden had expressed interest and would like her to audition. I asked her what she had told them and when she said that she was rather busy in Cardiff for the rest of the week and would be in contact when she had the time, it was patently obvious that this young singer with this fabulous voice would go far. And yet again, the rest is history.

My long days started very early in the morning, rushing around various parts of the City of Cardiff and interviewing the singers, one by one. They ended in presenting the programme 'live' from the St. David's Hall, as each day five singers strutted their stuff together with the orchestra. An international jury, headed by Dame Joan Sutherland and including many distinguished singers from around the world had to be interviewed too, so that the television audience could have some idea of what they were looking for in a so-called 'Singer of the World'.

There is an inevitable problem with this sort of competition and it was made very clear to me in the letters I received each year. People watching on television would complain to me that a favourite voice had not gone through to the final, their concern being based on the sheer entertainment value of an individual performance and by the fact that the voice had sounded perfect on television. I had an easy reply to offer and it was based on fact: there were singers who did indeed sound – and look – terrific on TV, mainly because they were singing into a close microphone. If a singer failed to go through, the likelihood was – and indeed the certainty turned out to be in many cases – that four rows back from the stage, the voice could hardly be heard over the sound of the orchestra.

I interviewed a Belgian baritone 'live' on one occasion and asked him about his present situation, saying that I had noticed he had given up a successful career as a painter. I felt sure the audience would like to know what sort of thing he painted. His reply reminded me that one lives and learns in that business: "Anything," he replied: "doors, ceilings, window frames!" I decided to do my research rather more thoroughly in future.

As I also presented many concerts for BBC 2 from Cardiff, I look back on my time with that department with the greatest of pleasure. Unfortunately, it was too good to last and it came to an end in a way which seems, in retrospect to be typical of the BBC's approach to man-management.

I was invited to present the fourth bi-annual singing competition and organised my diary for the year accordingly. This meant wiping out the whole of June, in order to spend time on preparation and research prior to the event, and then the ten days or so in Cardiff covering the competition. I duly signed my contract and looked forward to another enjoyable work experience. Not long before the month in question, the BBC had introduced a new voice to Radio 2 and was very keen to get his face as well-known as his voice. Here was a golden opportunity – a high profile programme seen by viewers all over the world and a fresh music presenter. Without so much as a by-your-leave, they asked him to present the competition and told me that my services were no longer required. Thank goodness I had signed the contract – having turned down any other work during that month of June – as they paid me a lot of money to stay at home and watch someone else present the programmes.

I was rather touched when they eventually realised their mistake and invited me back two years later. They say that lightning doesn't strike in the same place twice, though in my case, I found myself re-living that unfortunate experience. The then Head of Music asked me out to lunch a month or so before the competition and told me – straight out – that they had decided that, once again, I was to be dropped from this major commitment as they wanted my colleague from Radio 3 – Natalie Wheen – to do the honours. It then became abundantly clear that my television days were over. Not to worry, as I had had a good run and was happy to concentrate instead on my radio work. But it all seemed a bit carelessly cruel after I had given my all.

I've mentioned *Melodies for You*: this was the programme I had listened to as a child, when Eric Robinson was in charge. I always wanted to present that programme and my first opportunity came when my old friend and Radio 2 producer Alan Owen asked me to stand in for regular presenter Robin Boyle while Robin enjoyed his summer break. For four weeks I had the time of my life, only to be told afterwards somewhat patronisingly that my presentation was far too 'sophisticated' for a Radio 2 audience. Nonetheless, some years later, when – once again – Richard Baker ended his time on the programme, I was asked to take over and was thrilled to be able to step in. I spent a happy year on the programme until I became the victim of one of the most extraordinary pieces of BBC man-management I have ever encountered.

The plan each week was that the producer – one Bridget Apps – sent me the music she had chosen for the programme and I would then write the script, turn up at Broadcasting House and record a couple of programmes on one morning – self-operating the discs and enjoying every minute. After I had been on the job for a whole year (and was just beginning to feel comfortable) the music for the week failed to arrive and I called Bridget Apps to ask where it was. "Oh," she said, "Sheridan Morley's doing it". I said: "what, do you mean this week?" "No," she added, "he's taken over the programme." In a twenty-second phone call, I had been sacked – no thought for my feelings, no apology, and no suggestion that this had been handled rather insensitively.

The longer I worked for the BBC, the more I realised that this was typical of the sort of reward one gets for loyalty, dedication and devotion to the cause. I eventually – some considerable time later – had a letter from the Controller of Radio 2 saying that she had meant to write and tell me in advance. She gave me a farewell lunch – just the two of us – though I would have preferred to keep the programme. As Terry Wogan said in his autobiography: "It remains one of the greatest faults of BBC management. Nobody ever says anything to your face. Confrontation is a dirty word, much better to send a memo". As this simple lack of courtesy was extended to even the likes of Jimmy Young, Michael Aspel and – turning the clock back a very long time – even to Vera Lynn, what hope for a man like me? In the fifteen years of my Vienna presentation, the television people were very complimentary and seemingly grateful for what I was doing; apart from my radio producer, I don't remember a single word of appreciation from anyone at Radio 3 – no thanks, no comment, nothing.

Dear Vera Lynn – way back in 1949 – went to discuss future programmes with the BBC's Head of Variety – a little man sitting behind a very big desk. Instead of future plans he simply told her that her kind of music was finished – that the 'sob stuff' was no longer required. If she wanted to do any more, she would have to change her style. It's amazing to think that thirty years later she was still being true to herself and that people like me were lucky enough to work with her, both with The King's Singers on her own TV series and at the Royal Variety Show conducting the Huddersfield Choral Society as her 'backing group'. Thank goodness she stuck to her guns.

At the same time as presenting *Melodies for You* and *Brian Kay's Sunday Morning*, I started presenting another of my father's favourite music programmes – Radio 2's much-loved and very long-running *Friday Night is Music Night*. This was right up my street, with the amazing BBC Concert Orchestra as the backbone to a weekly helping of easy-listening music with guest vocalists, or as they were always called, Friday Night's star singers. I had always loved the format of the programme and once again felt immensely privileged to be part of it. I wrote my own scripts and made sure I never missed a moment of the afternoon rehearsal, being keen to make sure I knew what I was talking about. I marvelled at the skill of the musicians who could play any style and period of music at sight and genuinely seemed to be enjoying every minute of it. That enjoyment communicated itself to the faithful audience.

I remember going to Robin Boyle's last programme as presenter and asking him in the interval what it was that made him want to move on. His answer was quite simple: after all those years, there was nothing new he could possibly say about the overture to the *Yeomen of the Guard*! That was then up to me and to those who shared with me the opportunities to present the programme. When I started, the programme normally came from the famous Golders Green Hippodrome. It had an atmosphere all of its own. Sadly it was also showing its age and when a large part of the ceiling collapsed on top of where the principal bassoon and horn players would have been sitting had they been in session, the building had to be closed and the programme never came from there again. The equally famous Mermaid Theatre became a regular venue and soon established itself in the minds of the audience.

Later on, it was St Luke's Church – the home of the London Symphony Orchestra – that saw many of the broadcasts and it was there that I discovered yet another prime example of BBC management. After eight years of presenting the programme on and off, two members of the orchestra stopped me in the car park and told me that they always enjoyed my presentation and on the same day, one of the staff complimented me on being so attentive to rehearsals and so thorough in my scripting. It was good to hear, but I had a sneaking suspicion that maybe my days were numbered.

As the producer – the same Bridget Apps – left the hall, she said: "See you next time". That was the last I saw of her and the programme. The decision had clearly been made that 'outside' presenters were no longer affordable and that the show would be given to regular Radio 2 presenters including Paul Gambaccini, Ken Bruce and my old pal Aled Jones. The thing is that – yet again – nobody dared tell me to my face. Whenever I had phoned Bridget Apps, she would answer the phone immediately. Suddenly I was getting a recorded message every time I called. A friend told me that if I dialled in certain numbers before calling her, then my own number would not show up on her phone. I tried it and she answered immediately. I had clearly become yesterday's man as far as Bridget Apps and Friday Nights were concerned and she never had the courage or the courtesy to let me know. Again, I can't complain – I had enjoyed eight years on the programme and loved every minute.

Other programmes I enjoyed being connected with as presenter include *The Tingle Factor*, in which people talked about the various good things in life which hit the spot. I got to interview some wonderful people too: David Attenborough, John Julius Norwich, Eleanor Bron, Delia Smith and many others, including Robin Ray, who enjoyed the experience so much that he eventually took over the programme. Then there was *Comparing Notes* (another, like *Music in Mind* in which I succeeded Richard Baker).

The old adage: 'one door closes, another door slams in your face' became very true at that part of my life: *Melodies for You* and *Friday Night is Music Night* suddenly disappeared from my work schedule and I was able to concentrate on my two regular Radio 3 slots *Brian Kay's Light Programme* and the request programme *3 for All*. Not for long. This time I did get the phone call, as Controller Roger Wright called to say that all the four o'clock specialist programmes (including both of mine) were to come to an end. This time he offered no replacement and gave me only three months' notice. Suddenly, after many years in which I had been lucky enough to have so many regular programmes – literally thousands of them – on Radios 2, 3 and 4 – it looked as if my time had come and gone: the domino effect had taken over my life as a broadcaster.

I still find it extraordinary when people you have known for a long time, worked with over so many programmes and looked upon as good friends simply can't – as Wogan said – look you in the face and be honest with you. It's a poor reward when you've only done your best at all times to satisfy their demands. Hey Ho.

What upset me most was the way in which my departure was kept secret from my faithful listeners. I had to pre-record my last four *Light Programmes* as it was time for my annual trip to New Zealand. As it was the end of a seven-year run I thought it only reasonable to prepare my audience for the fact that the programme would be drawing to a close. At the end of each of the last four programmes I mentioned that time was running out and that I would consequently be including some of my all-time favourites in the remaining weeks. It seemed only fair that people for whom this weekly dose of what my colleague David Jacobs would have called 'our kind of music' should be ready for its disappearance from the schedules. While I was away, I managed to organise for those last selections to be recorded, so that I could listen to them myself on my return from New Zealand. It probably won't surprise you to know that Radio 3 had cut out all references to the programme's forthcoming demise, clearly in order to avoid any feedback from the devotees. At the end of the final programme it was simply announced that that was that: no more Light Music.

It was, in my humble opinion, a deliberately deceitful way in which to treat the audience, but then the BBC never seems to care what the audience actually wants or enjoys. It also made me look a bit silly, but there we are! Years before, I told my old friend and radio producer Tim McDonald at Radio 2 that I had become so busy at the BBC that I was thinking of giving everything else up. "Whatever you do," he said, "don't do that. There will come a time when you'll be out on your ear, however popular you and your programmes might be". How right he was and thank goodness I took his advice. Otherwise I would now be enjoying quiet retirement – the very thought of which is anathema to me.

There will have been plenty who were happy that I was removed: however large an audience one builds up over the years, there are always those who simply don't like the sound of your voice or the style of your presentation. One such wrote frequently to me (and indeed to almost all of my colleagues at Radio 3) hand-written notes which made his feelings perfectly clear in the un-friendliest terms imaginable. It never worried me in the slightest, and I was able to dismiss him (or maybe it was her?) as an opinionated coward, who didn't even have the courage to sign his name or give an address to which I could respond.

On a happier note, a last memory of my time at the BBC finds me in Paris, presenting for Radio 2 the World Cup concert at the Eiffel Tower, performed to a world-wide audience of millions by The Three Tenors. This was a privilege indeed: Jose Carreras, Placido Domingo and Luciano Pavarotti singing excerpts from the world of grand opera and Neapolitan songs with the famous Parisian landmark soaring high above them. The whole thing was to be televised at a later date, though broadcast 'live' on radio as it happened. A huge structure had been built to accommodate the television crew and presenter Desmond Lyneham with a vast picture window looking out onto the stage where the three giants of the musical world were to perform.

Alongside it – very much pushed to one side and squeezed in – was an infinitely smaller 'broom cupboard' with a tiny picture window through which the Radio 2 presenter could just about see what was going on. As luck had it, Lyneham had spent the whole of his coverage of the World Cup desperately trying to mention all those unpronounceable players and when it came to the big concert, he decided he'd had enough and didn't fancy struggling with equally unpronounceable operatic arias etc. This was very good news for me, as Radio 2 was given access to the big room with the huge window and I was able to have the best seat in the house with a million-dollar view of the concert.

The concert was a massive success, each of the singers leaving the stage between arias to watch the game on the television sets in their luxurious tented rooms, teasingly letting the audience know when they returned that a goal had been scored, without saying by whom! It was wonderful to watch the interplay between them and their conductor James Levine and there's no doubt that the vast assembled crowd, many of whom had paid unthinkable amounts for their seats, had a night to remember.

After the performance, my producer Alan Boyd and I wandered backstage to have a look at the amazing accommodation which had been prefabricated to give the superstar singers every comfort imaginable. There were three identical tented rooms, vast and unthinkably comfortable, with plush sofas, gold-plated crockery and cutlery, limitless quantities of food available and surroundings which complemented the vast amount of money that each singer was making from the gig. Within less than an hour, the whole structure and everything in it had been dismantled, put into one of a dozen or so juggernauts, ready to move on to the next time and place where the three were to perform. I look back on being there as a real privilege – one of the real perks of my time at the Beeb.

I have no regrets about eventually losing my connection with the BBC. I went on broadcasting regularly for Radio New Zealand on my annual visits to that beautiful country and after twenty-five years devoted service to the BBC I now enjoy being released from the deadline pressure of devising programmes and writing scripts. I had even had the good fortune, towards the end of my time with the Beeb, to be broadcasting from my dining room table in the Cotswolds, such are the wonders of modern science. I look back on that entire episode of my working life with the greatest pleasure. Mind you, with so many boxes to tick for broadcasters these days, I'm sure I would no longer get a job as a presenter, speaking properly, caring too much about grammar and sounding far too posh!

One of my father's favourite jokes was the one about the man who died from drinking too much French polish: it was a terrible end, but a beautiful finish! I often feel the same way about the demise of my 25-year broadcasting career.

CHAPTER TEN

Friends (and colleagues) pictured within

I take the title of this section of memories from Edward Elgar, who used the phrase to describe the characters he portrayed so brilliantly in his *Enigma Variations*. I have certainly been lucky in meeting, working with or getting to know some outstanding members of the music profession and some of those friendships go back a very long way.

Among the titles of my father's talks to luncheon clubs, WIs and so on were 'Is cruising all bunk', 'Where my caravan has rusted' and 'Farther in Law'. He also had one called 'Name-dropping as a hobby'. And that reminds me of a story concerning my 'twin' – Christopher (Lord) Patten (we were born on the same day) who was once asked by Margaret Thatcher to tell the colourful MP Norman St John-Stevas to stop dropping names constantly, as it gave a bad impression. Patten was then PPS to St John-Stevas and dutifully carried out the PM's instruction. When he passed on the message, St John-Stevas' reply was: "Funnily enough, The Queen Mother was saying the same thing to me only the other day"! The great harmonica player Larry Adler was also fond of dropping names at the slightest provocation: so much so, it was suggested that the title of his autobiography should be "Namedrops keep falling on my head"!

It was back in 1964 that Neville Marriner first brought his Academy of St. Martin in the Fields to King's College, Cambridge, in order to make recordings with the choir. His son Andrew (later a distinguished principal clarinettist with the London Symphony Orchestra) was one of an astonishing array of precocious talent which filled the front row of boy choristers. Among Andrew's contemporaries who went on to enrich our musical lives were conductor and violin supremo Roy Goodman (he of the top Cs in the famous King's recording of Allegri's *Miserere*) top bass Michael George, Jonathan Groves (son of conductor Sir Charles and one of London's leading musical agents), composer and conductor Jonathan Willcocks (son of Sir David), Andrew Darke (grandson of Harold 'In the bleak midwinter' Darke), Richard Suart (one of our finest Gilbert & Sullivan patter-men) and composer and conductor Bob Chilcott. It was a remarkable line-up of talent, fearless in its determination and quite brilliant in its boyish expertise.

So it was perhaps inevitable (with the family connection – apart from its outstanding qualities as an ensemble) that the Academy of St Martin's would join forces with the choir, as it went on to do with great distinction. The members of the Academy were not that much older than we choral scholars (well, there was certainly a gap, though not that great) and so we all had a great time making music together, creating opposing cricket teams, eating and drinking and generally having a whale of a time.

I've mentioned earlier that it was Neville who first dropped the name of the fledgling King's Singers to a couple of people who were to have a huge impact on our future (David Booth-Jones of the Hale Arts Trust and

Kenneth Tribe of Musicaviva Australia) and it was with the Academy that we made that official London debut concert on May the 1st 1968. Once the connection had been established, it was a further pleasure to be able to spend some time at the Dartington Summer School of Music when the Academy was in residence. In fact, The King's Singers were also to make an early appearance there, in spite of the fact that William Glock who ran the summer school did not like us at all. Luckily John Amis who ran it with him was far more enthusiastic and managed to persuade him that we were good box office. Much more recently, my week as conductor of the summer school choir (this was in 2013) coincided with the week when Sir Neville was training the string orchestra. It was so good to be able to spend a lot of extremely jolly time with him and his wife Molly over a bottle or two, largely reminiscing about the time we had spent there together forty years earlier.

That 1968 debut concert in London's recently opened Queen Elizabeth Hall is memorable for a variety of reasons, one of which concerned the Academy's double-bass player John Gray. On the day of the concert, The King's Singers began the morning rehearsal going through a selection of close-harmony arrangements which featured John on bass, while the other members of the Academy slowly assembled in the auditorium. We didn't want to say anything, but we couldn't help noticing that John seemed to have far more hair than he had had at the previous day's run-through! Halfway through our rehearsal, violinist Iona Brown suddenly shouted out – full voice: "Good God, is John Gray wearing a wig?" – thus breaking the ice for poor old John and giving everyone – including him – a good laugh.

Many years later – in the early 1980s – I had a call from Neville saying that he was about to record the music for a film version of Peter Schaffer's play *Amadeus*. Simon Callow had been asked to play the part of the playwright and actor Emanuel Schikaneder (Simon had been the original Mozart in the National Theatre production but was already too old (!) to play the part in the movie). Simon is a great actor with a wonderful speaking voice, terrific face and a host of outstanding roles to his great credit; but his singing voice is perhaps not altogether of the top rank. Neither was mine, but Neville thought it would be fun if I were to sing the part of Papageno, which Simon would be acting, and that he, Simon, would then mime to my voice.

I had recently left The King's Singers and reckoned that my singing days were behind me, so I suggested to Neville that a young, up-and-coming operatic baritone might be better suited to the task and glad of the publicity. "Oh no," he said, "that's not the point: we want it to sound like an actor trying to sing"! Well, I did the honours and my wife Gilly sang the part of Papagena (we had only just got married). It was our only experience of movie stardom and we both yearned for that year's Oscar as 'best dubbed vocalists'.

Neville and Molly own a beautiful pink, bow-fronted thatched cottage in lovely Lyme Regis and for many years I've had the pleasure of staying there to get away from things and to enjoy some top-quality sea air. On one occasion, Gilly and I drove down after I'd presented my Radio 3 Sunday Morning Programme to savour the delights of Lyme once again, out of season. We walked round the Cobb after a meal (always imagining that Meryl Streep might turn up, as she did famously in the film of John Fowles' *A French*

Lieutenant's Woman) and commented on how time appeared to have stood still in that particularly charming spot. There were fishermen's nets and lobster pots, old boats and things which looked as if they had been there for years. We thought it looked like a set for *Peter Grimes*. The next morning, as we opened the curtains and looked out over the Cobb, there were characters in tall hats and period costumes strolling towards the end where all the paraphernalia had been. They were filming Jane Austen's *Persuasion*!

And they had got to the bit where the fair Louisa falls down the precarious flight of stone steps known as 'the teeth'. We hurried along to watch the action and stayed happily for several hours as they took take after take until they got it right. After about six hours of filming they seemed satisfied. Imagine our amazement when the programme was broadcast to discover that what we had watched for all that time took precisely seventeen seconds of the programme! As they were filming, an old chap sitting in a boat – clearly an extra waiting for something more exciting to happen – was approached by an American tourist who asked him what they were doing. His reply: "We're making a film – it's *Persuasion* by Jane Eyre"!

When Neville's daughter Susie got married, they kindly asked me to be involved in the music-making and among the pieces we sang was Orlando Gibbons' anthem *O Clap Your Hands*. In the reception afterwards at the Savoy, no less a fellow guest than David Attenborough asked me what I could tell him about Gibbons. As he said it, I couldn't help laughing at the idea that this greatest communicator of the Natural World should be asking me about gibbons – then I remembered the capital G.

It is so wonderful to think that Sir Neville went on conducting to within two days of his death at the magnificent age of 92, a life so fulfilled and such a tremendous legacy. He used to consider his players to be his extended family and we felt honoured and delighted to be there on the periphery for over fifty years.

It was also because of the recordings we made at King's, Cambridge that I had the great pleasure of meeting Janet Baker for the first time. That will have been in the mid-60s when she was invited to join the choir for a recording of Handel's *Dixit Dominus* and Vivaldi's *Gloria*. When we performed the two works in the evening concert the night before the recording, Janet added the *Alto Rhapsody* by Brahms, with we choral scholars standing round her in a tight semi-circle and thinking we had died and gone to heaven, so exquisite was the glory of her voice – particularly in such close proximity. That morning, as I was collecting my music from the chapel to learn for the day, Janet walked into the chapel just to have a look and as there was nobody else in the building, I said good morning and told her how good it was to see her there. When she asked how I knew who she was, I mentioned that we both came from the city of York, that I was a choral scholar and that I was looking forward to her singing with us later that day. Neither of us was in a hurry so we talked for some time and during her visit – and on future occasions when she graced us with her presence – we were able to see a lot of each other. She even accompanied me when I drove to the college boat-house to collect my oar (the one with the painted handle!) and we had a good laugh trying to secure it to the roof of my battered old Hillman Minx.

Janet also came down to Dartington with the Academy where we would enjoy her singing and also play tennis with her and Neville Marriner and my old pal from King's, Tom Wheare. When she was making a recording in London with the Academy of Bach Cantatas (with John Shirley-Quirk and Robert Tear) I was able to go along to the sessions and see them all at work. I still have the original LP, along with the re-issue on CD. Many years later, I was asked to present a six-part series for BBC Radio 3 with Dame Janet and had the most fascinating time recording at her home in Harrow for a series which even she admitted had told her more about herself than she ever knew. She certainly told me a lot more about herself than I knew.

My most recent memory is of the day Janet generously agreed to come to the Leith Hill Musical Festival as guest of honour and presenter of prize-winning banners on the evening we were performing Elgar's *The Dream of Gerontius*. I felt sorry for Anna Stéphany who sang the part of the Angel that night, having to sing it in front of the finest angel of all time! Janet was most generous afterwards, describing Anna's voice as 'pure velvet from top to bottom'. Janet's own recording of Dido's Lament from Purcell's *Dido and Aeneas* – made when she was still in her twenties – remains for me a Desert Island Disc, even (dare I say – and I'm sure I have her permission to do so) surpassing the beautiful recording which Gilly made with The King's Consort. Janet is one of those magical singers for whom we have to hear only one or two notes to know precisely who is singing them, so uniquely beautiful is the sound. You can say that about only a small handful of world-class voices and for all of them, it is what makes them so special.

It must have been about 1980 when The King's Singers were touring the USA that we sang an afternoon concert of mainly 16th century Spanish music at the Metropolitan Museum in New York. Our American agent mentioned that among those in the audience were the celebrated pianist George Shearing and his wife Ellie. I asked if I could meet them and Bob introduced us as soon as the concert was finished.

I don't know about you but there have been times in life when I have been lucky enough to meet someone and to know at once that we seemed to have a lot in common. This was one such occasion and was to result in the closest of friendships which lasted for over thirty years until George's death and which continues to this day with Ellie. When George was the subject of television's *This is Your Life* I was invited to tell the story of how we met and how it was that we made such immediate contact:

At one point as we chatted, Ellie asked me where I lived in the UK. When I mentioned the Cotswolds, she said: "do we have a story for you?" Apparently, years before, George's agent had been organising a European tour and would call George and confirm – London's Festival Hall, Amsterdam's Concertgebouw, Ronnie Scott's and so on. Each time he called, George asked him to leave time so they could visit the Cotswolds. After about the sixth time of mentioning this, the exasperated agent said: "These Cotswolds, they must be very special friends of yours"!

They mentioned that they would visit 'their old friends' the Cotswolds the following summer and could I find them a hotel near to where we lived and maybe we could meet for dinner. That was no problem and we did precisely that. They had such a good time that they decided they would come back the following year and could we find them a smart country cottage for them to rent. Thus began fifteen years of five-month summer residency near to our home and the opportunity to see them constantly on their visits. They were the most wonderful company – George with his endless supply of appalling puns – not to mention his collection of outrageous limericks! – and Ellie's wonderful meals: we spent countless happy hours together year after year.

We also had the pleasure of visiting their home in New York and later, their holiday home at Lee, Massachusetts. The first time we went to the New York apartment, Gilly had not heard George play – in the flesh. I asked Ellie in the kitchen if George would mind playing for Gilly and she said: "you ask him". I was only being cautious, because you never really know whether or not to ask a professional to play when he's at home relaxing. I plucked up courage and George was only too pleased to oblige, giving us a private performance of his masterly variations on the tune of *Greensleeves*.

On one occasion when we were staying with them at the farm in Lee, Gilly and I had been shopping and as we approached the farm we saw to our horror an enormous black bear approaching the back of the farmhouse where we knew George would be sitting and reading his Braille book. Ellie was having a shower so we rushed through and managed to frighten the bear away before it came close enough to George to present problems. It had been opening all the bird boxes in the hope of finding some eggs. When we told George he put out his hand and asked how high the bear would have been if it was on all fours. As I raised his hand to a considerable height, George realised that he might have had a lucky escape

By the time George went to Buckingham Palace to be knighted by The Queen, he was already in a wheelchair and being blind, wore his trademark dark glasses. When the Equerry was briefing the recipients beforehand, he mentioned that they should not try to shake hands with the Queen unless she held out her hand to them. George replied – in a loud stage whisper: "Well she'd better have a bell on it"!

George made a CD with The King's Singers – sadly after I had left them – which remains one of the group's finest. The opportunity of working with one of the world's top jazzers taught the singers more in a few days about how to swing than they had picked up in a lifetime. The whole Shearing story is such a fascinating one, from his childhood in Battersea to his global stardom. He was the ninth child of a coal delivery man and used to say that his father was a coal porter – not *the* Cole Porter!

The 'Shearing Sound', featuring the famous Quintet, was all the more remarkable because this English man (as Ellie always says: British to the bone) showed the Americans how to do it, in his own sweet way. When the quintet eventually split, George could be himself and it is then, I think, that his true genius shone forth. His concerts and recordings alone or with just a bass player showed his remarkable inventiveness, his magical touch and the depth of his amazing musicianship. One of my favourite albums was issued after his death – produced by Ellie from private recordings he had made in his own New York apartment with bass player Don Thompson. It is the most remarkable sound, particularly when you consider how noisy New York city can be. The great thing is that – away from the pressure of a recording studio and playing on his own beloved Bösendorfer – the playing has a sense of relaxation and sheer enjoyment that would otherwise have been harder to create. Wonderful arrangements too and a terrific sound.

It would be impossible to count the number of times we have spent together, enjoying George's favourite food (roast lamb, with new potatoes and garden peas, washed down with a good Shiraz and followed by fresh raspberries and a chocolate roulade). On one occasion, we were joined in our Cotswold home by JoAnne and John Rutter: John had told me that he had always wanted to meet George. We usually placed George in the seat nearest the piano, just in case he felt the urge to tickle the ivories! Between courses, he suddenly turned round and played John's lovely *Nativity Carol*, complete with added Shearing harmonies! I can still see the look of total disbelief on John's face.

As a result of that dinner, John became involved in a special charity concert with my Cheltenham Bach Choir (I was the conductor of that very fine choir for nine years) at which George had so kindly agreed to play. I casually asked John if he might write something to celebrate the occasion and with characteristic generosity he agreed and composed his hugely entertaining and (as always) beautifully written set of what he called *Birthday Madrigals* – the anniversary in question being George's seventieth birthday. I eventually persuaded John to conduct the first performance and for members of the choir to be able to share the platform with two global superstars was something I am quite sure none of them (or me) will ever forget. When George first rehearsed with the choir, singing members were naturally a bit nervous of how the great man might behave. At one point I mentioned that some of the things George was playing did not quite match what was written in the score. Quick as a flash, blind-from-birth George said: "Brian, I'm so sorry – I've never been any good at sight-reading"! Immediately everyone laughed and relaxed and the rehearsal carried on with much enjoyment and huge musical satisfaction. When I queried how we were all going to come off together at the end of a certain passage, George complained that "from where I'm sitting, I really can't see your beat"! Great man. After George died, Ellie graciously and generously gave me several of his colourful sweaters and some of his jackets, including a dazzling red one which he had sometimes worn for concerts. On the rare occasions when I wear it, it is with enormous pride.

Another of our happiest friendships owes much to George and Ellie. I was shopping in our local grocery store in Burford one day when I saw someone who looked remarkably like one of my favourite actors and singers – Julia McKenzie. I had never forgotten seeing her in the flesh for the first time many years before when she starred spectacularly in the West End and on Broadway in *Side by Side by Sondheim* and later, at the National Theatre in *Guys and Dolls* – not to mention countless television programmes and series (*Fresh Fields, French Fields, Blott on the Landscape, Miss Marple* etc). As I waited at the checkout, she approached – it was indeed Julia – and we started talking. This carried on outside the shop when I asked her what brought her to Burford. She said she had just moved into a house in neighbouring Taynton with her husband Gerry, her Mother Kay and their golden retriever Cecily. I asked what Gerry did and she said he played the saxophone (she did not mention at that stage all the other amazing things he had done – that became

157

apparent later). I asked if he might know the name of George Shearing and Julia suggested that he would kill to meet him. As it happens, George and Ellie were coming to dinner the following night and I asked if Julia and Gerry could join us.

Thus began another particularly happy association between the six of us, meeting regularly at each other's houses and sharing many things we had and enjoyed in common. After fifteen years in Taynton, Julia and Gerry moved away from the Cotswolds, sharing their time between homes in London and Devon. On one occasion when we stayed with them in the West Country, we thought we would spend a morning at Greenway, the home of Agatha Christie, which is now National Trust and well worth a visit. By this time, Julia had become the latest incarnation of *Miss Marple* on television and it was fascinating to wander round the Christie house while people nudged each other, perhaps assuming that the National Trust employed 'Miss Marple' to be there at all times. In fact, the news that she had won the coveted part of Marple came by phone while we were all on holiday together in New Zealand: we did some celebrating that night. – and Julia had to learn the first script both on the beach by our holiday home and on the long plane journey back to Blighty.

You have to book in advance in order to look round the Christie house and we arrived five minutes before our appointed time and waited at the door. We had been chatting to the door keeper for some time when he looked at Julia and suggested that he might recognise her. She reluctantly agreed and as we eventually passed him to go into the house, Gerry said to him: "I was in *The Empire Strikes Back*" (which was true) but as he was heavily disguised as an airship commander, you would never know. He was only joking, as neither of them takes particular pleasure in being recognised.

Another friend and near neighbour in the Cotswolds was George Martin, another of our most distinguished musical knights and as delightful a man as you could ever meet. It was back in the 70s that he produced several of our King's Singers recordings, as well as being responsible for introducing us to Paul McCartney, in order to sing on his single of the Frogs' Chorus (*We all stand together*). To be produced by a man with such a remarkable sense of what is needed in order to create fine recordings was a massive privilege. It was an enormous pleasure to be with him in his studio as he was so immensely helpful, so full of ideas, and such fun to be with.

Many years later – well into this century – he came to a concert in the little church next to my house in Fulbrook, where members of my Burford Singers were taking part in a Christmas celebration. Afterwards he mentioned that he had written a piece of choral music and was looking for a choir to perform the UK premier. Might we be interested? Talk about an offer we could not refuse. He showed me the score and we agreed to programme it as soon as we could. It was called *Mission Chorales* and it had an interesting history. George had been asked to write the music for the 1980s film *The Mission* – set in the Amazon and concerning a group of missionaries who had travelled there in the hope of converting the natives to Christianity. He went to the Amazon to get the feeling for the music and to watch the filming, but the company suddenly ran out of money. Luck was at hand, in that the Italians came in with loadsamoney, but with the proviso that Morricone write the music.

George came home with his sketches, dropped them in a drawer and forgot all about them. It was years later while he was recovering from a small operation that he suddenly remembered them and asked his wife Judy to dig them out, so that he could do something rather than lying in hospital wasting time. He arranged the sketches into a twelve-minute piece, combining the *earthy* tribal music of the Amazonian natives with the *heavenly* music of the missionaries. It is beautifully scored for choir, soprano soloist, strings and oboe and I recommend it to any choir which is looking for something different to perform. We did indeed perform it in Burford Church (and again later with my Leith Hill Festival choirs) and it was a great success – particularly for George, who was there for both performances and was greeted appropriately by a wildly enthusiastic audience. George was one of the world's true gentlemen and, as I told Judy after his death in 2016, whenever I was lucky enough to spend an hour in their company, enjoying a cup of coffee with them at their home, I always drove away feeling that the world was a better place: a truly great man and a delightful couple.

Burford was also home to a man whose voice was universally known and loved as Tom Forrest in *The Archers*. Bob Arnold lived off the hill in Burford and came down to our local pub – the Masons Arms in Fulbrook – every Saturday and Sunday lunchtime to play cribbage with three of the villagers. To hear that voice resounding in the corner was like being in The Bull in Ambridge, so familiar was Bob's voice and turn of phrase. He was also a very distinguished folk singer and on one happy occasion, when I was presenting the Radio 2 Arts Programme, we recorded an entire two-hour edition in the pub, joined by members of the village who happily sat there listening to Bob telling wonderful stories and being given drinks on the BBC. Bob never stopped telling me how proud he was to have worked for the BBC for over fifty years – they don't make them like him anymore.

One of the best and most enjoyable lunch parties that Gilly and I gave was at our home in the Cotswolds. Our dear friends Ellie and George Shearing were with us again and we gathered together as many mutual friends as we could think of – folk whom we and the Shearings knew well and had worked with over so many years. Steve Race and his wife Lonnie were there: I had known Steve for a long time, meeting him first when told he was a close friend of the Methodist minister who Christened me. Later on, he became a great champion for the fledgling King's Singers, describing us from the start as "possibly the most arresting thing to happen to British music since Haydn's *Surprise* symphony!"

As we had previously introduced George and Ellie to JoAnne and John Rutter, it was lovely that they were able to be there too, driving over from their home near Cambridge. Happy to make their journey from Wavendon were Cleo Laine and John Dankworth. They had also been hugely helpful and encouraging in the early days of The King's Singers, inviting us to perform in the stables at their home as part of their so-called 'All-Music Plan' along with the pianist and arranger Richard Rodney Bennett. Cleo had sung with us on a number of occasions. As it happened, she and John had been driving in the States when they heard and instantly loved one of the great Rutter carols on the car radio, so they were delighted to meet him. Julia McKenzie and Gerry Hjert were on hand in the neighbouring village of Taynton and were very much part of the Kay/Shearing gang, so of course they joined us too, along with Humphrey Carpenter, the biographer and broadcaster who had years previously invited The King's Singers to record the jingles for Radio Oxford, where he was very much in charge. Also there were members of the Lough family: Ernest Lough and his wife and their TV producer son Robin and his wife Jessica along with Robin's brother Peter. Ernest was by then very much in retirement, many years after he had famously recorded (back in 1927) a Mendelssohn anthem for which he became world-famous as 'the boy who sang *O for the Wings of a Dove*'. It was one of those unforgettable sun-kissed lunches – round the pool at our home – that we wished had gone on forever. How my father would have loved to have included that cast list in his talk 'Name-dropping as a hobby'. Two can play at that game!

It reminds me that when Ernest died, the family graciously asked me to give the eulogy at his memorial service – in the Temple Church where he had made that famous recording all those years ago. I was honoured and delighted to do so, reminding people that, in spite of an illustrious subsequent career, he would always be 'the boy who sang *O for the Wings of a Dove*'. After the service there was a tea party in the Temple and one of the older members of that distinguished establishment asked if I was the chap who made the speech. When I admitted that I was indeed, he said: "Best we've ever had. Want to know why?" Yes please, I enthusiastically requested, to which he said, simply: "Short"!

Among our close professional singing friends are two of justifiably great distinction: the counter-tenor James Bowman and the tenor Ian Partridge. James was still at Oxford when

I went there to study for my Diploma in Education in 1967, singing in the choirs of both New College and Christ Church and teaching at the Cathedral choir school. Having eventually given all that up after moving to London he quickly took over from the great Alfred Deller as the country's leading counter-tenor, in view of not only the beauty of his voice but also its tremendous power. His was unlike any other male alto voice that anyone had heard and thanks to his strength of voice, his skill as a musician, his charisma and his sheer likeability and modesty, he set the gold standard for generations of counter-tenors to come: think of such star voices as those of Paul Esswood, Michael Chance, Iestyn Davies, Tim Mead, Andreas Scholl and a host of others, who, along with Deller and Bowman have kept this type of voice very much alive, after it had spent so many centuries audible only in church, college and cathedral choirs.

James and Gilly performed together frequently and made CDs together, often performing Pergolesi's wonderful *Stabat Mater* for soprano and alto. They would almost certainly have recorded it together, had James not already done so with Emma Kirkby. As it was, Gilly teamed up with Michael Chance and The King's Consort for her recording, which remains one of her finest. James and Gilly were about to embark on a European tour performing the Pergolesi when Gilly's mother suddenly died and when James was informed of the news he immediately jumped in the car and drove down from Surrey to the Cotswolds for lunch: a lovely and supportive gesture entirely typical of a great man and a dear friend.

I must have been still a student – and Gilly certainly was – when we both first became aware of Ian Partridge's glorious voice. His recordings of the Schubert Song Cycles

163

– with his sister Jennifer at the piano – were a revelation and a delight, and the only recordings at the time which could possibly stand up against the incomparable Dietrich Fischer-Dieskau. The partnership of Ian and Jenny – musical siblings seemingly joined at the hip – had a special magic to them and remain to this day among the finest of their kind. It was a huge pleasure to meet Ian so soon after I arrived in London in 1967 and joined the ranks of professional session singers. My first encounter was as a member of Simon Preston's New English Singers, with whom we made recordings and television programmes. He was also there as one of the John Alldis Singers and many other professional groups I was lucky enough to sing with, and to all of these he added his own very special sound: hear any of those recordings these days and Ian's presence always gives the tenor section an added brilliance, always binding disparate voices into one in a way that nobody else I can think of ever quite did.

Ian quickly became one of the Kay-Shearing fraternity and whenever George and Ellie – and Ellie to this day – were here in the UK, we got together as much as we could, exchanging endless 'old' stories, still – however many times we might have told them – roaring with laughter time and time again. Ian's fund of stories, never-forgotten from so many years in the business – are second to none and we have often tried to persuade him to write them down and publish them, as they would sell like the proverbial hot cakes. Whenever Ian and his wife Ann, along with Jennifer and her husband Bryan, met for a good lunch, out came the old stories again – with the occasional new ones – and reminded us all how good it was to get together and to recall just how lucky we all were to have spent our lives doing something which we enjoyed so much. Beats working any day!

Another of the most popular composers of choral music in the world today lives just five minutes away from us and it is great to have him so close at hand. I first met Bob Chilcott when he was one of those amazing choristers filling the front row of the choir at King's, Cambridge back in the 1960s, and where he famously sang not only that first famous solo verse of *Once in Royal David's City* on the Christmas Eve festival of nine lessons and carols, but also the treble solo on David Willcocks's King's recording of Fauré's *Requiem*, still one of the best-selling of all time.

Bob sang with The King's Singers for ten years (some time after I had left the group) before giving it all up and concentrating on composing and arranging, a decision of which we are all the beneficiaries. There are so many ways in which we are able to meet regularly, particularly as he lives just down the road. He is also a member of the Music Committee of the Leith Hill Musical Festival and my lovely Burford Singers agreed to invite him to succeed his late father-in-Law Sir Philip Ledger as our President, an invitation which he gladly and generously accepted.

Bob has an amazing knack at finding the perfect texts to set to music and his wonderfully outgoing, friendly nature has endeared him to choirs all over the world, particularly in his work with young voices, which, as he knows only too well, are the essential future for choral music. I shall mention the fabulous piece he wrote for me in my chapter on the Leith Hill Musical Festival. I seem to have said of so many of these *friends pictured within* how much laughter there seems to be when we all get together and it's impossible to think of Bob

165

without recalling the number of times we have completely exhausted each other – and those with us – by laughing ourselves silly – and why ever not. It's a tough old world and the more we can get some fun out of it the better.

My conducting friends and colleagues include one who did so much to establish the presence of female conductors on the podium, though we might have got off to a rocky start! Jane Glover was appointed to the London Choral Society while I was still Chorus Master, though shortly afterwards, my time with the choir came to an abrupt end. Luckily we were able to pick up the pieces when Jane became conductor of the Huddersfield Choral Society, by which time I was happily ensconced there. We enjoyed a number of years working together with that great northern choir and the partnership remains a fond memory.

How on earth Jane finds the time to write books, while enjoying such an illustrious and exceptionally busy career in many parts of the world remains a mystery to me. Her books on *Mozart's Women* and *Handel in London* are a must for anyone interested in those two great composers. Her style is so engaging and her experience in conducting so much of the music of both composers gives an extra special dimension to her writing. Gilly and I were lucky enough to be in Sydney when Jane was conducting Mozart's *Marriage of Figaro* at the Opera House and she arranged for us to be there for a dress rehearsal. Her main worry was not a musical one: by being in Australia for some time she was missing too many episodes of *The Archers*!

And what of my old friends The King's Singers? Well, four of us (Jeremy Jackman, Nigel Perrin, Simon Carrington and Yours Truly) have carried on making music, all of us conducting choirs and orchestras and carrying on performing mainly in the world of choral music. We meet when we can, though all being busy as ever, that can't be all that often. The group's various anniversary celebrations have given us golden opportunities, as well as the ever-growing number of 'round' birthdays!

We happily bump into Alastair Hume more often than most, as he is London-based with fingers in innumerable pies (including frequently playing the double bass in the English Festival Overture for my Royal Albert Hall concerts) and always full of life – along with his pride and joy, his vintage Lagonda. This he bought as a bit of a wreck back in the early days of The King's Singers and lovingly restored it over many years. He even generously drove it as the wedding car for my daughter Charlotte. Anthony Holt has lived in America for many years, where he reverted to his earlier life as a schoolteacher, though I hope he went on singing with that honeyed baritone voice. Alastair Thompson, like Bob, lives close to us, based in Oxford where he taught singing to students and the English language to visiting foreigners. Bill Ives was also based in Oxford for many years as Director of Music at Magdalen College, before retiring from that and concentrating on composing. None of us can quite believe that The King's Singers have now reached half a century, though I'm sure we all feel proud and grateful for the opportunity we had to start something up which has given so much pleasure to so many over so many years.

The subject of 'friends' is an interesting one. People assume that busy musicians must have countless friends though that's not necessarily the case: acquaintances yes and too many to number, though how many can be really described as friends? Apart from the sort of close colleagues already mentioned, it's easier to look upon neighbours as those one feels closer to. Those friends we make at school and university stand the test of time as we all grow older together, though in some ways, although we are surrounded by those many acquaintances, it can be a relatively lonely life on the road where one has to conserve one's energy for the job in hand. Having said that, there's no doubt that my life has been constantly enriched by true friends and neighbours and I don't remember feeling lonely as such at any stage of my life. I've often described Gilly as my dearest friend and I'm happy to stick with that and with the loving family to which I constantly refer.

CHAPTER ELEVEN

On the podium

I mentioned earlier that I had taken Tim McDonald's timely advice and not given up everything else in my life in order to devote all my energies to the BBC. The one thing I had continued to do was to develop a secondary career as a conductor – and I'm very glad that I did.

My first experiences coincided with my early time as a broadcaster, as shortly after leaving The King's Singers in 1982, I succeeded my brother-in-law Nicholas Cleobury as Chorus Master to the London Choral Society. This was a brave new experience for me and, as it turned out, an even braver one for the choir, as I was singularly short of experience when I started. But I learn fast and picked up as I went along, largely through working out what sort of things did and – more importantly – did *not* work in rehearsals. What made the association so special for me was that the conductor for whom I was preparing the choir was a young man called Simon Rattle! He was one of the most inspirational musicians I had ever met and although my relationship with the choir lasted only one year, it was long enough to benefit greatly from his expertise and boundless enthusiasm. We worked together on Britten's *War Requiem* and an all-Stravinsky programme and it was abundantly clear even then that he was going to end up with bigger fish to fry than the London Choral Society.

But for my conducting experience I could not have asked for a better start and although I was dismissed after that single year – the choir rightly decided it could not wait while I learned my job – it was in no time at all that the next step presented itself: and a glorious opportunity it was too. I had become involved in a charity called the Young Persons Concert Foundation, which existed to take full-size symphony orchestras into schools where there had never been any music. I worked closely with a group of enthusiastic 'big names' who helped to provide publicity and opportunity including the likes of singer Vera Lynn, conductor Geoff Love, composer Ron Goodwin, Judy Martin (George's wife), conductor Owain Arwel Hughes and many others. It was while I was presenting a concert which Owain was conducting that he casually asked if I might be interested in taking a couple of rehearsals with the Huddersfield Choral Society, of which he was then conductor. As a proud son of Yorkshire I was only too thrilled at the idea and readily agreed.

It happened that the regular Chorus Master at the time – Nina Walker from Covent Garden – could not do some of the rehearsals, so here was my chance to face one of the great choirs of the world, standing where Sir Malcolm Sargent had stood for so many years (from 1930 until his death in 1968) and experiencing at first hand that uniquely open-throated and thrilling sound. When I asked what I would be rehearsing, it turned out to be the *War Requiem* which I had so recently prepared for Simon Rattle. And so it was that, with some trepidation, though confident that I knew the score inside out, I ventured north and enjoyed an experience the like of which I had never had before or ever dreamt might come my way. One rehearsal led to another, as Nina Walker became increasingly busy at the Royal Opera House and before I knew where I was, I was rehearsing that great backbone of the Huddersfield Choral's repertoire, Handel's *Messiah*.

It was beginning to feel as if I might be being tried out as a possible successor to Nina and when I rehearsed *Messiah* I was given the acid test: a member of the contralto section (and what a section that was) put up her hand and said: "Mr. Kay, Sir Malcolm used to do it this way". It was clear that 400 questioning eyes were bearing down on me, waiting for my reaction. Someone was smiling down on me that day, as I simply said: "Sir Malcolm who?" – and stayed for ten years!

They were ten of the most enjoyable years of my musical life, even though it was pretty exhausting. Every Friday for ten years I drove a 320-mile round trip from my home in the Cotswolds, leaving after lunch, arriving in time for a quick meal (usually with my old and always-welcoming friends Carol and Richard Barraclough – the same Richard who auditioned me for the school choir all those years before) and then the rehearsal, and then driving back again. For part of those ten years I was also conductor of the Cheltenham Bach Choir, the Cecilian Singers of Leicester and the Mary Wakefield Westmorland Festival – as well as working full time as a member of the Radio 3 continuity team – heady days indeed – then I was young (-ish!).

The Town Hall in Huddersfield is one of the world's finest, with an acoustic which is perfect for large choral and orchestral concerts. And with a choir of over 200 to work with, the concerts I either chorus-mastered for or conducted were among the most enjoyable and rewarding in which I have ever been privileged to participate. There really is something about the sound of 'The Choral' that is unlike any other and many people have tried to explain why. One theory takes it back to the early days in the mid-19th century when the choir was formed; it was a time when mill workers got so used to having to talk very loudly to make themselves heard over the noise of machinery that they developed that uniquely open-throated sound which they could then use to great effect in their singing.

I also put it down to the simple matter of Yorkshire vowel sounds. The way a person speaks is bound to affect the way he or she sings – and the openness of the Yorkshire vowels is a natural gift when it comes to singing. In the same way that Italians make such good opera singers – because of the way they speak and the colour of their language – and the way that Americans make the best barbershop singers – ditto – well that also applies, in my experience, to the peculiarly Yorkshire vowels. I well remember Kathleen Ferrier's teacher Roy Henderson describing her open throat as 'a tremendous cavern': that perfectly describes the enormous resonating space which provided the necessary for her to make that remarkable sound; just so for the great voices of the north of England and nowhere more so than in Huddersfield.

Friday night was rehearsal night and when I started as Chorus Master I made it clear that I expected everyone to be there, in the same way that I was expecting to be there myself. I think I missed only six or seven rehearsals in ten years, due to circumstances beyond my control. Funnily enough, when I first mentioned that, Gareth Beaumont, one of the basses, suggested that it was all very well for me to say that. He reminded me that The King's Singers had sung in the Town Hall a couple of years previously – on a Friday night – and that most of the Choral had been there to listen!

But the great thing is that attendance was always remarkably good, as the weekly rehearsals of the Choral were an enormous part of people's lives. There were – and probably still are – people singing whose parents and grandparents were members, sitting in the same seats and singing from the same copies, such is the sense of tradition that the choir maintains. For them, without question, 'Friday Night is Music Night' indeed.

Mind you, on one occasion I was completely snowed up in my Cotswold village, to the extent that it was impossible to drive out at either end. On the Wednesday I phoned Jim Stafford, the choir secretary and explained the situation, adding that unless things improved dramatically, I might not make it to Friday's rehearsal. There was a short pause after which Jim simply said: "We'll all be there"! Luckily things improved enough for me to get out of the village and I left home at 7.30 in the morning, arrived at the King Street Mission at 7.15 in the evening, took the rehearsal, stayed the night and spent the whole of the next day driving home. Greater love hath no man than this! And sure enough, they *were* all there.

There had been a system in The Choral of re-auditions, which were taken by a large committee of people, not all of whom by any means were singers themselves. It was apparently a terrifying ordeal which singers approached in fear and trepidation. I thought that this was a crazy way of doing things and suggested that it should be the Chorus Master's job to test people for either admission to the choir or continuation of membership. I let myself in for it, as it takes a lot of time to listen to over 200 singers. But it made more sense and the committee agreed to a change of plan. When it was announced, there were gasps of horror, nobody wanting to have to sing alone in front of me. I explained that it was not a way of getting rid of people, more a chance to see and hear if any singers had problems with their voices that we might be able to solve. It turned out to be a fascinating experience, as one by one these glorious voices made me realise precisely why the overall sound of The Choral was so special.

It was during those ten years at Huddersfield that I learned so much about choral conducting and what works well or badly in training a large choir. I developed a basic technique which was based on two essential ingredients: solid hard work and lots of fun. If a choir cannot enjoy what it is doing, then it might as well not exist. And those good people of Huddersfield worked fantastically hard and where appropriate, laughed loud and long. I drove away from the town every Friday night and virtually sang my way back to the Cotswolds, so totally uplifting had I always found the rehearsal.

One of the perks for the Chorus Master was conducting the annual Christmas Concert, which was always accompanied by one of the great brass bands with which the north of England is so well blessed. Over the years I was lucky enough to conduct the Black Dyke Mills, Grimethorpe Colliery, Sellers International, Linley Band, Yorkshire Building Society and the Brighouse and Rastrick among others. The sound of 200 voices in combination with the pick of the country's finest brass bands in the Huddersfield Town Hall is simply thrilling and totally unlike anything else.

One year, Radio 2 decided it would like to record for broadcast Handel's *Messiah* in a famous and very splendid arrangement by Denis Wright for voices and brass. Two of

174

the top bands – Black Dyke and Britannia Building Society – assembled in the Town Hall under the magic baton of brass band supremo Harry Mortimer. The four soloists included my wife Gilly on the soprano line, the trumpet soloist was Maurice (*Star Wars*) Murphy and the broadcast created a great deal of special interest way beyond the confines of the north east. Sadly, at the next music meeting at the BBC, controller of Radio 3 John Drummond dismissed the whole thing as "profoundly depressing", in that it perpetuated "the cloth-cap image of music in the north"! Luckily it gave great pleasure to many more less-bigoted listeners, as well as giving an audience the chance to hear an amazing arrangement which otherwise would even more rarely have seen the light of day.

When Harry Mortimer came to take a Friday evening rehearsal, he casually mentioned that the last time he had heard the Choral was when he was himself playing the trumpet solo in a Malcolm Sargent performance of *Messiah*. As we reached the *Hallelujah Chorus,* the tears poured down his face at the sound, at the end of which he said: "You've made a happy man very old". He was once travelling on a train journey and reading through some brass band scores when the young lady sitting opposite him asked him about the music. When he told her that it was for brass band, she was very excited, as her father back in America was an enthusiast and she just wondered – and casually asked him – if he knew whether or not the great Harry Mortimer was still alive. Harry simply said that he believed he was and left it at that: such a modest genius.

Fast forwarding a number of years, we performed Britten's *War Requiem* again, this time with Jane Glover conducting.

By extraordinary happenstance, the performance took place at 7 o'clock on the evening on which the six o'clock news had announced that the Berlin Wall was coming down. I have never known an atmosphere like there was in the town hall that night. When that magical work came to rest on that final F major chord, nobody moved – for what seemed like an eternity. At moments like that I often think that there should be no applause, but that rather people should quietly drift away with their heads full of thoughts. In the end, someone could stand the silence no longer and began to clap, at which point the response was appropriately overwhelming.

I could happily have gone on spending the rest of my life commuting to Huddersfield and making music with all those wonderful people; but there comes a time when we must all realise that it is all-too-easy to outstay our welcome and that it is time to move on and give someone else a chance. I also believe that if you have not achieved what you would like to in ten years, then you never will. I was beginning to spend more and more time conducting concerts of my own and it became increasingly difficult to work as a 'Chorus Master', preparing major works for other conductors whose ideas on interpretation might well be different from the ones I was developing myself as a conductor. With great reluctance I gave up that privileged position in Huddersfield and moved on. I quietly hoped that the Choral might invite me back to conduct, and so it did.

1986 happened to mark the 150th anniversary of The Choral, which had been founded – funnily enough – in a pub in the town in 1836. There were many celebrations during that particular season, including a major programme for Yorkshire Television which involved a number of 'star' presenters with

Yorkshire connections including Michael Parkinson, retired soprano Elizabeth Harwood, John Dunn from Radio 2, actor Brian Glover and Welsh superstar baritone Geraint Evans. At one point in the programme, Gordon Langford had arranged a number of well-known TV adverts into a choral and orchestral medley, the climax of which was when the men of the choir had to sing "Tetleys make good tea"! Not sure the beer drinkers among them will have appreciated that. On another occasion I was lucky enough to conduct and present a major television special for Christmas. This took place in Ripon Cathedral and the Choral was joined by the Black Dyke Mills Band. Robert Hardy did some splendid readings and Janet Baker sang – divinely. Although I had known Dame Janet for many years, this was the one and only time I had the privilege of conducting her in performance.

I continued to conduct the Christmas concerts – right up until 2015 – and in 2004, on the occasion of my 60th birthday, I conducted a special charity performance of the Huddersfield Choral Society *Messiah* – the ultimate dream-come-true and one which led to my being invited again to conduct the two annual Christmas *Messiahs* – not surprisingly the hottest ticket in town and an honour indeed to be asked to take charge. Having trained the choir in that great work for ten years it was a special thrill to be able to conduct the performances, rather than handing over to someone else. The sound of The Choral is one I shall never forget and the joy of being part of it for so long remains one of the great highlights of my musical live.

But there were others: For nine years I was conductor of the Cheltenham Bach Choir, rather nearer to my home in the Cotswolds. That was another delightful experience and one which gave me so many opportunities to expand my ever-growing conducting repertoire. It was and remains a very fine choir, performing mainly in the Town Hall in Cheltenham – another marvellous venue for choral and orchestral music. With that choir I was, of course, preparing the music for performances which I would conduct myself and that makes a difference, as I can suggest my own interpretation right from the start. The choir was very well matched in terms of balance and happily accepted my desire in rehearsal for a mixture of dedicated hard work and good clean fun.

On one occasion I had programmed the *Five Songs of Nature* by Dvořák, beautifully written part songs which I remembered from having sung them years earlier as a member of the professional John Alldis choir. I was determined that we should sing them in the original Czech and casually asked the choir if any of its members happened to speak the language. To my great relief, a large number of hands were raised: I should have known, as many of the singers worked for GCHQ! That question as to whether or not to perform in the original language is always a tricky one, particularly when considering the Bach Passions, for example. I have generally performed these in English, as a two-and-a-half-hour work which tells a story should make the action entirely understandable to an audience. As they say: discuss.

I had a call one day from Lynne Holland in Leicester, asking if I knew of anyone who might like to take over the conductorship of a small but perfectly formed chamber choir of which she was a member. This was the Cecilian Singers of Leicester. As my wife Gilly's family lived in Oadby, I often broke my journey home from Huddersfield on a Friday night in order to see them. I thought about possible contenders for the Cecilian Singers and casually mentioned that, as I was going to be in Oadby the following Friday, would the singers like to spend the next day working with me – for fun – on the music they were preparing. They happily accepted the offer and we all met in Stoughton Church, brought sandwiches for a picnic lunch and enjoyed a very jolly day working on a variety of music. When they asked me at the end of the day if I might be remotely interested in taking up the job as conductor myself, I had no difficulty in saying yes, as I had found them to be such good company and such fine singers. I was also on the look-out for a much smaller choir than the ones I had been used to and this was my chance. So began another delightful chapter in my choral experience. The more intimate side of music making which a chamber choir offers is the perfect foil to the vast armies of singers I had worked with previously.

In the end, in 1991, it was time again to move on. My BBC work was taking over more of my time and as well as Huddersfield and Cheltenham I was also conducting the Mary Wakefield Westmorland Festival, based at Kendal in the Lake District. This had started out as a competitive festival and became the inspiration behind the Leith Hill Musical Festival, which was founded by the sister of Ralph Vaughan Williams, who wisely appointed her brother founder-conductor, back in 1905. 'Mary Wakefield' took place every other year and I was lucky enough to stay with them for five festivals, conducting such large-scale works as Elgar's *Dream of Gerontius*, Verdi's *Requiem* and Mendelssohn's *Elijah*.

After ten years the festival decided I had done enough, mainly – they told me – because they did not want any conductor to stay with the festival for longer than Sir Charles Groves. As he had done ten years, my time was clearly up. Again, I look back on my association with nothing but pleasure, moulding a 'choir' out of members of several in the district and sharing with them the unique pleasure of large-choir music.

Little did I know at the time that things were only going to get bigger and that one day, a choral force of some 200+ singers might seem relatively modest.

CHAPTER TWELVE

Music won the Cause

Way back in the late 1950s my family took holidays in the south west of England, in order to coincide with the Rydal School old boys cricket tour, which was based on the lovely town of Sidmouth. It was there that I met, for the first time, the conductor and later Charterhouse Director of Music Bill Llewellyn. To be honest, as an early teenager, I was somewhat star-struck. The reason was simple: Bill was conductor of the Linden Singers and they had appeared regularly on television. Back in the 1950s, if you were on TV, you were a bit special and so I was delighted to meet him. He had been at Rydal too and his sister was married to one of my own teachers at the school.

We stayed in touch over the years. Largely because he invited The King's Singers to Charterhouse and also included me in a line-up of soloists when he conducted Elgar's *The Kingdom* in a school concert. In 1986, when he was also conductor of the aforementioned Leith Hill Musical Festival he asked me to narrate his performance there of Honegger's *King David*. I was very glad to do so, partly because I loved narrating the work, but mainly because this was my first introduction to a festival which would become such a major part of my life in the years ahead. As soon as I entered the Dorking Halls in Surrey – where the festival is based –

I knew there was something very special about it. There was an indescribable 'buzz' about the place, in which 700 singers take part in an annual three-day competitive festival which carries on so splendidly the vision of its founder conductor Ralph Vaughan Williams.

RVW, as he is affectionately known in those parts, used to cycle round the villages and towns in the Dorking area rehearsing all the choirs: it was easy for him as he lived in Dorking and cycling round the neighbouring roads in those days was relatively safe and easy. He was determined that as many people as possible should sing and over the years, the festival grew; so much so that in 1931, RVW and the festival were largely responsible for building the Dorking Halls as a permanent home for the festival. Twelve towns and villages are now represented, producing some 700 singers in three divisions, each of which spends the winter months learning its music and one day around Easter time performing the results of its labours.

On the morning of each festival day, each choir competes against three others in five categories: madrigal, part song, male voices, female voices and small ensemble. Professional adjudicators then comment on their performances and award marks, so that one choir in each category will win one of the cherished banners or cups. After a break for lunch, the four choirs bury the hatchet and combine under the direction of the festival conductor and, together with a professional orchestra and soloists perform the main full chorus work which has been selected for the occasion. The next two days, another eight choirs take over and repeat the process. It is a tremendous social and musical event and the fact that there are still the same number of singers devoted to the festival

182

in the 21st century confirms its worth and helps to preserve RVW's original plan. As one of this country's leading choral composers it is inevitable that much of his music for choirs was written with the festival very much in mind. If that had not worked out the way he wanted, he would not have continued conducting the festival for over fifty years, right up to 1958, the year of his death.

After I had narrated Honegger's *King David* for Bill in 1986, he graciously invited me to join the Music Committee which is responsible for choosing the music for each festival. I was very glad to do so, as the President was my great friend and mentor Sir David Willcocks and the small but perfectly formed committee included two previous festival conductors William Cole (who succeeded RVW and even bought his house in Dorking) and Christopher Robinson. Bill had also included his number two at Charterhouse and conductor of the neighbouring Petersfield Festival Robin Wells. It was a committee well versed in the ways and means of the festival in particular and the wider world of choral music in general.

In 1995 Bill announced his intention to retire from the festival (as he had from Charterhouse) and a replacement would have to be sought. After the meeting was over I had a quiet word with the Chairman Deirdre Hicks and asked her if it might be appropriate for me to put my name forward. She thought it would and a meeting was arranged so that such an idea might be discussed. It was a very friendly meeting where all the right questions were asked, both by me and the festival representatives, and in the end it was agreed that I should succeed Bill as only the fifth festival conductor in ninety years. I was, of course, delighted and honoured, though I never thought I might be lucky enough to stay in that privileged position for over twenty years.

The job involves spending huge amounts of time delving into scores, both of the major oratorio works that form the backbone, and also the many hundreds of shorter pieces which might be suitable for the appropriate standard of each division in competition. It has been time well spent over the years and has resulted in an extremely wide variety of music, much of it by living composers. There has never been a year during my time when at least one major work by a living composer has not been included: it is both a duty and a pleasure to make sure this happens. It represents the future of choral music and avoids a festival such as that becoming some sort of museum piece.

I mentioned RVW cycling round the towns and villages; and Bill Llewellyn could easily make his way round (by car!) as he lived close at hand in Godalming. But for me to undertake such a plan, living 100 miles away would have been tricky and more time-consuming than I could possibly afford. So we came up with a scheme which worked well, even though it was a bit of a killer! Three times – once each in January, February and March – the choirs assembled in batches of 200+ on a Saturday and I rehearsed the entire festival programme in a day: one division 10-12, another from 1-3 and the last from 4-6: madness, but hugely enjoyable. On top of the three days of the festival itself, RVW instigated an annual performance of a Bach Passion, the St. Matthew and the St. John alternating, and more recently adding a third string in Handel's *Messiah*. To rehearse three major works and a Passion within the space of 24 hours with over 700 singers is quite a marathon, though I always found it a most exhilarating experience – nice work if you can get it.

Then came the festival itself, for which so many people in so many choirs had meticulously prepared under the direction of their own conductors. This, for me, became the most uplifting three days of the year, every year, with what I call all the right people doing the right things for the right reason. On each festival day I was present in the hall from nine o'clock in the morning until they closed the bar at the other end of the day. I needed to be able to hear each choir perform all the competition pieces and to note the various differences there might be in interpretation. It was then my job to put those performances together into one when I rehearsed it in the afternoon with the combined choirs and then performed it during the evening concert. It made for a very long day each day, but then I had to remember that the choirs had been singing all day as well and had every right to be even more exhausted than I was! For the *Passion* and *Messiah* performances the festival was joined by a 'Baroque' ensemble, with Theresa Caudle's magnificent *Canzona* providing glorious instrumental colours and buckets of expertise to complement the sound of 250 voices. For the festival itself, the English Festival Orchestra provided the backbone. That orchestra's ability to produce such marvellous sounds on one afternoon's rehearsal never ceased to amaze me. In any one year it had to master so many periods and styles and it did so with enthusiasm and sheer brilliance. One year alone the three days included Gershwin's *Porgy and Bess*, Weber's *Eb Mass*, RVW's *In Windsor Forest*, Haydn's *Nelson Mass* and Duruflé's *Requiem*: a mixed bag if ever there was one.

As that great English composer William Byrd said, way back in the 16th century: "Since singing is so good a thing, I wish all men would learn to sing." He had a vested interest, of course, in his hope that it was *his* music which would be constantly performed; but if you believe, as I do, that everyone has a voice and that nobody should be denied the opportunity to sing, then RVW got it absolutely right when he started and lavished so much time on the festival. He was the first to admit that he was not the world's greatest conductor. "I've told you before," he would shout to choir and orchestra, "don't watch my beat"! Apparently it was all in his eyes. The fact that I conducted the festival standing on the podium which was specially built to accommodate his considerable girth and that I used his own antique music stand added something rather special. On one occasion, after one of RVW's combined rehearsals, one of the singers went back to his own conductor and admitted: "RVW took it rather faster than you do, but don't worry", he said, "I sang it at your speed"!

What makes a great festival such as this work so well is the enormous amount of work which is put in 'behind the scenes', year in and year out. The whole thing is based on amateur enthusiasm and dedication to the cause. The festival's motto – *Music won the Cause* – is a quotation from Dryden's words which were set to music by Handel in his oratorio *Alexander's Feast* and it neatly sums up the devotion which so many people feel, a hundred and some years after RVW launched the whole thing. Those of us lucky enough to be part of it – as singers, conductors, secretaries, chairmen, programme note writers, librarians, sandwich makers, flower arrangers, box office managers and goodness knows what else – are all united in a common bond: that of enjoying to the full the life-enhancing power of music. And that goes too for the faithful festival audience, for which no effort is spared by all those mentioned above, and many more.

In my twentieth year as conductor of the festival, the committee decided to commission a major work in celebration and asked me for advice as to whom to approach. I had no hesitation in mentioning the name of my dear old friend Bob Chilcott, whom I had known since he was nine years old and standing in front of me as a chorister in the choir at King's. By the year in question – 2015 – he had already become one of the most popular composers of choral music in the world and I felt sure he would come up with something very special to celebrate my milestone anniversary.

And how right I was! Bob has always had a tremendous knack at choosing perfect texts and after I had suggested to him a fifteen-minute suite of Choral Dances, he put together a perfect selection of words on the subject of 'Time'. He began with the famous text by Henry VIII *Pastime with good company* – a text which he and I had so many times sung as members of The King's Singers. When the score finally arrived, I emailed him to say how thrilled I was with the music. His response was that he had just realised we had known each other for fifty years – what he touchingly described as 'pastime with good company indeed'. How good it is that he now lives just five minutes away from us in the Cotswolds.

The first performance of *Dances of Time* took place at the festival and as an absolute hallmark of a fine piece, it's fair to say that the four choirs which made up the 200+ taking part absolutely loved rehearsing and performing it. As the audience clearly loved hearing it too, I can only hope that choirs all over the world will have the chance to enjoy a work of which I feel extremely proud. I was delighted in 2019 to conduct the New Zealand premier of the *Dances* at the Teapot Valley Summer School near to our favourite town of Nelson in the South Island and again, the singers clearly loved the music as equally clearly did the audience. The President of the festival was another of my oldest friends, whom I have also known for fifty years, since we read music together at Cambridge. John Rutter very generously agreed to write what he called a 'choral flourish' in celebration and his setting of *Awake, ye heavenly choirs* will, like Bob's Dances, carry the name of the Leith Hill Musical Festival to all corners of the globe as choirs everywhere have the opportunity to perform it.

There is always a strange feeling when one finds that one has been replaced and following my decision that my twenty-first year as festival conductor should be my last, I heard that – yet another old friend and former King's chorister – Jonathan Willcocks was chosen as my successor. As his father Sir David was for many years President of the festival, it feels a bit like keeping it in the family, but there is no doubt that with what I would call typical Willcocks flair, the future of the festival will be firmly assured. If this sounds a bit like a Cambridge *Mafia* at work, then all I can suggest is that the class of the mid-60s if you will was a wonderful breeding ground for so many of us who went on to make our life in music. The privilege of having come under the influence of so many fine teachers and performers in those rarefied surroundings and at that impressionable age remains something for which all of us remain profoundly grateful. Continuity and tradition are both very important, but there will always be fine musicians who can help not only to preserve that sense of tradition, but can also bring to it a sense of development – as I was always encouraged at the Leith Hill festival – by evolution rather than revolution.

I was deeply touched by the extreme generosity of the festival organisers, not only throughout my twenty-one years, but also as I left. They gave me a rip-roaring send-off, with a particularly jolly party the day after my last concert. Entertainment was provided by my dear old friends Instant Sunshine (with their inimitable send-up of The King's Singers an inevitable highlight) and the gifts with which I was showered remain real treasures: a beautifully hand-made leather music case (crafted by one of the singers) a case of wine, a huge bunch of flowers for Gilly and the most amazing book, in which all those seven hundred lovely singers had contributed their thoughts and reminiscences. It is a work of art, superbly and sumptuously bound by a world-class bookbinding cousin of Liz May, the festival's tireless administrator. Every time I dip into it I have to have a stiff drink by my side as the comments of so many people whose company I enjoyed for so long are deeply moving. As if that were not enough, shortly after I received a cheque in the post which represented what was left of the amazingly generous contributions from all the choristers. It was large enough for us to buy what we had wanted for so long – a new and beautiful table and chairs for the kitchen. This means that we can think of the Leith Hill Musical Festival with affection and gratitude every time we sit down to a meal.

Intermission
Three

French Maestro Pierre Monteux was interviewed as he approached his ninetieth birthday and was asked what – apart from his music – had given him most happiness in his long life. He replied: "The ladies in my life have given me a great deal of happiness; and so have my model railways." After a short pause he added: "but now that I'm getting very old I have had to give up my model railways!"

When another great French maestro Pierre Boulez was asked how he managed to get by on only four hours sleep a night, he replied: "I sleep fast!" Boulez was once asked if he thought his music was "too modern" for the time. His answer speaks volumes: "It's not that my music's too soon; the audience is too late."

When I was in China on a conducting tour with The Really Big Chorus, we were entertained to a performance of Chinese Opera. It is a fascinating form of entertainment though much of it goes over Western heads, due in part to its extreme length and the fact that the dialogue – such as there is – is in Chinese. However, help was at hand, as there was a large board on the stage with English subtitles to keep us in the picture. At one point a rather vicious-looking creature appeared and shouted something rather frightening to the others on the stage. A quick look at the board and it was clear that they were the right words, though not necessarily in the right order, as it read: "What are you doing here on earth?" Close!

In the bazaar in Istanbul, the first thing I saw was a man holding up a board full of rather smart-looking watches and a huge sign which read: 'Genuine fake Rolex'!

And for some considerable time, there was a sign on the M40 which never failed to raise a chuckle, until sadly they took it down, as a new service station had been built. It said, quite simply: EMERGENCY WC – 26 MILES!

While I was singing at Westminster Abbey as a lay-vicar (1967-1971), my fellow bass Kenneth Tudor (such a funny man) asked me if I'd ever met a previous incumbent of the Deanery – the man in charge of the Coronation, Dean Don. I said that I hadn't and asked if he was still alive: "O no," said Ken, "Dean Don's Merrily on high"!

During my years as Chorus Master of the Huddersfield Choral Society I plucked up courage and asked if I could possibly conduct the annual performances of Handel's *Messiah*. The response cut to the quick: "A Chorus Master knows his place and it's not on the podium". Nonetheless, my wish was eventually granted, though I had to wait several years.

Did George W. Bush really say "the trouble with the French is that they have no word for *Entrepreneur*"? I hope so.

My distinguished broadcasting colleague Richard Baker was once stopped outside the BBC by an autograph hunter who asked: "Are you the chap who reads the news on telly?" When Richard proudly admitted that he was, the response was: "sign here – newsreaders make good swaps!"

On one occasion when I was invited to the Director General's Christmas party in the Council Chamber of Broadcasting House, there were many of us enjoying his very generous hospitality (bravo the licence fee!) when I suddenly spotted a small man going round with the drinks doing what looked like a very good imitation of Norman Wisdom – pretending almost to drop the tray and generally fooling about. Imagine my excitement when I realised that it was indeed that funniest of funny men – another childhood hero of mine, and right there as a fellow guest, unable to resist 'performing' to the delight of everyone there.

I well remember the day that the great Finnish composer Sibelius died. It so happens that Sir Malcolm Sargent had conducted Sibelius's fifth symphony the night before and that the performance had been broadcast to many parts of the world, including Finland. The announcement in one of the national newspapers the next morning came up with the unfortunately worded headline: Sibelius dies after hearing Sargent conduct fifth symphony!

When Vaughan Williams wrote a concerto for Larry Adler to play on his harmonica, he arranged for the virtuoso player to visit him and to go through the score. All went well until a certain point in the piece where Adler admitted that what

RVW had written was unplayable – explaining that to do so would involve blowing and sucking at the same time. The composer looked at it closely, thought about it for a while and then said :"You don't like my music". Adler insisted that this was not the case, but that there was no way round this particular problem – and that otherwise he *loved* what the old man had written. VW thought again and then proudly announced "I'll write that bit again and if you still don't like it I'll rewrite the whole thing for bass tuba"!

Of course, not everyone loved Vaughan Williams's music: Sir Thomas Beecham clearly didn't enjoy VW's *Pastoral Symphony* and at a rehearsal he gave the distinct impression that all he was prepared to do was to beat time. After a while he noticed that the orchestra was no longer playing. When he asked why, the Leader pointed out that the symphony had finished. Beecham turned over the last page, saw that it had and said: "Thank God"!

I can hardly bear to write this, but when my great mentor Sir David Willcocks died, in September 2015, I turned on BBC Radio 3 the following morning and heard his recording of Handel's Coronation Anthem *Zadok the Priest*, played in tribute. After a short reverential pause, the breakfast programme announcer then calmly said: "The choir of King's College, Cambridge, conducted by the *immortal* David Willcocks, who died yesterday". Can't get the staff!

Our dear friend George Shearing never liked being called a jazz pianist – even worse, a blind jazz pianist: he was a pianist, full stop. He used to play concertos as well as jazz and composed a great deal, including two sets of wonderful Shakespeare settings for choir, piano and bass. These display his great love of two principal influences – English madrigals and the music of Delius. He used to say "I have been credited with writing over 300 songs, many of which have ridden the bumpy road from relative obscurity to total oblivion: this," he said, before playing *Lullaby of Birdland*, "is the other one."

On one of our King's Singers trips to New Zealand we had to fly from Christchurch to Timaru, where the landing strip was being resurfaced. As a result, we had to fly in a hedge-hopping DC3 – in its time a great workhorse of a plane, but one which had clearly seen better days: it was a case of 'chocks away' as the be-goggled pilot pushed the starter button and off we went in clouds of smoke. We never reached much of an altitude but somehow we made it safe and sound. As we tottered down the steps, Al Hume, somewhat green round the gills, couldn't resist wondering "What the hell must a DC1 have been like?"

I mentioned the venerable old-timers who inhabited the choir stalls of Westminster Abbey during my time as a lay vicar: the one who kept us all amused was fellow bass Ken Tudor. He was habitually late for rehearsals, which didn't go down well, particularly in the time of Sir William McKie, who as organist had a fairly low tolerance level if things weren't going too well. The last time Ken arrived late, MacKie was on the verge of saying that enough was enough, but what could he do when Ken breezed in brandishing a steering wheel and announcing that he was driving round Trafalgar Square when the thing came off. "As far as I know," he said,

Gilly on our wedding day,
February 1983

Wearing my Sunday Morning
waistcoat, created by Joan Lilly
and including favourite composers
and my Radio 3 signature tune

With Charlie
on her wedding
day, April 2002

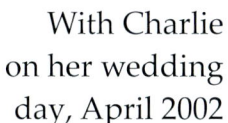

With Charlie and
Jonathan at my 70th
birthday celebration
lunch at Ditchley Park,
May 2014

With Sally and the children, a short-lived beard and a real 1970s shirt and collar, 1976

Jonathan, Hamilton and Marianne at home in New Zealand, 2020

Dom, Sophie, Freddie and Charlotte with dogs Indy and Trixie at home in Dorset, 2017

Cutting Gilly's magnificently designed 70th birthday cake

70th birthday celebration lunch in May 2014, wearing the late George Shearing's dazzling jacket

In Auckland New Zealand with Henry "Blowers" Blofeld after a very jolly lunch with our friends Angela and Hylton Le Grice

Enjoying a good laugh, as always, with Neville Marriner

Three little maids with red wine: Julia McKenzie, Ellie Shearing and Gilly

A night at the opera: Gilly at Glyndebourne with Ellie and George Shearing

With composer Bob Chilcott at the Leith Hill Musical Festival

Synchronised conducting with John Rutter at Leith Hill

Must have said something funny to make Instant Sunshine laugh at my Leith Hill festival farewell party, 2016

Only Vaughan Williams is missing from 100 years of Leith Hill Musical Festival conductors. *L-R:* BK, Sir David Willcocks (president), Bill Llewellyn, Christopher Robinson, William Cole

Presenting *An Evening with Brian Kay*

Party time with Gordon Kaye *('Allo 'Allo)*, Jean Boht *(Bread)*,
Val Doonican and Elaine Paige

At the celebration lunch for George Shearing's knighthood
with George and Ellie, Gilly, Jon and Lou Gardey

Backstage at
Symphony Hall in
Birmingham with
Cleo Laine and John
Dankworth, Barrie
Forgie (BBC
Big Band), George
Shearing and bass
player Neil Swainson

Conducting choir, orchestra and audience in the Burford Singers
Coronation Jubilee Concert, 2013

Conducting and presenting a Yorkshire Television Christmas special
in Ripon Cathedral with the cathedral choir, the Huddersfield Choral
Society, the Black Dyke Band, Dame Janet Baker and Robert Hardy

"the car is still going round and round in circles!" Needless to say, he got away with it, though it was a close-run thing.

When David Willcocks and the Bach Choir commissioned a setting of the Mass from composer Paul Patterson, David suggested to Paul that he should not forget the choir's chairman Leo Rothschild, who was noted for the strength of his low notes. "Find a suitable moment for the basses to go down as low as possible," was his advice. Paul found the perfect moment, taking the bass department, including Rothschild, down to a low Eb on the words "and the rich he hath sent empty away."

When my sister Heather was wondering what to eat in a restaurant one lunchtime she asked the rather young waitress to find out what was *soup du jour*. The girl went to the kitchen to check and when she returned, she said "It's soup of the day"!

Our dear friend Julia McKenzie told us a wonderful story about the occasion she was asked to sing for The Queen during the celebrations for one of Her Majesty's great anniversaries. In the line-up of stars being presented after the event, one of Julia's fellow artistes suddenly presented The Queen with a book of raffle tickets for her daughter's school fete. Funnily enough when the big day arrived, it was the Queen whose ticket was pulled out of the hat first: her prize, dry-cleaning vouchers!

An elderly gentleman who had sung in choirs all his life was reaching the end of his time on earth and fearing the approach of the grim reaper he prayed to his Heavenly Father asking: is there a heavenly choir I can join when the trumpets have sounded for me on the other side? His reply came swiftly: the good news is that there is indeed a heavenly choir; the bad news is that you are expected at this evening's rehearsal!

That reminds me of the story of an elderly clerical gentleman who awoke one morning, checked the obituaries in the paper and read his own. Somewhat perturbed he phoned the Bishop and explained. After a short pause, the Bishop asked: "where are you ringing from?"

I love the story about Her Majesty the Queen visiting the town of Wigan and sitting next to the Mayor at lunch. Halfway through he politely asked: "I don't know what to call you". Her reply could not have been more charming: "You could call me Ma'am or you could call me your Majesty, but it hardly matters as you've called me 'luv' three times already!"

How can you spot a real musician? Leonard Bernstein had an answer: it's someone, he said, who can listen to the *William Tell* overture without thinking of the Lone Ranger! When I told that to my Radio 3 audience on one occasion, a listener sent me another definition: It's a man, he wrote, who hears a beautiful woman singing in the bath and puts his *ear* to the keyhole!

A friend of mine visited one of our great cathedrals shortly after it had installed a new state-of-the-art sound system, whereby wherever you were sitting, you could hear what was being said far away at the high altar coming through a small speaker in the seat in front of you. This was fine when it worked, but as the precentor got to the bit where he should have said 'the Lord be with you', he realised that something was amiss and turned to his colleague and said quietly 'there's something wrong with this' and the congregation dutifully responded 'and also with you'.

CHAPTER THIRTEEN

The Really Big Sing

Among many other pieces of good fortune to come my way has been my apparent habit of following on from someone well established in one or another form of the business of which I've been privileged to be a part. When it comes to broadcasting, I seemed to inherit a number of opportunities from that great-voiced music presenter and former newsreader Richard Baker: there was the Radio 4 series *Music in Mind*, the Vienna *New Year's Day Concert* for radio and television, Radio 2's *Friday Night is Music Night* and *Melodies for You*, all of which I took over from him. When it comes to choral music, there have been many times when the work of my mentor Sir David Willcocks has eventually come my way.

Back in the 1970s, a Canadian-born lecturer at Imperial College in London called Don Monro had what seemed – even to him – to be a crazy idea. Nothing ventured, he walked round the corner to the Royal College of Music and told the then Director – Sir David – that he wanted to put on a performance of Handel's *Messiah* in the Royal Albert Hall, hoping to attract a large number of singers for whom this would be a wonderful opportunity and an unforgettable experience. Would Sir David be interested in conducting it? It would not involve rehearsal for the singers, they would simply turn up and sing. Don imagined that he would have his head bitten off at the very idea, but to his great delight, Sir David keenly agreed. And so started The Really Big Chorus singing 'Concerts from Scratch'.

This grew and grew until before long it had well earned the title 'Really Big' and to this day, almost 4,000 singers turn up year after year to enjoy the experience. The performance takes place usually on Advent Sunday each year and remains one of the most remarkable gatherings of unrehearsed amateur singers anywhere in the world. On top of that annual treat, there are two other occasions in the year when such gatherings take place, also in the Royal Albert Hall – one in May and the other in July. The organisation also arranges trips abroad, weekends of singing with the opportunity to visit exotic locations, and these include – every other year – a cruise, on which singing is mixed with sailing, sight-seeing and having a lot of fun. There is also an annual summer school which attracts singers from all round the world.

In 2005, I received a call from Don Monro asking if I would like to be involved, sharing with Sir David the task of conducting some of these performances. Of course I would be delighted, never expecting that within a few short years I would have succeeded Sir David as Principal Conductor.

My first trip abroad with the choir was to Halle, the birthplace of George Frederick Handel. It was an extraordinary experience, made the more so by the fact that I conducted *Messiah*, standing next to the font in which Handel was christened. That added a certain *frisson* for us all and inspired us to give of our best. Next came Salzburg; for some reason or other I had never been to that beautiful city and eagerly looked forward to the opportunity. 350 people signed up to come and sing Mozart's Requiem in the Cathedral – again with the added excitement of using the Cathedral Orchestra, which Mozart himself had conducted in that same magnificent building.

The trip also included two notable options for the times when we were not singing: we either visit Mozart's birthplace or tramp around the surrounding hills pretending to be Julie Andrews in *The Sound of Music*. We flew to Munich on the Thursday and completed the journey by coach. The following day involved sight-seeing, a three-hour rehearsal with choir and piano and then the evening 'feast', complete with 'entertainment' from members of the party.

Before the feast we were invited by the Mayor to a drinks welcome in the former Archbishop's Palace. A string quartet delighted us with a spirited performance of *Eine kleine Nachtmusik* before our host gave us a few words of welcome. He was delighted that we had chosen to visit "the city that is Mozart" and hoped we would enjoy the occasion. Don Monro nudged me and said: "respond". On that spur of the moment I thanked the Mayor for his kind words and couldn't resist adding: "not wishing to spoil your evening, Sir, I have to tell you that outside Salzburg, Mozart's music is very little known"! He had to laugh because 350 singers had generously done so.

On the day of the concert we assembled in the enormous space of the Cathedral, surrounded by the famous four organs, one of which adorns each corner of the transept and for which Mozart had composed his four-organ music. The rehearsal passed happily and we dispersed to our various hotels to eat and change. As we left the cathedral

Don reminded me that we only did these concerts for our own amusement; audiences were usually pretty thin, but if anyone did turn up, there would be a collection for local charities. The thought of performing in such a vast space without much audience might have worried me, but then I told him that as I would have my back to the audience in any case, such things need not concern me too much.

After a good meal I changed into my tails and made my way back to the cathedral. Imagine my surprise and delight when I got there and found 3,000 people occupying every inch of the building! They made a pretty good collection that night! The fact remains that the seats were free – no cost – and as the Salzburg Festival had recently taken place, where tickets cost an arm and a leg if you can get any, the idea of a free concert obviously found favour. This made it an amazing and unforgettable experience for us all and we were delighted to go again three years later for another go, this time singing Mozarts' *Vesperae Solennes de Confessore*.

The next excitement for me with The Really Big Chorus was my first opportunity to conduct massed voices in the Royal Albert Hall. It is a building I have known and loved for most of my life, having sung there with The King's Singers, listened to everything there from the final concert of the original Swingle Singers to so many Proms concerts, presenting them for Radio 3. But to conduct there was something I never imagined could possibly come my way.

This first time was to be a performance of Carl Orff's *Carmina Burana*, with some 2,500 singers and a vast orchestra. The orchestra alone fills the arena (where the Promenaders stand) and the choir fills the stage, up each side of the organ – floor to ceiling – and round both sides

201

of the arena a good half way to the back of the hall. It is an awesome spectacle and one which never ceases to thrill everyone present, myself included. I was allowed a two-hour morning rehearsal with the choir and a piano, then a three-hour afternoon rehearsal with choir, soloists and full orchestra. The evening performance knocked me off my feet, and so started an association which continues with the greatest pleasure to this day.

The first cruise I conducted was round the Baltic. The organisation had been before and had endured pretty rough seas. Gilly and I need not have worried. For the entire trip the sea was like a mill pond as we visited such delightful ports of call as Visby, Tallinn, St Petersburg, Helsinki and Stockholm. We did not have long to enjoy the delights of the Hermitage in St Petersburg, but we did manage to scratch the surface, going from room to room and seeing so many paintings we had known all our life. When we asked how long it would take to go round the entire collection, looking at every item, we were told that the latest estimate would be nine years!

One thing which makes these overseas trips so hugely enjoyable is that the TRBC organisation works tirelessly to make sure we can (a) relax and (b) concentrate on the music and when it comes to the cruises these are masterminded by the hyper-efficient team of Tony Hastings and his wife Annie, who make sure we want for nothing. They also run the annual summer school, which has become such a major feature of TRBC. Don Monro's widow Ann is very much part of the team (she originally had the unenviable task of sending out tickets to all 4,000 singers for *Messiah* and for the two other annual RAH concerts, a somewhat burdensome job now undertaken by Annie). Trevor Ford and his wife Marianne Barton who run the English Festival Orchestra which always plays for the Albert Hall concerts are also very much on hand: it's a formidable team and the singers are always and quite rightly hugely appreciative of the vast amount of work which goes on endlessly and devotedly behind the scenes.

Trips abroad carry on year on year, including such exotic places as Beijing, where we performed Handel's *Messiah* in the Forbidden City Concert Hall. We weren't really allowed to, as performing Christian works was not entirely acceptable in China. The posters and tickets all said: 'A work by Handel', though they all knew perfectly well what it was, as they stood up quite naturally for the *Hallelujah Chorus*!

Other outstanding memories include Haydn's *Creation* in Cape Town, Mozart in St Petersburg (a bit more time to look round this time), Karl Jenkins' *The Armed Man* in Dubrovnik (particularly emotional singing a Mass for Peace in a city so recently ravaged by war) – and again in Krakow, the day after visiting Auschwitz, and visits to Madeira, Prague, Malta, Guernsey, Tenerife, Granada, Sorrento, and Lisbon, New York (Fauré's Requiem on the fifteenth anniversary of 9/11), Mallorca, Athens and Riga with cruises to the Aegean, the Mediterranean, the Black Sea, the Nile, the Yangtze (with a concert in Hong Kong) the Rhone, the Danube, the Seine and the Douro. I thought my international touring days had long gone, thirty years after I left The King's Singers, but how wrong I turned out to be.

I fondly recall such moments as sitting in the garden in Prague where Mozart had sat on the evening before the first performance of *Don Giovanni* and hurriedly composed

203

the overture. In St Petersburg I had a rehearsal with the local orchestra and this took place in an imposing-looking building on the other side of the square from the Hermitage. The facades of those buildings are hugely impressive and I looked forward to having a good look inside. Imagine my disappointment when I found that there was nothing remotely impressive behind those closed doors. What might well have been a fine interior in pre-Revolution days was now a bit of a wreck: holes had been punched through the walls so that electric wires could pass through, the ceilings were peeling and the rehearsal facilities so totally unsatisfactory that I could not imagine any British orchestra tolerating such surroundings – not to mention dreaded 'health and safety'.

Other 'scratch' performances I have conducted in the Royal Albert Hall have included Elgar's *Dream of Gerontius*, Verdi's *Requiem* (four times and counting), *The Armed Man* (ditto), Haydn's *Creation*, *Requiems* by Mozart and Fauré, *Glorias* by Vivaldi and Rutter and the first performances of two new works by Karl Jenkins commissioned by and specially written for Don Monro and The Really Big Chorus – *Gloria* and *Gods of Olympus*. We also gave a hugely enjoyable Gilbert and Sullivan Gala Concert, filled with 'shreds and patches' from many of the much-loved Savoy Operas. When we first performed the Karl Jenkins *Gloria*, the composer was interviewed for television. He is well aware that he's known as a 'Marmite' composer and when the interviewer asked what we would make of this new piece, he rather charmingly replied: "If you like my music, you'll love it." After a moment's pause, he graciously added: "If you don't, you won't"!

But the Big One – the Royal Albert Hall 'Scratch' *Messiah* – is one which Sir David was understandably reluctant to hand over, as long as had the health and strength to carry on, having done it for some 35 years. Eventually my time came and he graciously handed over. My first was in 2010 and it is an annual treat to which I now eagerly look forward. The sight and sound of 4,000 people giving their all (whether they really know the music or not!) is unique and the accumulative volume is genuinely awesome.

People share boxes with singers they have known for many years and there is always a scramble to get the best seats in the hall for singing. Some of those are a long way away from the conductor and it means that I must use enormous gestures throughout in the hope of making myself seen and keeping those vast forces as together as possible. After the first time, I awoke the next morning and told Gilly that I could hardly move my arms! But I was already looking forward to the next time. Gilly also told me that when 4,000 people turned over a page, it felt like a tsunami of wind running round the circular hall.

There is little doubt that when things get tough – as they do during a recession and the following years of austerity – people turn to singing as a wonderful way of re-charging the batteries. It is as much a social exercise as musical and binds folk together in a uniquely life-enhancing way. Much of my life is spent conducting choral workshops, where singers like the idea of meeting for one day, working hard on a piece of music and giving some sort of 'performance' at the end of the day. There are so many pressures on people's time these days that there is an increasing reluctance to give up one night every week to preparing for concerts (though thankfully many still do) and to enjoy that sense of achievement in the course of a single day or maybe a weekend offers an alternative satisfaction. Musical summer schools provide something similar, where a residential week of music-making has a similar effect.

The Really Big Chorus started an annual summer school in 2014 and this has grown into another of those events that have become so important for so many regular singers, concentrating on such works as Duruflé's *Requiem*, Rutter's *Gloria*, Brahms's *German Requiem*, Mendelssohn's *Elijah*, Elgar's *Dream of Gerontius* and Handel's *Israel in Egypt*. The excitement of putting together major works such as those in just three days of intensive rehearsal remains one of life's great joys. A lot of fun too.

Nearer to home, in the Cotswold village of Fulbrook, just over the bridge from the town of Burford, where I've lived since 1977, over 100 local people form the Burford Singers. It's been around for a long time and has presented a high level of performance over the years in the town's outstanding church. Yet again it was my good fortune, in 2002, to be asked to take over as conductor. The choir had been steadily built up over the years by my predecessor and former professional session-singing colleague Brian Etheridge, a fellow Kingsman. Here was a great opportunity to make music with like-minded friends and neighbours and for that reason, among others, it has been something really special in my musical life. In a similar way to Vaughan Williams's insistence that nobody needs audition to take part in the Leith Hill festival, so the Burford choir prides itself on being a non-audition organisation. In the old days, anyone could walk in off the street and join in; but more recently, owing to the limited space for performers in both the rehearsal room and on the concert platform, the limit has had to be set at just over 100 members.

At one point we had a waiting list of sixty people, all keen to join and be part of this very fine local choir. In the end we decided that there should be some sort of 'voice-assessment' – not an audition as such, but an opportunity for me, as conductor, to check that each applicant at least has a voice and appears to be reasonably musical. We are blessed with such a fine venue for performance and also with a fiercely loyal audience, which so much enjoys seeing and hearing friends and neighbours singing.

Young professional soloists are always keen to join us, often enjoying an opportunity to try out repertoire works away from the London critics. As I audition prize-winning soloists every year for my Royal Albert Hall concerts, I have managed to build up a substantial list of fine young singers and to be able to invite them to adorn our efforts. And they never seem to mind coming to the Cotswolds.

My thinking, when devising the annual programme, has always been to ensure that every concert has something different about it – that is to say that no two consecutive concerts are remotely similar. In this way, the interest of the singers and the audience (and the conductor!) is maintained and over the years it is possible to cover a wide variety of musical periods and styles: a performance of Bach's *St. Matthew Passion* followed by an evening of Gilbert & Sullivan, for example, with Mozart to follow that and then a programme including a major work by a living composer. As far as the audience is concerned, it is always a matter of building up trust, of creating that feeling that whatever is on the bill, it will be worth turning up for. Including works by living composers is a vital part of the business. Yes: the well-known great works come round from time to time – in fact, rather often – but including something new is essential, particularly if it means hearing something contemporary.

If the 'modern' works are carefully chosen (and performed alongside something familiar) then music-making need never stand still, and composers can enjoy a chance for their music to be heard. It is then trying to find a balance: music which will 'stretch' singers without putting them off, as they will have to spend many weeks – months even – on any set programme. Nobody is going to enjoy all types of music, though none of us will know how we might respond to something new without giving it a try. It is up to the conductor to make a calculated guess as to the likely suitability of any piece.

Works by living composers we have performed in Burford include John Rutter's *Gloria, Magnificat* and *Feel the Spirit,* George Shearing's *Music to Hear,* Richard Blackford's *Mirror of Perfection,* George Martin's *Mission Chorales,* Philip Ledger's *Requiem,* Jonathan Willcocks' *A Great and Glorious Victory,* Morten Lauridsen's *Lux Aeterna,* Bob Chilcott's *Requiem* and *Dances of Time,* Paul Carr's *Requiem for an Angel,* Cecilia McDowall's *Fancy of Folksongs* and Karl Jenkins' *Gloria* and *The Armed Man.*

Add to that Duruflé's *Requiem,* Haydn's *Nelson Mass, St Nicholas Mass, Harmonie Mass Mariazeller Mass, Te Deum, Spring* from *The Seasons* and *Creation,* Mendelssohn's *Elijah* and *Hymn of Praise,* Bach's *St Matthew* and *St John Passions, B Minor Mass,* Motets *Singet den Herrn, Wachet auf* and *Lobet den Herrn* and *Magnificat,* Vivaldi's *Gloria,* Handel's *Messiah, Judas Maccabaeus, Israel in Egypt, Sing unto God* and *Coronation Anthems*, Orff's *Carmina Burana*, Bernstein's *Chichester Psalms*, Purcell's *Come ye Sons of Art*, Charpentier's *Messe de Minuit pour Noël*, Mozart's *Requiem, Coronation Mass, Bb Missa Brevis, Great C Minor Mass* and *Vesperae Solennes de Confessore*, Brahms' *German Requiem*, Vaughan Williams' *Serenade to Music, Fantasia on Christmas Carols* and *Five English Folksongs*, Poulenc's *Gloria*, Finzi's *In Terra Pax*, Monteverdi's *1610 Vespers*, Fauré's *Requiem*, Beethoven's *Mass in C*, Schubert's *Masses in C and G*, Rossini's *Petite Messe Solennelle*, Elgar's *Dream of Gerontius*, Dyson's *Three Songs of Praise*, Gounod's *St Cecilia Mass*, Puccini's *Messa di Gloria*, Stainer's *Crucifixion*, Britten's *War Requiem* and gala concerts from Grand Opera and Gilbert & Sullivan and you can see that we seriously play the field.

You might well ask how a choir of 100 singers can perform – in Burford Church – a work like Britten's *War Requiem*. Well, the simple answer is that it can't – and we didn't. What we did, in 2018, was to join forces with another choir (the Surrey-based English Arts Chorale, of which I happen to be President) and produce a body of singers 140-strong, just about enough for a work of this scale. It was the first time we had undertaken such an idea and it turned out to be one of the most exciting projects I've ever been involved with. I well remember hearing the broadcast of the first performance of Britten's choral and orchestral masterpiece in May 1962 while I was in my penultimate year at school. There had been so much hype in the newspapers about this premier celebrating the opening of the new Coventry Cathedral that I felt I must listen and see what all the fuss was about.

The performance – like so many first outings – was not good: as Britten himself said: "orchestra second-rate, chorus deplorable, acoustic lunatic and cathedral staff waging Trollopian clerical battles but with modern weapons"! Four years later we were lucky enough to perform the work in the chapel at King's College in Cambridge with Britten conducting the chamber ensemble and David Willcocks the choral forces and main orchestra. This immensely powerful 'pacifist' Requiem remained part of my life through the occasions I was lucky enough to act as Chorus Master, to Simon Rattle in London and both Owain Arwel Hughes and Jane Glover in Huddersfield. So finally to have the opportunity to conduct it myself seemed like the icing on a considerable cake.

And what a thrill it turned out to be, both for me and the choirs. We spent the best part of six months getting to the heart of the matter and apart from the initial concern at the music's difficulty and whether or not we could ever crack it, the singers quickly accepted what a wonderful work it is and gave everything they could, both in preparation and performance. One thing which lifted everything even higher was that we gave two performances, first in Winchester Cathedral and then in our neighbouring Tewkesbury Abbey – two glorious venues which gave us the opportunity to sing away from our usual surroundings. We were incredibly lucky too to be able to be joined by three outstanding international soloists: soprano Linda Richardson (whom I first heard when she was a student at the Royal Northern College in the 1980s and who has sung for me so many times and with such distinction), the tenor James Gilchrist (who put more into those wonderful Wilfred Owen texts than anyone I have ever heard and had the audience hanging on his every word) and the bass Quentin Hayes (Royal Opera House principal and, as it happens, a native of Witney, just down the road from Burford). We were truly blessed. A very fine orchestra too, largely members of the RPO with dazzlingly brilliant young wind players from the Royal Academy of Music.

The full score is amazingly complex and I spent a considerable part of each day for the best part of eighteen months with my head buried in the score until I knew it virtually by heart, an essential thing when conducting a work of such complexity. And I was fortunate to have my own full score in which I could mark every detail which would need my close attention on the day. As luck would have it, the ABCD (Association of British Choral Directors, of which I was founder chairman and am now a vice president) held one of its auctions to raise money. Britten's publisher Boosey & Hawkes generously presented to the auction a one-off fully and beautifully bound conductor's score of the *War Requiem* and I was determined that it should come my way, knowing that I was about to conduct it.

The bidding began in October and ended at midnight on New Year's Eve. I ran neck-and-neck with my old friend Andrew Potter (the founder of ABCD and former head of music at OUP) as the deadline approached. Andrew assumed that I would be out partying on New Year's Eve so threw in a last offer on the morning of December 31st. Little did he know that at 11.59 and 59 seconds that night I would be sitting at my computer making dead sure that the prize was mine. And what a treasure that full score is, now fully marked up in perpetuity and longing – like its owner – for a chance to do it all over again.

There is nothing quite like singing together as a group: there is no doubting the therapeutic benefit of a communal pastime such as this. It has to be fun as well as being good for the brain and the sheer thrill of being part of that great C major chord on 'Praise' in Elgar's 'Praise to the Holiest' from *The Dream of Gerontius*, the rolling magnificence of the Sanctus from Bach's *B Minor Mass* or the joy of Handel's mighty *Hallelujah Chorus* and even that magical pianissimo ending to the *War Requiem* really does take some beating when it comes to life-enhancing moments. And the splendid thing about it is that you don't actually have to be a great singer to do it. For people like me to be given the opportunity to conduct such moments is a privilege indeed.

I was asked, some time ago, if I would become a Vice President of the Royal School of Church Music and I was honoured to be able to accept. When asked why, I suggested that as everything that has happened to me in my working life stems from that moment in 1962, when David Willcocks appointed me a Choral Scholar at King's College, Cambridge, I have a great deal to be thankful for and it's pay-back time. It has been good to be able to devote so much of my life to encouraging others in the special reward that comes from church music and from singing in a choir.

The occasions when I've been able to conduct massed voices for the RSCM have given me as much pleasure as I hope I have given to others. Such occasions have also taken me back to my various roots, having enjoyed the luxury of conducting evensongs in St. Paul's Cathedral, Westminster Abbey, Salisbury and Liverpool Cathedrals and – for me, the big one! – King's College chapel in Cambridge. That was a dream I never expected to see fulfilled.

It was Trevor Ford who issued the invitation for the Vice Presidency and he has also been a major part of all my musical work since I left the BBC. He and his wife Marianne Barton run the English Festival Orchestra (and a great deal else besides) and that orchestra played with me for twenty-one years at the Leith Hill festival. It was partly as a result of that association that The Really Big Chorus came my way, along with the many workshop opportunities that have resulted from the involvement of so many thousands of singers in my Albert Hall concerts and our various trips overseas. It has really been a case of one good thing leading to another as far as I'm concerned and my gratitude to so many is boundless.

CHAPTER FOURTEEN

En famille

I have stressed time and time again the importance to me of family life: it is what I was brought up to and I've always considered it to be right at the top of what matters most in life. My seventieth birthday in 2014 was a good time to reflect on my good fortune and to gather round us as many of the family as we could manage. We took the beautiful Ditchley Park stately home for a celebration lunch and although inevitably many of our freelance musician friends were busy at the time, we gathered sixty family and friends for quite a party. My son Jonathan and his wife Marianne flew over from New Zealand, along with their son, 8-year-old Hamilton (who stayed with his other grandmother) and my daughter Charlotte and her husband Dom came from Dorset, leaving 11-year-old Freddie and 8-year-old Sophie behind.

Gilly masterminded the whole thing brilliantly and had commissioned a magnificent cake: the top of it was a replica of one of my gold discs, complete with the HMV emblem in the middle – dog and speaker included – His Master's Voice! Around it were four figures – all expertly made out of icing sugar – BK as a Choral Scholar, complete with cassock and surplice, BK as a King's Singer, suitably decked in 70s attire – flared trousers and long sideburns – BK as broadcaster, sitting at the Radio 3 console, headphones and all, and finally BK as conductor in full fig. It was a work of genius and aroused much comment.

After an hour and a half's champagne reception, we all sat down to a sumptuous lunch, having been greeted on arrival in the great hall by my dear friend Shelley van Loen and her quartet playing adorable Palm Court music. They played after the lunch too and eventually had us all dancing. At the end, one of my guests thanked them for their playing and said how much he had enjoyed it. She asked if he was a musician and when he said yes, she asked what he played. He told her he composed and arranged a little and at this she was only too keen to ask his name. She rather hoped the floor would open and swallow her up when he said John Rutter!

Ditchley Park is one of the most beautiful locations imaginable and one that I know well as for the several years I've presented and conducted concerts there as part of the Dean and Chadlington Festivals. These have been put together by star guitarist Craig Ogden and his mezzo soprano wife Claire Bradshaw, who live in the village of Dean, across the road from former Prime Minister David Cameron's country home. Through their contacts in the musical world they have always managed to attract top quality artistes to perform at the annual gala concert and those nights at Ditchley have been very special, with an audience enjoying the beauty of the surroundings and the inevitable Glyndebourne-type picnic interval.

It was wonderful to be able to gather together for my birthday bash my two brothers and my sister, assorted cousins and a wide variety of friends from across the years. Ellie Shearing had recently arrived for her annual stay and had brought with her a dazzling red jacket which had been one of George's performing outfits. It turned out to be ideal for the lunch party and gave folk a chance to describe me on arrival as 'understated, as ever'!

I've mentioned earlier how I met Gilly and how her presence has enriched my life more than I can say. She had studied law at Warwick University and having achieved her Bachelor of Law degree, the university agreed that she clearly didn't want to be a lawyer but would rather become a singer: too right. There was at the university a Benefactors' Fund and from that they gave Gilly money to go to London each week to have singing lessons with John Carol Case, the much-loved baritone who had also taught me years earlier while I was at King's, Cambridge. He encouraged her to apply for the Royal College of Music and she was given a scholarship to study singing for two years, meanwhile having to earn her living as a free-lance singer in order to pay for her keep. The law degree was not entirely wasted as many years later she became a Magistrate and sat in Oxford, Witney, Banbury and Bicester as a JP for over twenty years.

Gilly (Gillian Fisher) had a beautiful, clear Baroque soprano voice and her emergence from the Royal College coincided with the huge explosion of interest in so-called 'authentic' or 'historically aware' performance practice. As a result, she became very much in demand and enjoyed many years traveling the world as a distinguished solo concert singer. As word got round, she became increasingly busy, not only because of the sheer beauty of her sound, but also because she was so lovely to work with: people simply asked her back time and time again. Long since her 'retirement' from the concert platform, there are still many recordings available on CD (and Spotify) to remind us of that beautiful voice (see Appendix VII). Now she only ever sings in church – as long as when I'm playing the organ, I transpose the music down a little to make up for having to give forth at half past nine on a Sunday morning. She remains the most wonderful wife, my dearest friend and – having been there and done it all herself – a fantastic support to her itinerant musician husband. She also served as Chairman of the Fulbrook Parish Council for ten years, so I think it's fair to say she has done her bit! She's also wonderful at house-keeping, keeps me extremely well-fed, only rarely allowing me to accompany her on the weekly Waitrose run.

When we got married we spent a week's honeymoon in Kenya and as we arrived at Heathrow to check in, we gave our passports to the man in charge, who immediately questioned why our tickets were in the name of Mr and Mrs Kay, while Gilly's passport clearly said Gillian Fisher. "We got married yesterday" was our inevitable and truthful reply. "You'd be amazed how many people say that" said the suspicious official. "Yes, but we did," we added. "Ditto", he replied. "And I suppose you have your marriage certificate with you?" Needless to say, we had left it at home. This was beginning to look serious when I suddenly remembered that Gilly's father had put a mention of the wedding in a national newspaper. "Hold it right there", I said, and rushed to the nearest newsstand. Finding the announcement and showing it to the rather bemused man, a smile at last appeared on his previously authoritarian face and he said "in that case, you can go to the VIP lounge and enjoy some champagne!" Needless to say, and with some relief, we were only happy to oblige.

Older brother Barry spent his working life in Martins (later Barclays) Bank, ending his years as manager in Ripon where he has continued to live in happy retirement. Like Father he was a member of the York Amateurs and married Eleanor from within its ranks. Funnily enough, although he was the only one of the four of us not to take up music professionally, on the occasion of his marriage the local paper pictured the two of them under the heading 'opera singers wed'. In 2016 we celebrated their golden wedding.

Younger brother Graham could easily have been a full-time professional singer, following his undergraduate years as a choral scholar at St. John's College, Cambridge. Instead, he decided on a safer profession as a solicitor and followed Father into the family firm of Newbald Kay and Sons, sitting in the same chair at the same desk in the same room as Father did for so many years. He very sensibly kept singing as a hobby and, possibly as a result, continues to have a fine baritone voice which he uses constantly both as a chorister and as a soloist. He also turns his hand to conducting and a fine musician he remains.

Sister Heather, as I have said, sang for a living, reaching her peak as a member of the world-famous Swingle Singers. I well remember Ward Swingle describing Heather to me as 'very much my kind of girl', by which I assume he meant singer! – though anyone could easily fall for her charms. And as a Swingle Singer she was very good indeed – out of the top drawer. She eventually met and married conductor Nicholas Cleobury, keeping her life firmly in the world of music and through Nick's brother Stephen, keeping up the long-held family connection with Cambridge and King's.

Talking of retirement, some of Father's brothers died within too short a time of retiring, as so often happens; Father was determined not to go the same way and so he retired at the age of 58. He still died at 65, but he had been able to enjoy several years of blissful retirement. Mother lived on – like her mother – until aged 93 and astonished us all by having a new hip at 92. On the day of the operation, the surgeon paid her a visit and got a cool reception. She asked him what time he thought it was and when he said it was eleven o'clock, she scolded him somewhat firmly, making clear that she had expected her operation to be at 9.30. She was as amused as we were when he told her that it was, and she'd had it! They don't make them like that anymore.

My son Jonathan started his working life as one of 10,000 civil servants working at Abbey Wood in Bristol for the Ministry of Defence. He and his wife Marianne honeymooned in New Zealand in 2002 and having driven all-round the country wisely decided that they would prefer to settle there. They bought a house in Christchurch, never dreaming that within a few short years the city would be devastated by earthquakes. As a result of the inevitable destruction, he would never have been out of work, had they decided to stay. But after twelve years they relocated to the charming town of Cambridge on the north island and to a beautiful house with a large swimming pool, surrounded by a stud farm – a delightful spot for them and one which clearly suits them perfectly.

Consequently, of our three grandchildren, Hamilton is a born and bred Kiwi, with all that that entails. New Zealand is a wonderful place for a child to grow up and he seems to enjoy all the available benefits – playing saxophone and drum kit, skiing, judo, sailing, rowing, swimming and the sort of quality of life which only that beautiful country provides. He also shows a distinct talent for acting and has already made his mark with the local theatre company. Although they are so far away (thank goodness for Skype and Facetime) I do believe he enjoys a terrific start in life. Thank goodness too that we are able to fly out and see him most years.

Freddie and Sophie, the other two grandchildren, live in a beautiful village in Dorset where my daughter Charlotte's husband Dom is a Lt Colonel in the Royal Lancers. He has served with the army in Northern Ireland, Bosnia, Iraq, Afghanistan and Mogadishu, a wonderful record of service to his country. He and Charlie are two of the happiest people I know and not without reason: a lovely home and two equally lovely kids. Freddie is mad keen on all sports and particularly cricket. He takes part in special cricket sessions with the other Freddie (Flintoff), scoring runs at a splendid rate and turning into a fine spin bowler: Freddie, your country needs you. Sophie is a born performer: as our dear friend, actor and director Gerry Hjert always said when we showed him photos "that girl sure knows where the camera is." I think she fancies a career on stage in one form or another, but who knows? Only time will tell. Freddie enjoys his singing and with his school choir (from King's in Bruton) he took part in my Royal Albert Hall *Messiah* performance in 2016 – a great thrill for both of us. It's not an easy life being an army wife and Charlie certainly wasn't born to it; but she's taken to it as a duck to water, at the same time as having developed a fine career as a photographer, particularly of young children. And with so many young army wives around, that's a pretty healthy job to enjoy.

And that leaves me. But then you've heard enough about me already. When Gilly was asked in interview to sum me up in three words, she generously suggested "multi-talented, modest and funny". I was touched by the thought on all three counts, though when I think about it, if it comes to 'multi-talented' I've certainly been lucky enough to have fingers in a number of pies over the years, moving seamlessly from one career to another and hopefully contributing to each. It seems a little odd to call me 'modest' when here I am writing at length about myself, though – as whenever I give a talk about my life in music – it is always with the intention of creating some general impression of a life as a professional musician and broadcaster rather than necessarily blowing my own trumpet. I'm proud of what I've been lucky enough to do, though I genuinely do not hold myself in very high esteem. People have often said that, when broadcasting, I clearly very much enjoyed the sound of my own voice: nothing could be further from the truth. I have always found it extremely hard to listen to myself and when I think of all the great broadcasting voices over the years, I am truly modest enough to believe that I do not belong in such company. As for 'funny', I've always enjoyed a good laugh and maybe I inherited some of my father's gift of the gab. I'm certainly fun-loving and these days, you have to take it where you find it.

One of the things I very much enjoyed in my early career was being involved in charity work, most particularly as a member of Scope, or as it used to be called in those rather less sensitive days, the Stars Organisation for Spastics. That excellent organisation ran three homes, properly and professionally administered and greatly supported by so-called 'stars' who could give of their time and enthusiasm in order to encourage others to be generous with their time and money. Again, I'd like to think there was something in the genes, as Father was one of those people who would have done anything for anybody.

The general committee of the SOS would meet at regular intervals at the organisation's headquarters in London's Park Crescent and offer whatever helpful support seemed appropriate. It also gave a lot of people in the entertainment business a chance to get together in a good cause and to enjoy a good lunch. The distinguished chairmen in my time included such film-star luminaries as Anthony Quayle, John Mills and Roger Moore and the rank and file members created very impressive gatherings. To be able to meet and enjoy the company of many of the great stars of the day was a great privilege and my memory bank is filled with names like Vera Lynn (who worked tirelessly for the SOS over so many years), broadcaster David Jacobs, big-hearted Arthur Askey, band-leader Geoff Love, actresses Hayley Mills and Sylvia Sims, funny-man Dickie Henderson, farce-king Brian Rix, the incomparable Eric Morecambe, Coronations Street's 'Albert Tatlock' (Jack Howarth) and 'Elsie Tanner' (Pat Phoenix) and many more. These people all had considerable 'clout' when trying to enlist the support of punters, who would flock to meet them in order to make huge sums of money for the cause.

I spent several years in such delightful company but in the end had to leave it to others when I became too busy. At least I had been able to do my bit and enjoyed a few years as chairman of one of the homes which Scope ran, enjoying the chance to get to know well those who lived there.

People often ask what sort of music I enjoy listening to and these days, I must admit it isn't much. It's hard to explain, though when you have spent twenty-five years of your life listening to music as a job, constantly playing CDs, timing pieces to slot into radio programmes and then thinking and writing about them, it comes as a relief when you don't have to do it anymore. I used to listen to music non-stop but am now infinitely more selective as to what and when. I *hear* music all the time: it's there in my head as I suffer dreadfully from 'earworms' which are the bane of a musician's life. As I prepare for conducting a concert, the music goes round and round and blotting it out becomes increasingly difficult. It is a serious occupational hazard and if anyone knows of a cure, I'd be very glad to hear of it. I've only to hear a snippet of something familiar first thing in the morning and it can plague me for the rest of the day – and night, of course, often making sleep difficult.

CHAPTER FIFTEEN

Home,
Sweet Home

'Location, location, location' is the cry of the estate agent (and occasionally of the politicians) and as far as I'm concerned, that is the secret of finding the right place to live – assuming you are lucky enough to be able to do so. I have certainly been fortunate in that respect, even going back as far as childhood. The life of an itinerant involves being so often away from home, that 'where one hangs one's hat' assumes an even greater importance.

I mentioned earlier my rented (£4 a week) flat in the South Lambeth Road, back in the late 1960s; that was not my first flat in London. When I moved from Oxford in 1967 I joined forces with fellow choral scholar Martin Lane, the original top alto in The King's Singers, who had also moved to London in order to further his hopes. We found a conveniently-priced (ie dirt-cheap) floor of a house in the Lots Road (the wrong end of Chelsea) with one bedroom and a sitting room with the other bed in it, a gas ring for cooking and a shared bathroom with the other occupants (unknown to us and whom we never met) of the house. It was simply ghastly and we hated it. We took turns in sleeping in the back room, as the traffic noise from the embankment road which passed within inches of the front door precluded any chance of a good night's rest. I even remember waking myself up in the middle of the night, standing in the middle of the room and screaming at the traffic to shut up. Nothing was offered by our 'landlady' in order to improve our surroundings and after a relatively short time we did a midnight flit, disappearing into anything that might be an improvement.

Our luck was in, as another old friend from Cambridge had just taken a lease on a large seven-bedroom flat in Westminster and was looking for two people who might take a room each. We moved in at once and life improved beyond measure. It was next door to Westminster Cathedral and must now be worth squillions. But for five pounds a week it was heaven. It was also wonderfully central and with my being able to walk along Victoria Street every day to fulfil my singing obligations to the choir of Westminster Abbey it was just perfect.

After a year or two there, I happened to be talking to a friend who knew that someone he knew (the violinist John Bacon) had just been appointed Leader of the BBC Welsh Symphony Orchestra and was leaving town. He had done up a one-bedroom flat just over Wandsworth Bridge and was looking for someone to take over the lease. At £4 a week, that was a pound less than I was paying in a flat which was beginning to feel rather crowded, so I jumped at the chance. Those were the days when you could park anywhere in the street, knowing that even my much-loved MGA would be safe.

In 1970, when my first wife, Sally and I were married, it was time to invest in a mortgage and inevitably that meant moving further afield than easy reach of central London. The answer was a two-up, two-down detached house on the outskirts of Kingston-upon-Thames near Richmond Park.

That we bought for the princely sum of seven thousand pounds. Having the key to the door of my own house was a wonderful feeling, even if – with the arrival in 1973 of son Jonathan – that particular house would clearly not be big enough for long. It lasted two years before we moved to the three-bedroom, double garage detached house in a cul-de-sac in Ewell Village – the one we eventually sold to the drummer in *Hot Chocolate*.

It was there in 1975 that Charlotte was born and the family was complete. The day she returned from hospital just 24 hours old I left for two months in Australia and New Zealand – there's the glamorous life of an itinerant musician for you! Even though we were in commuter belt, Ewell did feel like a village and it suited us very well for four or five years. I was beginning to travel a lot with The King's Singers, so it was hugely important that the family I left behind was comfortably placed. But after a while, it occurred to me that it was taking almost as long to drive up to London from Surrey as it would from somewhere further away and more truly countrified.

One fine day in 1977 The King's Singers were performing at the Playhouse Theatre in Oxford and in the break between rehearsal and the evening meal I wandered out into the street. Right there next door was an estate agent and on impulse I went in and asked if by any chance they had any five-bedroom houses in Cotswold stone, with an acre of land somewhere rather pretty for £30,000. As the man behind the desk said, my luck was in as one had come in that very morning in the village of Fulbrook, just outside Burford. Could I stretch to £33k? I thought it wise to have a look at it first, and the following day I did exactly that, being instantly attracted to that most beautiful part of the country. I did my sums and decided we should give it a go. And that's how my association with Fulbrook began.

With the *Hot Chocolate* drummer firmly installed in that perfect commuter's house in Ewell, we settled into a new life in what could easily have been a strange place. But the day we moved in, we found – on the back doorstep – a cake, a bunch of flowers and a card which read: "Nobody's going to get in your way, but we're all here if you need us". It was typical of the friendliness of a Cotswold village and we immediately felt at home. One of the two village pubs – the Masons Arms – became a regular watering-hole, where I soon felt very much at home-from-home. We had a large croquet lawn which took a bit of looking after and an orchard which had some vegetables planted by the previous incumbent. Jonathan, then just four years old, had never seen such things and happily walked along the row of carrots, pulling each one out, deciding it wasn't big enough and then pushing it back in again! We also inherited a chicken house with six chickens, which provided the best eggs I have ever tasted. Clearly life here was going to be different from the suburbs of London.

While I was wandering round the empty house waiting for the removal lorry to arrive, I suddenly heard the most horrendous noise. I had hoped for complete peace and quiet in the country, but clearly this was not to be. I rushed out to see what it could possibly be and there – at a height of about 2,000 feet – was CONCORDE! I couldn't believe my eyes. But sure enough it was there again five minutes later and I began to think I had made a terrible mistake. I need not have worried. It was merely doing take-off and landing exercises from Brize Norton airfield, which lies a few short miles to the south of the village. It was a glorious sight, even if it was a hideous sound. It just so happened that they were doing those exercises that very day. What a start.

Well that turned out to be the first of *eight* houses in Fulbrook, eventually (in the year 2000) ending happily next to the church and churchyard. It's a Norman church which, at 900 years old, is even younger than the carbon-dated 1,000-year-old yew tree which proudly stands outside. It's there that I play the organ for services whenever I'm at home on a Sunday. It is an easy walk into Burford (round-trip two miles) for the morning paper and nearby are all the best supermarkets, spread between the neighbouring towns of Witney, Carterton and Stow-on-the-Wold.

Not long after I moved in, I was introduced to an old chap in the pub who offered me a charming thought. I've 'eard about you," he said, in that lovely Cotswold burr: "You're what we call around here an importation – and an importation you'll remain until you've lived 'ere forty years. Then you'll be an *old* importation"! It's always good to know one's place. I celebrated my graduation to 'old importation' with a village party in 2017.

The houses in the village we've lived in are all different and the reasons for moving have been equally varied, including up-sizing, down-sizing and even one 'neighbour from hell'. The first – that £33,000 one way back in 1977 – was full of small rooms and one of the major contributions I made to its future was knocking two of them and a passageway into a large drawing room, complete with an open fireplace at each end. Rather like the old family home in Upper Poppleton, it had only one bathroom and adding another would have been beyond my means at the time. Fortunately the house now belongs to my old friend Simon Park (the 'Eye Level' one-hit wonder) who with his wife Jan have transformed the whole place into an extremely *des res*. Goodness knows what he paid for it, but when he made a speech at his house-warming party he said he was sick of my telling him that I paid for the house what he'd just spent putting in a second bathroom.

When my family split up in 1980, I bought a small cottage next door to the house, with the idea of retaining a bolt hole in the village while I moved to a flat in Camden Town for a couple of years. Bill Newman – the demon barber of Burford – and his wife Maggie who had been born in that cottage and died there 75 years later, lived there as sitting tenants. They were not altogether happy tenants of the previous owner and when I went and told them that they had a new landlord – me – Maggie got all excited and cried: "Oh Bill, get out the apricot wine." For the next few years they went on paying me the princely rent of £1.05 a week! When Bill finally moved out – having found another love following Maggie's death – we eventually had to rebuild the cottage from top to bottom and had a wonderful time doing it.

Another memory typical of village life occurred when I had been up to Yorkshire to spend the run-up to Christmas with the children and my parents. We drove down to Fulbrook on Christmas Day itself and in order to avoid worrying the immediate neighbours I called Bill and Maggie and warned them not to bother if they suddenly saw the lights on in the house: we were coming home. Imagine our delight when we arrived back after a long, cold journey to find that Bill had taken the trouble – on Christmas Day – to go next door and light the fires in our various fireplaces.

We arrived home to find the house full of light and warmth. It was a wonderfully generous gesture and one for which we were extremely grateful.

A builder in Burford called Albert Nash (good name for a builder) once took the dogs for a walk on Christmas morning and when he got home, his wife told him that 'someone in Fulbrook' had a burst pipe, though sadly, she couldn't remember who had called. Again, with amazing generosity, Albert walked all the way to Fulbrook – in the freezing cold – and went round every house he'd ever worked in as a builder until he found the person in question. They don't make them like that very often these days, though fortunately that same spirit still exists in the country.

When Gilly and I were preparing for marriage, we were asked if we'd like to rent a house in Fulbrook which belonged to the family of the local doctor – the Sharpleys. This gave me the opportunity to show Gilly the village and to meet some of the neighbours, without putting any pressure on her to consider living where I had lived before. It took very little time for her to be won over by the charms of Fulbrook and its residents and having been in that rented house at the time of our wedding, we quickly looked for somewhere else in the village to buy. We found a small cottage in a beautifully leafy lane and this became our first married home, where we stayed for a few short years.

After a while we felt the need for something bigger. We were both working from home and a small cottage can become rather constricting. A large converted double-barn came on the market – right in the middle of the village – and although we were horrified at the thought of the price (£175,000) we decided to have a look at it. It was owned by an apparently well-known singer/songwriter called 'Lonesome Dave Peverett' (don't ask!). The long landing was lined with – not gold, but platinum discs and in the carport stood a Roller. Clearly this was out of our league. Nonetheless, he opened the door, showed us the downstairs sitting room and then asked what we thought. We asked if we could see more of the house and he showed us round the whole of the downstairs, clearly somewhat bored by the whole process. He was almost upset when we asked if we could see upstairs! It was an odd technique, but it clearly worked, as we bought it! We lived there for only eleven months and at the time of writing it's just sold again – asking-price exactly one million pounds.

During the time we were there I had a rather unpleasant experience: I'd been up to London to make a couple of radio programmes and stayed late in order to be interviewed by the great Brian Matthew on his Radio 2 programme *Round Midnight*. During the afternoon I began to feel a headache – something mercifully I never have ('well, hardly ever') – and by the time I drove home I was feeling distinctly unwell. I told Gilly, went to bed and then the sweating started. It went on for a few days, during which my head seemed to be splitting. Eventually we called the doctor who informed me that it was viral meningitis and that I was what our Australian friends call 'not a well person'. I lost a stone-and-a-half in a week (useful, but not the ideal way to do it) and only then gradually gathered strength as the virus passed. But it was a sobering experience and one I could have done without.

At that time, Jonathan and Charlotte were living with their mother in Humberside and approaching serious exam time. So we sold the barn and bought a house in my old home-city of York. It was a Victorian terrace house near to the river and needed everything doing to it. It had been used as a boarding house for university students and needed a lot of TLC in order to return it to its former glory.

We lavished no end of effort, including having to fight the planners over removing a hideous 1950s fireplace in the drawing room in order to reinstate a marble surround which we discovered at a reclamation centre and which was so perfect for the room, it could almost have been there from the start. We won in the end and the restoring of the entire house took many months.

At the same time we had done up what we called Newman's cottage in Fulbrook and spent a lot of time commuting between the two. We loved being in York – near to my mother who was still there in Upper Poppleton – and once the house was finished, it was a lovely place to live. I was beginning to work more at the BBC and had to get used to the idea of commuting to London by train.

Gilly was by then singing all over the world as one of our leading baroque sopranos and there were almost times when we would wave to each other from opposite sides of the M1 as we moved between York and Fulbrook – sometimes missing each other at either end altogether. It dawned on us that this really wasn't going to work and that we clearly belonged in one place – preferably the Cotswolds. We decided to sell the York house and move back down south. The removal firm which had brought our possessions up to York came to move us back and the same man who had lugged all our stuff up and down stairs in a tall terraced house greeted us with the words: "I knew you wouldn't stay here long."

And so we settled back into our Cotswold cottage and tried to decide what to do next. The cottage was clearly too small but behind it was a large barn which had been converted into two cottages. One had a swimming pool and each had a lovely south-facing walled garden. Once again our luck was in as the lady who owned the one with the pool decided to move on, so we bought that and used it as guest bedrooms and a work-place for me. The two cottages we now owned were separated by a courtyard. That worked really well until the owner of the other half of the barn also decided to move on, which gave us the chance to buy that, knock the two into one house and then move the whole operation across the courtyard, using the old cottage as a rental property once again.

It was fun having a swimming pool, but also an extremely expensive luxury. In a bad summer it probably cost us about £20 a swim. Having knocked two cottages into one, we had the advantage of separate staircases at each end, with a perfect self-contained guest area approached by a different staircase from our own. In many ways it could have been perfect.

But one day we were enjoying a quiet drink by the pool when our neighbour – in a very large house with vast lawns the other side of our garden wall – presented his four-year-old son with a new motorbike. As the not-surprisingly rather excited small boy began charging round the vast lawn, followed by two barking Dobermanns, we realised that this was not a good sign. There was no way we could live – and work – in a place like that, with unlimited noise at all times of the day and night. It was clearly going to be time to move again.

We found our ideal home in the leafy lane where we lived when first married and sold the barn ready to move. Having offered the full amount for the house we wanted, the owner somewhat mysteriously refused to sell it to us. Panic! We were now about to be homeless. Luckily Tricia Murfitt, a dear friend in the village, whose husband had sadly died, had met and decided to marry another villager – Tony Picking, Prince Philip's sometime personal pilot – so we quickly asked which of their two houses they were going to sell. Neither, was the answer. But Tricia would happily let us rent her house if that was any help. It certainly was and after having lived in and rented it for eighteen months, she finally decided to sell it and gave us first option. We were able to buy a house we had already lived in and knew well, and we happily remain there to this day, only too happy and lucky to be in such a wonderfully warm and friendly village. And we ain't moving again, so that completes the tour of the Kay properties.

CHAPTER SIXTEEN

The Land of the Long White Cloud

It all started in 1972 – that's to say my love affair with New Zealand. The King's Singers had never sung outside the UK since our official London debut on May 1st, 1968, when we were invited to spend three months touring Australia and New Zealand. It was a remarkable offer and one we could hardly refuse. The trip began in New Zealand and apart from the rigours of the journey in those distant days – 48 hours door to door, flying in the recently built jumbo jets London-Frankfurt, Frankfurt-Bahrain, Bahrain-Kuala Lumpur, Kuala Lumpur-Singapore, Singapore-Sydney and finally Sydney-Auckland. – this was to be a truly wonderful and eye-opening experience. We had been told that New Zealand was like England in the 1950s – as the old joke used to say: "We are now landing in New Zealand – please put your watches back twenty-five years!" It's certainly the case that in most of the hotels we stayed – almost all single-storey affairs in those days – there were still framed photos of the Queen and Prince Philip behind the reception desk: not any more.

What struck us most – and immediately – was the warmth and friendliness of those who had been detailed to look after us. After our first concert in New Plymouth, in the North Island, we were invited to someone's house and asked what we might like to eat and drink. Might a piece of steak and some wine be acceptable? We happily rallied round, followed by a giant Pavlova and were made to feel entirely at home. When the phone rang, it was organisers from the next town wanting to know (a) were we any good and (b) what did we like to eat and drink. The result was that, everywhere we went, we were treated to similarly generous hospitality and began to think that this touring business might suit us rather well. And our hosts everywhere could not have made us feel more welcome. We felt completely at home. It has felt like that ever since.

When we arrived in the North Island town of Tauranga, we were lucky enough to enjoy a day off and were invited to the home of two supporters of the concert club (The Chamber Music Federation of New Zealand) – Claudia and Reg Jarman. They gave us a lovely supper and we chatted away very happily, until we noticed some croquet hoops in the lawn. When asked if we ever played, we explained that we had recently been at Cambridge University, so we were well familiar with the basic technique of that rather vicious game. These genial, silver-haired and so friendly people offered us the chance to prove our skills, and proceeded to wipe us off the court, way into the middle of the next week!

But they were to play a very important part in my life, as they suggested that when we got home again after the trip, we should contact their son Richard, who had married Sally – 'an English rose' – and was living near Bradford. As it happens, one of our first concerts back in Blighty was in the Huddersfield Town Hall, so we inevitably made contact. So began a friendship unlike any other and one which was to transform our lives for Gilly and me twenty-five years later.

By 1998, Gilly had sung in most countries and had

already 'retired' from the concert platform. But she had never been to New Zealand. I suggested we might have a holiday there and contacted Sally and Rich Jarman, who by then had returned to live in Auckland. As soon as we said we were coming, they said they would pick us up at the airport, give us two days at their Auckland home to rest from the flight, followed by two more days at their beach house in the Coromandel. This was at the paradise beach of Whangapoua and, again, this was to prove somewhat life-changing for us. Their kindness and generosity proved that although much had changed in New Zealand since 1972, that same old warmth was still there, and how.

After our time at the beach, we said we would hire a car and drive round more of the country. Not at all, as they had just won a car in the lottery and we could borrow that. We couldn't believe our luck and off we went. Everywhere we drove we were knocked out by the loveliness of it all and vowed that we would return a soon as we could. We had already agreed to visit South Africa the following year and so it was that we found ourselves back in NZ in the year 2000, enjoying yet again the hospitality of our friends and soaking up all that wonderful sunshine which makes such a difference to those visiting from the UK in the middle of our bleak midwinter.

This was to be the life-changing bit. We joined Sal and Rich again at the beach in Whangapoua and after a few days we had a crazy idea: what about buying a place right there in 'paradise'? Rich, who has a wonderful way with a drink, called an estate agent friend and invited her round for a gin – this was 4 o'clock in the afternoon: business, Kiwi style. She dutifully responded and we talked about property in

Whangapoua. There is, she said, a queue of people wanting to buy places on this most desirable beach – where should we be in the pecking order? Where indeed did we live? When we said 13,000 miles away, she concluded that we would be so many places down the list that we might as well forget it! Another gin and we thought that was the end of that.

The following morning, Gilly and I went for our usual power-walk and as we reached the end of the road skirting the beach, a lovely old chap was banging in a sign outside his house, which said "For sale – private treaty – apply within". We applied within and an hour later, the house was ours! That's the way to do business in NZ. We had been encouraged by Sal and Rich, who said that if we didn't buy it, they would. We exchanged contracts *by fax* (now there's a thing!) and we were away.

As we took off from Auckland airport for the UK, we looked at each other and wondered what on earth we had done, buying a beach house so far from home. We stopped in Sydney en route for home and spent a few days with our dear fiends Jean and Dick Taylor. When we explained what we had done, they insisted that it would be the best decision we'd ever make. Thus emboldened, we took off for home in the best possible spirits.

The thought of a 'second home' raises all sorts of issues, particularly when it is on the other side of the world. But we were to enjoy five glorious years globe-trotting from home to home and relishing the prospect of spending many English midwinter weeks in the sun-kissed beauty of the Coromandel. We would spend every day walking the beach and the harbour road, watching kingfishers and herons at work, listening to tuis, bell birds, song thrushes, fantails and even possums scratching around at night. We would barbecue constantly, go from neighbour to neighbour enjoying that special brand of Kiwi friendliness and wondering why – when the time came – we ever went back home.

Another joy of our association with the 'Land of the Long White Cloud' came – yet again – as a result of following in the footsteps of illustrious colleagues and friends. Sir David Willcocks had become involved in an organisation called the Teapot Valley Summer School of Music, run by Carl Browning and his wife Inga. I had known Carl from the days when he used to live in Huddersfield – he had founded, along with conductor Mike Brewer, the amazing National Youth Choir of Great Britain – and he would mention from time to time that if David ever 'retired' from Teapot, it might be good if I were able to step into his voluminous shoes. Chance would be a fine thing, I thought. As the years went by, and David's time had come to an end in this context, I was indeed able to become involved and I have enjoyed conducting there on four occasions. Singers from all over NZ – and beyond – come to the summer school and we work for a week preparing for a couple of concerts – starting from scratch and building to an exciting musical climax. It takes place in the beautiful Teapot Valley, not far from the lovely South Island town of Nelson – a favourite for Gilly and me, with its own delicious micro-climate and an old-world charm which delights us both. It is also within easy reach of the Abel Tasman and of Golden Bay, which must surely be one of the most ravishing places on God's earth.

There is such enthusiasm among 'amateur' singers the world over and the Teapot Valley summer-schoolers are no exception. There are no fewer than twenty-six rehearsals –

often four a day – during the week's preparation for the two concert performances. One year, things were going so well that I suggested we take an evening off and relax. No such luck – all they wanted to do was *sing*! The only drawback with the Teapot Valley location is that it is entirely teetotal. This, of course, would have suited my grandfather down to the ground, though after a hard day's work, I'm always glad of a pint to put back what the day has taken out. Luckily there's a rather splendid pub close by – one which rejoices in the oxymoronic name *The Honest Lawyer*! My grandfather would have appreciated that too, having founded the family firm of solicitors.

On my most recent visit to the summer school, in 2019, I was privileged to conduct the New Zealand premier of those delightful *Dances of Time* which Bob Chilcott had written for my Leith Hill Musical Festival twenty-year celebrations. I could not have been more pleased with the way the singers and the audience took to this lovely work and I can only hope that those taking part will have persuaded the conductors of their own choirs to add it to their repertoire.

Another close and very rewarding musical experience for me in New Zealand has been the opportunity to work with other choirs. My first was the Orpheus Choir of Wellington. Many years ago I was asked to conduct a concert in the capital city's Michael Fowler Centre – an entire evening of Mozart, including the Clarinet Concerto and the *Requiem*. Again, so much enthusiasm and a great sound. The same can happily be said of the Auckland Choral Society, with which I have enjoyed three particularly enjoyable occasions. It's conductor for many years – Peter Watts – generously invited me to conduct a performance of Haydn's *Creation* in Auckland Cathedral. That led to an opportunity to bring together several choirs from the district when the Choral Society mounted a massed-voices performance of Carl Orff's *Carmina Burana*. And a great shout it turned out to be! Nor was that the end of our association, as when current conductor Uwe Grodd took a sabbatical, I had the special pleasure of conducting two Christmas performances of Handel's *Messiah*. That was in Auckland's magnificent Town Hall, with an excellent chamber orchestra – Pipers Sinfonia – and the hall's great organ – recently rebuilt at enormous cost and played by John Wells. Way back in the 1960s, while I was at King's Cambridge, John had applied for the coveted position of organ scholar and as a member of the choir I sang at his audition. He got the job and succeeded Andrew Davis in the post.

As far as working is concerned, the other side of my good fortune has been the opportunity accorded me by the Radio New Zealand Concert programme. Over many years, whenever I've been in the country, I have recorded a number of programmes, which have then been broadcast – and frequently repeated – until I came again and refreshed the available content. It started out as a series called *An Englishman Abroad* and with an all-purpose title such as that I was able to include virtually anything I liked. There followed special programmes of choral music, life-stories with music which I wrote and presented on the subject of lives I particularly admired – Noel Coward, Ivor Novello, Flanders & Swann and Gilbert & Sullivan, and speciality programmes about – for example – the Vienna New Year's Day concert, which, for some reason (presumably because it would have to be 'live' in the middle of the night!) is never broadcast in New Zealand. There has been enough of my recorded material over the years – including programmes of Light Music and interviews with conductors – to keep *Concert fm* on air for months! I feel very privileged to have been able to keep that happy association going for so long.

But the work side of things is only a small part of the story. I love being able to do it, but the main attraction of being in New Zealand so often is the sheer beauty of the country, the constant friendliness of the people and the quality of life that goes with it. I always return to the UK (sometimes reluctantly, as it's still the bleak midwinter when we arrive home from a blissful antipodean summer break) feeling ten years younger – and these days, every little helps!

The other great attraction of New Zealand, apart from the outstanding natural beauty of the countryside, is the quality of the wines. Over the years we have visited and sampled a considerable number of New Zealand's magnificent vineyards and we have certainly done our bit to bolster the local wine industry. The areas where the grapes are grown tend to be in some of the loveliest parts: I think of Hawkes Bay where two of our favourites – Black Barn and Craggy Range – are within easy reach of the fascinating *art deco* town of Napier; of several in the Marlborough region surrounding the town of Blenheim – with, among other things Sir Peter Jackson's irresistible museum of World War One and Two aeroplanes; and another beauty – conveniently close to the Teapot Valley where the summer school takes place – the Neudorf vineyard. Several have become centres for musical performances with operatic soirées and pop concerts which help – as if it were needed – to spread the word about the excellence of the Kiwi wines.

There's little doubt that if push came to shove, the Land of the Long White Cloud would be the only place on earth that we could even think of settling in, as an alternative to the sheer beauty of the Cotswolds and with immediate family at both extremes, we could easily end up with sharply divided loyalties. Not much chance of its happening, though it's good to be able to consider the choice. We just remain grateful that the country fondly known as *Godzone* plays such a major part in our lives.

CHAPTER SEVENTEEN

Hard Times

There is no point in pretending that everything in life (mine or anybody's) has been a constant bed of roses: such deception would inevitably be counter-productive, however self-indulgent it might be to gloss over times of stress. Having said that, I've always felt like a glass-half–full man.

The time when my first marriage broke apart is an obvious case in point: it goes without saying that that represented a seriously low point in my life. Everything I had been brought up to suddenly seemed to go out of the window, leaving me feeling lost and adrift. It was made even worse by my having to carry on fooling myself and everyone else as an apparently happy-go-lucky King's Singer. Suddenly there seemed no point in having spent all that time on the road at the expense of family life, which really should have come first. Such is the nature of insecurity felt by all freelance musicians that life and work can easily fall out of balance. It's really tough on the children too, though fortunately, at 5 and 3 respectively, Jonathan and Charlotte were a bit young to realise quite what was happening in their lives at the time.

Charlotte was born on February the 24th, 1975 and she came home the following morning. Within a few hours of her arrival I was on the road again – this time back to Australia and New Zealand with The King's Singers for two months.

Home-coming from afar after so long was no easy task. Lovely as it was to be home, the family had fully adjusted to life without me and I almost felt as if I was interrupting a well-settled situation. It took only a few days to sort that one out but missing the first two months of a new child's life is very hard on the emotions.

A death in the family changes things and my father's untimely death was extremely hard to take, largely because of all the good times we could have had and the so many things which remained unsaid between us. I was at the start of a six-week tour of South Africa with The King's Singers in 1980 – five concerts a week with virtually no gaps (though we did manage a couple of days and nights animal-watching in the Kruger Park). We had had a big party one night and got to bed pretty late and, dare I say, probably too well-oiled. I had instructed the hotel reception not to put through any calls until late midday and was somewhat disturbed when the phone rang at 7.30 in the morning. Having hollered down the phone that I was unhappy to be woken, I heard the soft voice of Frank Abel (the husband of my mother's cousin and a Port Elizabeth-based government architect) who had been given the unenviable task of letting me know that my father had died – a heart attack in his cabin on board the P&O ship *Canberra*, shortly before starting out from Southampton on a lecturing cruise. He was only 65. There are times in life when one feels intense loneliness and this was surely one of those, particularly as I was unable to leave my colleagues in the lurch by going home for the funeral. My absence would have made the rest of the tour impossible. I so wanted to be back in the bosom of my family at such a tough time for us all. The singers all knew my father, so there was plenty of natural support during the dark days which followed.

Losing one's job is never easy and the times when the BBC has turfed me off programmes has taken some of the gloss off the business – particularly when done as uncaringly as previously described. Nobody likes to feel rejected, though each time one door has closed, another one seems to have opened and for that I must always remain grateful. What bugs me is that insensitivity with which the Beeb dumps folk, however dedicated and loyal they might be. I even saw in the paper a tweet from the singer Tom Jones when he was suddenly dropped from a popular TV programme: "shocked and disappointed about *The Voice UK*," he wrote, "I was told yesterday. No idea, no conversation, no warning. 'Twas ever thus."

The worst experience I had at the BBC was when I was presenting the Radio 4 programme *Comparing Notes*. Someone had the bright idea that I should interview Sir Edward Heath – the former Prime Minister with a penchant for music. I very much looked forward to meeting him and above all, to visiting his beautiful home in Salisbury's Cathedral close. I already knew the house, as it had belonged previously to the family of David Booth-Jones who had given The King's Singers such a leg-up in the early days.

I arrived at the gate of Arundells to be greeted by an armed policeman and shown into the small room where the interview was to take place. My producer and assistant set the microphones up as we awaited the arrival of the great man. When Heath eventually appeared – characteristically late – I attempted a little introductory small talk. I mentioned that I knew the house before and that my friends had built a rather nice summer house in the garden. "Ghastly thing," barked Heath: "I pulled it down the moment I got here." I quickly got the feeling that this wasn't going to be easy. I should have read in advance, rather than later, John Campbell's vast biography of the PM, as this would have prepared me better. The subject of Heath's personality keeps recurring: "crusty old curmudgeon ... baleful presence ... stiff, unsmiling iceberg ... a priggish bore ... impervious, solitary, thick-skinned, elephantine"– oh dear.

We staggered through a difficult hour: I wasn't happy and Heath would clearly rather have been doing anything else. When my producer announced that we'd got everything we needed, Heath simply rose rather heavily from his chair, walked to the door and without even turning round said simply: "Someone will show you out". I could hardly believe that a man of such stature could have been so astonishingly rude and I realised then just how Margaret Thatcher must have felt all those years when, having lost out to her, Heath carried out the longest sulk in political history. I still can't believe that a former Prime Minister could behave in such a way – after all, he had agreed to do the programme when he could easily have said no.

In Michael McManus's fascinating 2016 Heath biography – *A Singular Life* – he quotes Michael Heseltine after a visit to Arundells, where he found Heath – at home as opposed to the public persona – to be "a human man, full of warmth, magnetism, wit and humour, charming and relaxed". Clearly it wasn't my day. He also describes a visit to the house by Lynn Barber: "When I left," she said, "the policeman at the gate beamed and said 'Oh I can tell it went well. Look!

247

He's come to the door to see you off. He only does that if he likes someone!'" Ah well: can't win them all.

My happy years as Chorus Master to the Huddersfield Choral Society included one particular incident which was considerably less happy than others. And what made it worse was that it cast a long shadow over the 150th anniversary celebrations of the choir. That came in 1986, by which time I was well established and was enjoying my working relationship with Owain Arwel Hughes, the Principal Conductor.

The way the choir worked was that all the preparations for the concerts, recordings, television appearances and so on were the responsibility of the Chorus Master, who took the weekly Friday evening rehearsals before the eventual arrival of the conductor who would then place his own stamp on the performance, knowing – or rather hoping – that by then, the choir would be word and note perfect following many weeks of rehearsal. The anniversary year naturally placed a huge strain on everyone, with more concerts than usual in Huddersfield, London and Cardiff, along with special television programmes and radio features.

The repertoire for the choir naturally revolved around the sort of works best suited to a gathering of over 200 extremely powerful Yorkshire voices and there was inevitably a fair amount of repetition of the best-known and most well-loved oratorios, requiems and masses. As I was there every Friday, week after week, I became very close to the choir, enjoying what seemed to be a very fruitful relationship. So much so that members of the choir would talk to me about their concerns, as I was the only professional musician to be regularly present.

When Elgar's *Dream of Gerontius* came around again for the umpteenth time, there were those who thought it was time for a change of repertoire and they told me so in no uncertain terms. I considered it my duty to act as a go-between, passing on to the Principal Conductor any concerns or worries that might seem important. When I told Owain of that particular worry, I'm rather afraid he took it the wrong way and thought that I was (a) getting too close to the choir and (b) over-stepping the mark by making repertoire suggestions which he rightly assumed were his business – as always in Huddersfield – in consultation with the committee.

This was all very unfortunate, all the more so because Owain decided that it would be better if I were replaced as Chorus Master: although I was merely trying to be helpful, I was, he thought, simply getting above myself. The committee thought otherwise and its members were keen that I should stay. It soon became a matter of "him or me" and this led to an extraordinary general meeting, news of which made the national newspapers and local television. Owain was much loved and had produced many memorable performances over a number of years, so there were heated arguments on both sides. In the end, what had been such a good relationship inevitably came to a premature end, though not in the way that Owain would have hoped. I was much relieved to be able to continue doing the job I so much enjoyed, though the affair had naturally left a nasty taste in the minds of us all. It was all totally unnecessary and wasteful and I look back on the whole business with infinite sadness.

I wouldn't think of 'fighting the flab' as being a particularly difficult area of life but I have always had to bear this in mind. Always having enjoyed a good glass of wine and being very fond of the best kinds of draught beer, there have often been times when a certain amount of care and attention has been the order of the day. I'm sure it's true for most people that holidays are always a tricky area when it comes to potential over-indulgence and our annual trips to New Zealand have usually put temptation firmly in the frame! I'm always keenly aware of the need to fight the battle of the bulge, attempting to avoid what our old friend George Shearing used to refer to as 'the girth of the booze'!

In the life of a singer, one of the greatest difficulty is looking after one's body as much as one's voice. The perils of constantly flying round the world in air-conditioned sealed tin cans is fraught with danger to the voice, as is being in enforced close contact with people, so many of whom are likely to be full of germs a singer could well do without. In my time with The King's Singers, this was a constant worry, as when one of us caught a cold, there was a very good chance it would pass down the line, living as we did in such close proximity to one another.

I well remember being in the middle of a British tour when we were performing five concerts a week for several weeks on the run. This involved a huge amount of travel with inevitable tiredness making it ever more difficult to fight off infection. On one occasion, during a concert in Edinburgh, I could feel my voice gradually disappearing as I had clearly succumbed to some ghastly bug. If any one of us lost his voice completely, the livelihood of the other five was put at risk. This was one of the reasons I eventually gave up smoking, not that I had been a serious inhaler. As I came off stage at the end of the concert, I immediately phoned the famous ear, nose and throat man Norman Punt in London, asking if he could see me the following morning. This was fine for him, though for me it meant another early morning flight when I would probably have been better served resting before the next leg of the tour. What he actually did to me I shall never really know, except that it meant that my voice returned in time for that evening's concert – having flown back north to join my colleagues. I'm sure it was not the wisest way to deal with loss of voice and the long-term implications might well have been basically unhealthy; but when push comes to shove, it's a case of needs must.

As Gilly would agree with me, after she had given up singing, the relief of not having to worry so much about losing one's voice is enormous: the first thought on waking every morning used to be one of wondering what sort of shape my voice might be in, and then having to look after it throughout the long day before a concert begins. When I turned to broadcasting, the worry became a great deal less, knowing that with the close proximity of a microphone, one can usually fudge it if the voice is below par. It's an occupational hazard and one simply has to get used to dealing with it as best as one can.

One of my worst conducting experiences happened in the city of Naples. I was there with The Really Big Chorus and we were to perform Mozart's much-loved *Requiem* with soloists and an orchestra recommended by the local Conservatoire. Almost everywhere we've been on these trips, we've been very well served by local musicians and we've got used to feeling safe in the hands of people we've met for the first – and often, the only time. So we approached Naples with no sense of foreboding! The largely student orchestra had been recommended to our tour leader Tony Hastings and we agreed an afternoon orchestra and soloist's rehearsal.

When we arrived at the meeting point there was no sign of the orchestra's own conductor, and the time agreed for the rehearsal was fast approaching. We eventually tracked him down by phone and he arrived – by which time the rehearsal should already have started. "Let's have a coffee", he generously suggested. I assured him that I would prefer to get on with the rehearsal and reluctantly he forgot about the coffee and led us to the rehearsal venue.

As we approached the hall, I could hear – through an open door – what sounded like a school orchestra on a bad day playing anything but Mozart. Imagine my horror when I realised that this was to be the very orchestra I was to conduct. I'm not sure if they had ever played any Mozart before, but they certainly had very little idea of style and the basic requirement of 'all the right notes in the right order' was not a concept with which they appeared to be familiar. When it came to the trombone solo which introduces the *tuba mirum*, it became abundantly clear that the soloist was a member of a brass band! Not only that, but throughout many of the movements, he littered the proceedings with wrong notes, though he was by no means the only one. There was nothing for it but to 'keep calm and carry on', which I did with some considerable difficulty. Things went from bad to worse with the arrival of the soloists – young singers clearly full of their own supreme confidence and raising in me a glimmer of hope: that was until they opened their mouths. The soprano – a student of singing at the Conservatory – made the ghastliest noise I think I've ever endured at close proximity, and worse, she got most of it – the Mozart *Requiem* remember – wrong.

On the night, there was such a vast crowd wanting to hear the performance that many had to stand and many were turned away. Some of the late-comers spotted four chairs in front of the orchestra with nobody sitting in them and thought – these will do and took them. They were, of course, the four chairs which had been placed for the soloists. Consequently, when the soloists and I entered, there was nowhere for them to sit and they had to stand throughout. Frankly, I had absolutely no sympathy for them at all: not being able to sit seemed to match their not being able to sing. Fortunately the Really Big Chorus singers who had come with me from England were not to be deterred and saved the day by singing quite splendidly and giving the performance of a lifetime. The orchestra was so bad that I have never before or since had to encourage a choir to sing as loudly as possible for a long as possible in the hope of drowning out those who accompanied them! Perhaps I shouldn't have worried: the audience cheered us to the rafters and went home clearly a lot happier than I did. Hey Ho: some you win.

I guess we all have dreams we could well have done without: one from which I have frequently suffered, and suffer still, finds me sitting in the radio studio and broadcasting to the nation and suddenly realising that not only is the next CD nowhere to be found, but there appear to be no more CDs of any kind in the studio still with an hour of the programme to go. It's always on the day when my producer hasn't turned up and I'm doing the business all on my own! The sense of panic and helplessness has often resulted in my waking up in a cold sweat.

Another finds me about to go on stage – to sing or to conduct, it's all the same – and for unaccountable reasons

I have left changing into my performing kit until the last possible moment. That's when I find that I've brought the wrong shirt, or the wrong bow tie and in the frantic last-minute rush I can't get my very wrong socks off and the right ones on. I know that the seconds are ticking away, the orchestra has tuned, the expectant hush has filled the hall, and there I am in a panic. At the last minute, when all is almost done, I start to tie my shoelace and the lace breaks (that has actually happened twice – both times at the Royal Albert Hall). It worries me how often both these dreams recur, though waking up and finding I was only dreaming comes as a merciful relief.

CHAPTER EIGHTEEN

Keep Calm and Carry On

This well-worn adage gives me a chance to wrap things up and to try and summarise why on earth I've spent all this time reminiscing. I find myself caught between Dorothy Reynolds' "We said we wouldn't look back" and Janet Baker's "Good thing to do some stock-taking". Constantly looking forward is all well and good and has always been my main concern. But the opportunity to re-consider how things came about and whether or not it all makes any sense is an enjoyable one, if a little self-indulgent.

Towards the end of my time with the BBC, when I was broadcasting to the nation from my dining room table (such are the wonders of modern technology) I realised just how much energy and time I was saving by not having to travel in order to do my job; and that reinforced my feeling of good fortune that I have never had to commute, never go through the daily grind by car or train, never to be crammed into a tube or had to stand on a train all the way to London (or wherever) as so many people must. Being able to do most of my work in the large and fully equipped shed at the bottom of my garden has been a blessing and one which I have learned to appreciate more and more.

And then there is the good fortune of having as a hobby the various jobs at which I've spent my entire working life.

Professional musicians are extremely lucky in their chosen career and if things go according to plan, they can enjoy their work hugely at the same time as knowing just how much hard work is involved in constantly trying to give of their best. And it is hard work: it might not look or sound like it, though there is so much truth in the notion of art concealing art.

It can be a somewhat lonely profession. Sir John Barbirolli wrote this about his dear friend, the singer Kathleen Ferrier: "Quite often she would talk to me wistfully of the loneliness attaching to an artist who had reached the position she had attained in the musical world. On the one hand, the popular conception of glamour – adulation and endless entertainment; on the reverse side of the picture the constant travelling, memorising in train, ship and plane, and the enervating – exhausting process of having to appear at your social best, when body and soul cry out for peace and rest, the heart for the simple satisfactions of family life."

There is so much truth in that and I remain grateful for being naturally gregarious at the same time as recognising that audiences expect and deserve to have access to you as a human being. As long as it doesn't go too far, so that supporters become overwhelming, then communicating with those who enjoy what you do is a vital part of the job, however little you might feel like it at the time. I have mentioned the so-called glamour of this profession earlier and there is no doubt that it can have its seemingly glamorous side; but it's fair to suggest that it can come at a price, whereby, for example, in a certain way one's life is not one's own. Being recognised can be a perk and it can also be a pain in the neck. It's hard to imagine having to live your entire life in a goldfish bowl to the extent that soap stars and footballers must have to: lovely to be appreciated for what you do, but even better to be left alone to enjoy the simple pleasures of life without constant interruption.

One of so many distinguished musicians I was delighted to meet was the great Italian conductor Maestro Guilini. I was asked to interview him in his suite at the Connaught and naturally approached the hotel in some trepidation. His rooms were on the top floor and the nerves began to jangle as I made my way up in the lift with my producer. I really need not have worried, as he was the most utterly charming man. We enjoyed our official chat (well, at least, I did!) and then it was time to say goodbye. He saw me to the door and when I reached ground floor, I looked up through the atrium and there he was still standing there and waiting to wave goodbye. If he was that charming with me – and he certainly was – then no wonder all those great musicians and singers he worked with revered him so deeply. Wonderful man.

Another chance meeting with a famous conductor (carefully arranged) came when The King's Singers' agent – Richard Armitage at Noel Gay Artists – fixed for us to sing to Arthur Fiedler in his suite at the Savoy. Fiedler had been conductor of the Boston Pops Orchestra for so many years and it was Richard's hope that he might be interested in engaging us to sing with the band. We sang a couple of close harmony arrangements for him and seemed to make no impression at all – he was clearly wanting to get on with something else. Fair enough, when you think that musicians of all shapes and sizes must have wanted him to listen to them and to give them a job. It was pretty clear that nothing would come of it, though at least we had set foot inside a suite at the Savoy! It was all the more exciting for us when his successor at the Pops – film composer supreme John Williams no less – *did* invite us to take part in one of the orchestra's coast-to-coast TV shows, broadcast live from Symphony Hall in Boston. But you couldn't have had two more different encounters than I did with Guilini and Fiedler and I know which one I preferred.

And then there is the sheer tiredness of it all, the physical and emotional exhaustion which suddenly comes upon you at the busiest of times. Looking back to those hazy, crazy days of 200 concerts a year with The King's Singers, having to perform at your best every day and then always being expected to enjoy some serious après-concert with all and sundry makes me feel well and truly knackered even now just thinking about it! But we were young then and any kind of likely exhaustion would have been overwhelmed by the feeling that we were basically having a very good time.

I remember Janet Baker explaining to me that she retired from performing at such a relatively early age because her body told her to: she never had to bother about her faultless technique – she could always rely on that – but there comes a time when your body screams at you to stop and it would be foolish to ignore such warnings. It happened to me once, years ago, when I had quite clearly been overdoing it. One morning my legs simply gave way and I collapsed in a heap, seriously wondering if my time had come. It was only excessive tiredness, but I took it as a warning and have tried to be more balanced in my life-work relationship ever since. Having said that, I still find it hard to stop! If you really enjoy what you're doing, then do indeed keep calm and carry on. Of course as you get older, it is easier to create that better balance, to be able to order your life more carefully and when it comes to that, it helps a lot being your own boss.

Apart from my two years as a staff announcer at the BBC back in the 1980s, I have never been other than self-employed, even though at the time of The King's Singers I had to operate as a member of a team. Having said that, there was never any formal agreement or contract between the six of us, everything being done by some sort of gentlemen's agreement. Mind you, however much you feel like your own boss, in the world of the freelance it is always hard saying 'no': you are always aware that your next job could be your last. It was only when I reached my seventies (in 2014) that I finally learned how to say no and to be much more choosey about the work I was prepared to take on. Even now I do think very carefully about turning down an offer of work, though I'm getting better at it.

I suppose I've been particularly lucky in that I've been able to jump from one career to another a number of times – fifteen years with The King's Singer, then twenty-five with the BBC and now full-time conducting: one thing has generally led to another, with no real chance of getting bored with a single job. As a broadcaster, sitting in a small dark room talking to yourself, in the hope that someone out there is listening, can be a fairly lonely existence; and the pleasure of then standing up in front of choirs of all shapes and sizes acts as the perfect foil and puts to an end any feeling of sameness in work, of the sort that so frustrated my father in his daily grind at the solicitor's desk. How he would have loved to call it a day and move on to something else, something infinitely more enjoyable and fulfilling. In a sense he did, eventually, by retiring early (luckily he could afford to) and making use of his fabled gift of the gab – again, facing an audience, rather than sitting on his own in the office. I simply could not have coped with that sort of life.

For my work with the BBC I was lucky enough to be rewarded with a Sony Award on two occasions, including the coveted Gold Award in 1996. The presentation show at the Grosvenor House Hotel in London was packed with radio and television people – from both sides of the footlights – and it was all fronted by Ned Sherrin. When my name was read out for the big one, I approached the podium with my producer at the time, fellow broadcaster (and what a great one too) Piers Burton-Page. When I shook hands with Ned Sherrin, his only comment was "which one of you is Brian Kay?" That's the great thing about radio – nobody needs to know what on earth you look like. When I won the second award a couple of years later, another of my distinguished colleagues, Jeremy Nicholas, congratulated me and said "Watch it, too many awards and you'll be out!" And how right he was, as it was not so long afterwards when my time came to be replaced.

I hope I am old enough and wise enough to know that in broadcasting, as in almost everything else, it is not possible to please all the people all the time: all those who broadcast for a living know perfectly well that for all the folk who enjoy what they are doing, there are going to be at least an equal number who do not. They might not like your voice, your choice of music, your presentation style or your programme format. The great thing about radio is that you can always turn it off if you're not getting the quality you expect, or that it's being presented in the way you simply don't enjoy. During my many years with the BBC I kept in my wallet a letter I received from a listener who clearly thought I had no idea what I was talking about and was totally ignorant of the English language and of grammar. Nonetheless, he clearly listened, as he wrote me a short hand-written letter of complaint, as it happens correctly pointing out a minor error. I have the letter in front of me as I write. After detailing my offence, he delivered the *coup de grâce*: "God damn you," he rather charmingly wrote, "for an ignorant, over-paid, conceited son of a syphilitic bitch". Apart from the appalling slur on my parent's character, it seemed to me a somewhat excessive way of expressing his disappointment at finding a well-meaning broadcaster clearly not up to his own standard of excellence. Another listener lapsed into doggerel which, although similarly unsatisfied by my efforts, at least made me laugh:

> There ought to be a warning
> 'gainst Brian Kay's Sunday Morning:
> Three hours to pass
> with Brian Kay
> Means a pain in the arse
> for the rest of the day.

It takes all sorts. Needless to say, I kept calm and carried on. One time when I had to do just that was during my years presenting BBC Proms from the Royal Albert Hall for Radio 3. I was asked one year to present a performance of Bach's *St Matthew Passion*, conducted by the American Scott Joplin exponent and early music specialist Joshua Rifkin, a minimalist performance given – somewhat strangely considering we were in the vast space of the Royal Albert

Hall – one to a part. I was a little concerned about taking it on as I was already booked to conduct a fireworks concert in Cholmondeley Park in leafy Cheshire the night before. Radio 3 kindly agreed to provide a driver so that I could drive up to the BBC on the morning of the Cheshire concert, leave my car at the Beeb, be driven there and back, stay in my usual Saturday night hotel next to Broadcasting House, grab a short night's sleep and be at the RAH early on the Sunday morning to prepare for the 'live' broadcast of both my own Sunday morning programme and the afternoon Prom.

This was all well and good in theory, but unfortunately the driver provided was not ideal, to put it mildly. He drove me up to Cheshire without any trouble and spent the afternoon of my orchestral rehearsal and the evening of the performance watching cricket and relaxing. So far so good. We left the park shortly before 11 o'clock and already tired by my efforts I looked forward to sleeping in the back of the car all the way to London. Unfortunately, he got completely lost looking for the M6 and even when he finally found it, he drove at about 60 mph, constantly opening his window to take in gasps of air in an effort to keep himself awake. Needless to say I was not able to relax or sleep and eventually arrived at Broadcasting House completely exhausted. After a very short night in bed, I turned up at the RAH, rehearsed, presented my three-hour radio programme and then the four hour Prom and eventually had to drive home to Oxfordshire where Gilly was waiting with a very welcome dinner. Again, I had no alternative to keeping (relatively) calm and carrying on, though it was a tough call.

Two very different people provide food for thought on this subject: Winston Churchill used to say "If you're going through hell, keep going" – and, of course, his famous "Keep buggering on"! and then there's the song which Vera Lynn used to sing: "If you're up to your neck in hot water, be like the kettle and sing."

When I was clearing out a whole attic full of memorabilia recently I came across the programme of the Royal Variety Show of 1978, when we King's Singers were invited to take part on the express request of Her Majesty the Queen Mother. The afternoon rehearsal on such occasions is a real scramble to give all the 'acts' a chance to run through their spots, when those shows are always far too long with so many people wanting to be part of it. But it was a great opportunity to cram the official glossy programme full of autographs, with the idea of giving it to the children. Many of the names on that occasion are long gone, but it was a wonderful feeling to be surrounded by the great and the good of the entertainment world: Arthur Askey, Harry Secombe, Anne Shelton, Gracie Fields, Max Bygraves, Nana Mouskouri, Lulu, Showaddywaddy and many more. After the TV broadcast, 'live' from the London Palladium, our agent gave us dinner along with the Head of Light Entertainment Bill Cotton Jr. I then had to drive home, arriving in the wee small hours of the morning, only to rise again after a very short sleep to take Jonathan (then just five years old) to school. There's the glamorous side of the business for you.

If I were ever to appear on *Desert Island Discs* I would probably be asked – as so many are – how I might cope on this mythical island. There's no doubt that I would not be of any practical use to myself, as any attempt at serious DIY usually ends in failure. I might be all right on my own, at least for a while, as even now when I go for a long walk, it gives me a chance to think and not to be distracted, though I would soon tire of it, no doubt. Another problem is that I tend to be, by nature, an extremely tidy person, believing that a well-ordered existence greatly helps the business of getting on with life. I like to know where everything is and I don't thrive on mess! After a lifetime of travelling around the world and gathering souvenirs of all sorts, it is so easy to become overwhelmed by a house full of knick-knacks of all shapes and sizes and the only way to keep that under control, in my experience, is to move house every so often and have a good throw-out. It is extremely cleansing and makes one realise that a touch of minimalism is not such a bad idea after all.

So there you have it: my gallimaufry of memories both musical and – for me – life enhancing. My stock-taking has been fun and there will be much more that I could have included if my memory were a bit stronger. But there's very little that I would have changed and I consider myself truly blessed that my entire life has been spent sharing and celebrating the sheer joy of music: music, my life indeed.

BBC Music Magazine

Brian Kay's Light Programme remains a part of my broadcasting career of which I feel particularly proud, as it gave a golden opportunity to thousands of devotees for that kind of largely neglected music to indulge their preferences and recall music which had been so popular back in the 1940s and 50s. Without doubt, a sense of nostalgia accounted for its popularity, though we discovered as the seven-year series progressed that more and more young people who were hearing it for the first time were clearly enjoying it afresh.

After a while, as the programme established itself on Radio 3, I was asked to write down some thoughts on the state of the art for the BBC Music Magazine – itself a hugely successful and long-running publication, to which I had regularly contributed with my so-called *CD Starter Collection*. I am grateful to the magazine for allowing me to recreate it here. It's title was *Light Music in the post-war period*. It began:

What exactly is Light Music? That is the question most frequently asked by newcomers to my weekly Light Music programme on Radio 3. The best definition I can suggest came from Andrew Gold, who was Head of the BBC Light Music Unit in the late 1960s. "Light music," he said, " is where the tune is more important than what you do with it." By the time he came up with that helpful definition, the swinging 60s had, perhaps inevitably, condemned such relaxed, tuneful and mainly orchestral music to virtual extinction. Only now, forty years on, is it enjoying a healthy revival, thanks to the determination of a number of record companies and the combined efforts of unstoppable enthusiasts and technical wizards who are able to breathe new life into the old 78s which made such music so readily available in the good old days. The simple fact that during the first four years of *Brian Kay's Light Programme* some 600 composers have been included is testament to the astonishing quantity of available Light Music.

But what concerns us here is what happened in the years following the Second World War, when the BBC broadcast such enormously popular programmes as *Music While You Work*, *Grand Hotel* and *Friday Night is Music Night*, which still flourishes today, over fifty years since it first hit the airwaves. Mention of the BBC is essential in this respect, as the war years represented a golden age for the wireless, when news was so important, comedy series lightened the load and people worked or played to the sound of music. The long-running and enormously popular *Music While You Work* was specifically designed to encourage greater productivity in the mass production of weapons of war, by providing a diet of rhythmic music as a constant accompaniment to the monotonous regularity of manual labour – the whole enterprise neatly summed up by using Eric Coates's spirited march *Calling all Workers* as the signature tune.

The sort of music that was played reflected to a great extent the relaxation music which had dominated pre-war years, a legacy which stretches back to the days of the silent movies, when cinemas the length and breadth of the country had groups of instrumentalists to play along with the action, and resident composers who could put together the right kind of music to reflect the on-screen drama.

Another essential ingredient was the proliferation of seaside and hotel orchestras, dance bands and smaller ensembles which provided background music in the major shopping emporia, and on a more purely commercial side, the music publishers who built up vast collections of 'library' music to feed the insatiable desire for this kind of easy listening.

In the days of austerity which immediately followed the war, the need for this kind of relaxation became even greater, combined with feelings of nostalgia for what had gone before. The BBC with its broadcasting monopoly was very much on hand and employed no fewer than eight full-time orchestras around the country producing a whole host of programmes every day of the week. These included the BBC Concert Orchestra – the only one to survive to this day – which was formed in 1952 from what had previously been the BBC Theatre Orchestra.

The seeds of that transformation came towards the end of the war with the desire to create an orchestra 'capable of putting over the finest light music to great effect'. The number of players was gradually increased and in 1952 the BBC Concert Orchestra as we know it finally emerged, specifically to play music of 'proven popularity for' or 'likely to have an appeal to' a mass audience. Major names associated with the orchestra in those days, as permanent or guest conductors, included Stanford Robinson, Gilbert Vinter, Charles Mackerras, Vilem Tausky and Sidney Torch.

Two major developments took place in the early 1950s with the arrival of *Friday Night is Music Night* and the annual BBC International Festivals of Light Music which were held each summer in London's Royal Festival Hall. These presented great opportunities for the commissioning of new works and the chance for Light Music to develop beyond the legacy of the pre-war years in the hands of a new generation of composers and conductors including the likes of Malcolm Arnold, Ernest Tomlinson, Sidney Torch and Robert Farnon (who had settled in the UK after leading the Canadian Band of the Allied Expeditionary Forces alongside Glenn Miller in America and Britain's George Melachrino). Some of the great names of the recent past were still around including Haydn Wood and Eric Coates, the man generally regarded as 'the uncrowned King of Light Music'.

There's no doubt that the BBC's policy on commissioning new music across the board was a tremendous help and inspiration to a large number of composers, giving them the chance to come up with new ideas in sound and style. Where Coates had scored a bulls-eye with his marches and waltzes, this younger generation began to look for ways of combining the tradition they inherited with the benefits of modern technology and a desire to up-date in keeping with a changing world. George Melachrino's close harmony style, Robert Farnon's astonishing ear for orchestral colours (Andre Previn described him as 'the greatest living writer for strings', even though he began life as a trumpet player in Percy Faith's orchestra) and the 'cascading strings' sound which Ronald Binge created for Mantovani all helped to develop our listening habits and to bring Light Music firmly into the second half of the 20th century.

As television began to dominate home entertainment alongside radio, the need for signature tunes for programmes of all sorts gave watchers and listeners the chance to become even more familiar with the sort of Light Music which turned out to be ideally suited to the purpose. *Desert Island Discs* is unthinkable without the introductory music of Eric Coates's *By the Sleepy Lagoon* (even though that particular piece was actually inspired by the fading light of Bognor Regis across a calm sea!); how different our daily dose of *The Archers* would be without Arthur Wood's *Barwick Green*. When another Coates gem was used for both radio and television's *In Town Tonight* 20,000 people contacted the BBC in the hope of discovering the title of the music and the *Knightsbridge March* became an instant and enormous hit. As the need for more signature tunes grew, so those publishers' collections of 'library music' came into their own, as well as being much in demand for film sound-tracks, which became another vital outlet for the best of our Light Music composers.

The question remains as to what exactly Light Music is and where it belongs at the start of the 21st century. What does so-called 'light' music actually mean and how does it differ from so-called 'serious' music? There's no doubt that the finest composers on the 'lighter' side take their music-making every bit as seriously as their apparent counterparts and in their way, with their natural affinities, they should surely be respected every bit as much. The fact that 'easy-listening' by its very nature doesn't challenge the brain in the same way as symphonies, concertos, oratorios and chamber music need not mean that it should be condemned to the side-lines or looked down upon from a great height. On the contrary, the contribution it makes and has always made to the lives of countless millions is, in its way, equally important.

Why else would 16th century composers have turned to writing madrigals, or Bach and Handel have written dance music, Brahms been captivated by gypsy fiddlers, and composers from Sousa to Sullivan determined to give a mass audience what it clearly wanted? It is a matter of supply and demand and even in a world that – since the end of the Second World War – has changed out of all recognition, that demand remains as potent today as it did in the heady days before the pop and rock revolution of the second half of the 20th century. That violent change in the overall sound of music has inevitably had an effect on the way broadcasters schedule their programmes. Gone are the Light Music Festivals and with the exception of the Concert Orchestra, so are those BBC Light Orchestras.

But there is a distinct feeling of nostalgia for times gone by which drives more and more people of a certain age to revert to the kind of thing which excited them in the days of their youth. Having said that, as there are composers – young and not quite so young

270

– determined to continue developing Light Music for a new generation, the future looks brighter than it has for a long time. And now that so much of the Light Music of the past is available once again in the most contemporary of formats, the threat of its extinction from a few years ago is greatly reduced and likely to remain so. In fact, there is far more Light Music available today on commercial recordings than there ever was during the supposed 'golden age' and this clearly indicates a thirst for it among the record-buying public.

Younger listeners are tuning in; where older ones turned away and sought pastures new, they are returning; and with the help of those adventurous record companies and, as always – hopefully – the BBC, Light Music at its brightest and best will surely survive well into the 21st century and beyond.

When Dame Ethel Smyth was introduced to Eric Coates, she apparently said: Ah yes, the man who writes tunes – or words to that effect! I don't imagine she was being particularly complimentary, though there's no doubt that far more of Coates's deliciously tuneful music is heard these days than the works of Dame Ethel. There's nothing wrong with good tunes and I always assume that those who knock them are consumed by envy, that they cannot manage to write anything half as good. The point about composers like Coates is that the best are great craftsmen: nobody perhaps better than Coates in this field. His scores are a joy to read and – like all the finest composers of musical history – there's never a wasted note or a note that's out of place.

I would say the same thing about two other top rank tune-smiths I've been lucky enough to work with over so many years: Gordon Langford and John Rutter. Langford made numerous wonderful arrangements for the King's Singers at the start of our career, doing more perhaps than anyone to create the sound and the style of our ensemble singing. During my years presenting *Friday Night is Music Night* there were many occasions when the BBC Concert Orchestra played Gordon's masterly arrangements and medleys and I was always moved to say that every student of orchestration should be made to look at his voicing for every department of the orchestra. The same is true of Rutter: he is, of course, loved all over the world for his choral music, but this overlooks his genius as an orchestrator. Look, for example, at his choral and orchestral work *Feel the Spirit* – perfect arrangements of negro spirituals which he wrote for the amazing mezzo Melanie Marshall. Look beyond the vocal and choral writing to the subtlety with which he handles the orchestra. It is a work of pure genius. Those who disparage natural melody-makers will always look down on the achievements of those whose music gives so much pleasure (think of Sullivan and Lloyd Webber) though in doing so, they overlook the brilliance that lies behind their achievements – a sure case of art concealing art'.

(Courtesy: *BBC Music Magazine*)

Choral Conducting Repertoire

Bach JS	B Minor Mass
	Magnificat
	St John Passion
	St Matthew Passion
	Cantata 50 – Nun ist das Heil
	Cantata 140 – Wachet auf
	Cantata 79 – Gott der Herr ist Sonn und Schild
	Motet: Singet dem Herrn
	Motet: Jesu meine Freude
	Motet: Lobet den Herrn
	Motet: Komm, Jesu, Komm
Bach CPE	Magnificat
Beethoven	Mass in C
	Choral Fantasia
Bernstein	Chichester Psalms
Richard Blackford	Mirror of Perfection
Howard Blake	Song of St Francis
Borodin	Polovtsian Dances (Prince Igor)
Brahms	German Requiem
	Liebeslieder Waltzes
	Alto Rhapsody
Britten	Hymn to St Cecilia
	War Requiem
Bruckner	Motets various
Paul Carr	Requiem for an Angel
Christopher Brown	The Circling Year (1st performance, Wembley Stadium 1983)
Charpentier	Messe de Minuit pour Noel
	Te Deum

Bob Chilcott	Singing by Numbers
	Jubilate
	Dances of Time (1st performance,
	Leith Hill Musical Festival 2015)
Coleridge-Taylor	Hiawatha's Wedding Feast
Duruflé	Requiem
	Quatre Motets sur des Themes Gregoriens
Elgar	The Dream of Gerontius
	The Musicmakers
	Songs From the Bavarian Highlands
	Coronation Ode
Fauré	Requiem
	Cantique de Jean Racine
Finzi	For St Cecilia
	In Terra Pax
Anthony Le Fleming	Cantate Domino
Gershwin	Porgy and Bess
	(Andrew Litton concert version)
Gounod	St Cecilia Mass
Handel	Messiah
	Israel in Egypt
	Coronation Anthems
	Dixit Dominus
	Judas Maccabaeus
	Alexander's Feast
	Dettingen Te Deum
	Sing unto God
	Foundling Hospital Anthem
Haydn	The Creation
	The Seasons (Spring)
	Te Deum
	Harmoniemesse

	Missa in Angustiis
	Nelson Mass
	St Nicholas Mass
	Mariazeller Mass
	Paukenmesse
	Missa Brevis in F
	Missa St Johannes de Deo
Michael Haydn	Mass in honour of St Ursula
Honegger	King David
Hummel	Mass in Bb
Karl Jenkins	The Armed Man
	Gloria (world premiere, Royal Albert Hall 2010)
	Gods of Olympus (world premier, Royal Albert Hall 2012)
Morten Lauridsen	Lux Aeterna
Philip Ledger	Requiem
William Llewellyn	Requiem: On Earth in Concert Sing
Cecilia McDowall	A Fancy of Folksongs
	Ave Maris Stella
George Martin	The Mission Chorales (UK Premier, 2012)
Mendelssohn	Elijah
	Lobgesang – Hymn of Praise
	Lauda Sion
	Hear My Prayer
Monteverdi	1610 Vespers
Mozart	Requiem
	Regina Coeli, K 127
	Coronation Mass
	Vesperae Solennes de Confessore
	Mass in C Minor
	Missa Brevis in Bb
	Regina Coeli

Orff	Carmina Burana
Parry	Blest Pair of Sirens I was Glad
Paul Patterson	Magnificat Millennium Mass
Elis Pehkonen	Gloria (1st performance – Cheltenham Bach Choir)
Poulenc	Gloria
Puccini	Messa di Gloria
Purcell	Come ye Sons of Art away Te Deum Queen Mary Funeral Sentences Ode to St Cecilia
Alan Ridout	Canticle of Joy
Rossini	Petite Messe Solenelle
Rutter	Requiem Magnificat Feel the Spirit Birthday Madrigals Gloria
Schubert	Mass in C Mass in G Magnificat
George Shearing	Music to Hear
Richard Shepard	There was Such Beauty
Stainer	Crucifixion (CD recording, Chandos)
Stanford	Songs of the Sea
Sullivan	Boer War Te Deum HMS Pinafore

Tallis	Spem in Alium
Tippett	Spirituals from A Child of Our Time
Vaughan Williams	Sea Symphony
	Serenade to Music
	Festival Te Deum
	5 Mystical Songs
	5 English Folksongs
	Mass in G Minor
	Christmas Fantasia
	Three Choral Hymns
	A Cotswold Romance
	In Windsor Forest
	O Clap Your Hands
	Dona Nobis Pacem
	100th Psalm
	Garden of Proserpine
	Toward the Unknown Region
	Benedicite
Verdi	Requiem
	Four Sacred Pieces
	Opera Choruses gala programme
Vivaldi	Gloria
Walton	Coronation Te Deum
Weber	Mass in Eb
Jonathan Willcocks	A Great and Glorious Victory
	Magnificat
David Willcocks	Sing!

Choirs conducted, including

Auckland Choral Society (New Zealand)

Bach Choir (London)

BBC Singers

Berkshire Choral Festival Choir (Sheffield, Massachusetts)

Bradford Festival Choral Society

Bristol Bach Choir

British Federation of Young Choirs

Burford Singers

Cecilian Singers of Leicester

Cheltenham Bach Choir

Derbyshire Singers

Dudley Combined Choirs

Edinburgh Royal Choral Union

English Arts Chorale

Hallé Choir

Harrogate Choral Society

Hertford Chorus

Huddersfield Choral Society

Leicester Philharmonic Choir

Leith Hill Festival Chorus

London Choral Society

Mary Wakefield Westmorland Festival Choirs

Northern Sinfonia Choir

Nottingham Choral Trust Choirs

Orpheus Choir (Wellington, New Zealand)

Really Big Chorus

Royal Choral Society

Southampton Choral Society

Southend Choral Society

Sussex Chorus

York Musical Society

Orchestras conducted

BBC Concert Orchestra
BBC Philharmonic
Britten Sinfonia
Canzona
Cotswold Chamber Orchestra
English Festival Orchestra
English String Orchestra
English Symphony Orchestra
Hallé Orchestra
London Festival Orchestra
Manchester Camerata
New Cheltenham Chamber
    Orchestra
Northern Sinfonia
Orchestra da Camera
Orchestra of Opera North

Regency Sinfonia
Royal Academy of Music
    Orchestra
Royal College of Music
    Orchestra
Royal Philharmonic Orchestra
Royal Scottish Academy of
    Music Orchestra
Young Persons Concert
    Foundation Orchestra
European Sinfonietta (Seville)
Orchestra Accademia (Venice)
Virtuosi Pragenses (Prague)
Cape Town Philharmonic
Riga Festival Orchestra
Athens Philharmonia

Brass Bands conducted

Black Dyke Mills Band
Brighouse and Rastrick
Desford Colliery Band
Feathers Band
Grimethorpe Colliery Band

Lindley Band
Sellers International
Yorkshire Building Society
    Band

Presidencies, Vice Presidencies and Patronages

Association of British Choral Directors (Vice President)
Bampton Classical Opera (Patron)
Birmingham Bach Choir (Patron)
Bristol Bach Choir (President)
Cambridge Concert Orchestra (President)
Derbyshire Singers (President)
English Arts Chorale (President)
Huddersfield Choral Society (Honorary Patron)
Joyful Company of Singers (President)
Leith Hill Musical Festival (President)
Market Harborough Singers (President)
Morecombe Promenade Orchestra (President)
Royal School of Church Music (Vice President)
Southampton Choral Society (Patron)

Gillian Fisher Discography

Handel: Italian Duets
With Patrizia Kwella (soprano), the King's Consort, Robert King
Hyperion CDA 66440

Handel: Il Duello Amoroso
With Patrizia Kwella (soprano), London Handel Orchestra, Denys Darlow
Hyperion CDH 55136

Handel: Music for Royal Occasions
With the King's Consort, Robert King
Hyperion CDA 66315

Handel: The Triumph of Time and Truth
With Emma Kirkby, Charles Brett, Ian Partridge, Stephen Varcoe
The London Handel Orchestra, Denys Darlow
Hyperion CDD 22050

Handel: Coronation Anthems / Foundling Hospital Anthem
With Winchester Cathedral Choir, Brandenburg Consort, David Hill
Argo 440 946-2

Pergolesi: Stabat Mater
With Michael Chance (counter-tenor), the King's Consort, Robert King
Hyperion CDA 66294

Purcell: : Royal and Ceremonial Odes
With James Bowman, Michael Chance, Charles Daniels, John Mark
Ainsley, Michael George, Charles Pott, the King's Consort, Robert King
Hyperion CDA 66314 – re-release on Helios CDH 55327

Purcell: Hail Bright Cecilia / Who can from joy refrain?
With the King's Consort, Robert King
Hyperion CDA 55327

Purcell: The Complete Odes and Welcome Songs
With the King's Consort, Robert King
Volume 3 – Hyperion CDA 66412 / Volume 4 – Hyperion CDA 66456
Volume 5 – Hyperion CDA 66476 / Volume 6 – Hyperion CDA 66494
Volume 7 – Hyperion CDA 66587 / Volume 8 – Hyperion CDA 66598

Various: Great Baroque Arias
With James Bowman, John Mark Ainsley, Michael George,
The King's Consort, Robert King
IMP PCD 894

Purcell: Timon of Athens and Dioclesian
Monteverdi Choir / EBS / John Eliot Gardiner
Erato ECD 75473

Purcell: The Fairy Queen
With Lorna Anderson, Ann Murray, Michael Chance,
John Mark Ainsley, Ian Partridge, Richard Suart, Michael George
and The Sixteen, Harry Christophers
Collins Classics 70132

Acknowledgements

It's been a lot of fun writing this book and throughout the long and sometimes frustrating process of relying on rather distant memory, my wife Gilly has been my strength and stay and has encouraged me at every step of the way and for this I remain profoundly grateful. My thanks too to my daughter Charlotte and granddaughter Sophie who helped enormously with the photos and Charlotte's husband Dom who taught me how to overcome considerable laptop problems.

Two dear friends – Sally Jarman and Julia McKenzie – along with my sister Heather, took the trouble to read the text through in the early stages and to offer invaluable suggestions and corrections and neighbour and historian Allan Ledger offered gratefully accepted encouragement and enthusiasm as well as an introduction to my publisher.

To all of them my thanks, along with my old publishing friends Marcus Clapham and the late Clive Reynard who very generously offered the benefit of their expertise in the early stages, helping me to remove dozens of unnecessary exclamation marks before insisting that the book was certainly worth producing. And when along came Alan Gordon Walker from Umbria Books, the fate of my manuscript was sealed and without his tireless assistance in reading it, editing it, chasing it and publishing it, it may never have seen the light of day. My special thanks to him and his designer, Louise Millar, and indeed, to you, for being kind enough to buy a copy.

Index